WHEN WORLD HURTS TOO MUCH

IDENTIFYING AND MANAGING NEURODIVERGENT STRESS, ANXIETY, AND TRAUMA.

ASH BANKS

When the world hurts too much. Identifying and managing neurodivergent stress, anxiety, and trauma.

Written by Ash Banks.
Cover Illustration by Auggy Dailey.[1]
Cover design by A.R. Banks.

ISBN: 9798391523376

For updates, new releases, and totally unrelated stuff I just happen to be writing, please check out:

https://www.amazon.com/Ash-Banks/e/B08TMMNPZH
https://www.amazon.com/A-R-Banks/e/B09JHP4FT5
https://www.amazon.com/Robin-Banks/e/B01MU5VWGL
https://godsbastard.wordpress.com/

Just in case you're curious, this book was written while listening to "Modern Country" by William Tyler stuck on repeat. It's good music for when I need to brain hard, but I need to stay relaxed while doing it. Also, one of the tunes is called "Highway Anxiety" and another one "The Great Unwind." Is that apt or what?

---

[1] https://www.mrsgendered.com/#/

For Lou Kennedy, who started it,

and Emma Brown, who didn't know what she was getting into.

"The truth will set you free, but first it will piss you off."

-Quote often attributed to Gloria Steinem, but wrongly so.

CONTENTS

Preface

Content warning: suboptimal parenting. You can skip this bit without missing anything.

I was four or five years old when my mom left me in the sea. Spoiler alert: I didn't die. I'd like to say that I didn't get hurt, either, but that would only be a half truth.

Although we lived by the sea, it was our first holiday at a real seaside resort. It was a good holiday, mostly, but there was a major hitch. The seaside I was used to was either covered in concrete or pebbles. I had never had to deal with sand before; I don't think I'd ever even touched it, to be honest. The sandpit in the local play area doubled as a cat litter tray, so I wasn't allowed in there.

Sand was alright, mostly. I quickly discovered that I could cope just fine with it, as long as my feet were dry. When my feet were wet, however, the feeling of the sand glomming onto my skin was something I just couldn't tolerate.

After a few failed attempts at convincing me that I was freaking out over nothing, my mom gave up and agreed to carry me back to our deck chair when I emerged from the sea. That was quite a concession on her part; she had told me quite clearly some time earlier that I was too big to be carried, and that was that. So we went to the beach twice a day, every day, we had our swim, and then she carried me back to safety. As soon as my feet were dry, my ability to walk unaided was restored, and the rest of the day proceeded in a normal fashion.

That worked just fine, until the day when my mom's friend came to visit us. Said friend had a child a year younger than me, who was already deemed a much superior specimen by all who knew us. I can't really blame the adults in my life for coming to that conclusion, because I was a mess. I was already in the process of developing what would shortly become a paralyzing degree of social anxiety, performance anxiety, and an insecure attachment style. I was intellectually ahead of my peers, but my mom's attempts at making me follow an actual curriculum so I could skip the first year or two of elementary school had failed abysmally. On the other hand, my physical skills lagged behind those of my peers – a problem that my mom attempted to solve by forcing me to take up gymnastics. When that not only didn't fix me, but caused me to develop an all-consuming fear of any physical task requiring balance, everyone around me pretty much gave up. I was a substandard child, and that was that.

The one thing I had going for me was that I was A Good Child. I did as I was told, I never spoke out of turn (or at all, if I could help it), and I could be relied upon to sit quietly in a corner for extended periods of time without requiring supervision or any kind of engagement. If you parked me in the vicinity of books, you could forget about me for *hours*.

Alas, Good Children are not supposed to have tantrums. According to my mom's friend, that was what I was doing. I was acting out because I wasn't getting my way, and the only way to respond to children misbehaving in such a horrific fashion was to ignore them or punish them, ideally both. My mom was being too soft, and her softness was reinforcing my bad behavior and would likely ruin me forever.

Many details of my early childhood have been lost to time and a subpar memory, but I can remember the change in my mother's expression when she heard all that. For a brief moment, she looked unsure, and then she looked ashamed. Then she didn't look like anything, because she turned around and walked away from me.

I stayed stuck there, in the sea, and watched her go. I don't know how long I was there for, or what I did. I can't remember whether I cried, screamed, or just stood there. I can remember, though, the moment when I realized that she wasn't coming back for me. Nobody was. Nobody was going to help me. My choices were either to stay in the sea indefinitely, or to deal with what was coming: the horrific sensation of the sand crawling into every crevice of my skin, consuming my toes, flooding my entire body with horror and dread. The next bit of memory is missing, but I must have made it back to our deck chair, because I am writing this from dry land.

I was a substandard child in many respects, but I had a pretty advanced approach to problem-solving. Once I realized that I needed to be able to walk out of the sea unaided, I worked out how to do it. I spent the rest of our holiday digging holes in the sand, filling them with water, and systematically training myself to tolerate the feeling of dry sand on wet skin. You start with a little patch, somewhere not very sensitive, and work your way up. By the time our holiday ended, I could submerge both my feet in water, place them on the sand, and endure the resulting reaction.

This is important: I didn't learn that dry sand on wet skin doesn't really feel horrible. It did and it still does. I taught myself to ignore that sensation and carry on.

Unfortunately, I learned another lesson: that when my needs and problems didn't match those of other people, they would not be respected. I learned not to rely on the adults in my life to help me when I struggled. I learned that even mentioning those struggles would result in disbelief, shame, and punishment. I never, ever wanted to do anything that would make my mom walk away and leave me in the sea again, literally or metaphorically, so I didn't. Or I did my best not to, anyway.

I didn't always succeed, because my body has a whole bunch of quirks. Aside from a whole bundle of sensory issues, my joints are unstable, my blood pressure is ludicrously low, my blood sugar level is on a rollercoaster, and I am allergic to more things than I care to list. So, try as I might, I carried on falling over, twisting and dislocating various parts of my anatomy, getting dizzy, going faint, and having allergic reactions.

That was unfortunate in and of itself, but it wasn't the worst part. You see, the whole being-left-in-the-sea incident didn't just teach me a lesson. It taught my mother something, too. It taught her that accommodating my needs might result in public shaming – something she absolutely would not tolerate, no matter the cost. It taught her that if she ignored me long enough, I would stop demanding things from her. It taught her that if she didn't help me, I would eventually help myself.

Unfortunately, she then proceeded to apply those lessons across the board. Whenever I behaved abnormally, I was clearly just acting out. If I fell over and hurt myself, it was my fault for messing around. If I smelled something that triggered my allergic rhinitis and mentioned it, I was making a fuss. If I then started wheezing, I was having a tantrum. If I said that I was dizzy or faint, I was trying to manipulate her. If I actually fell over or passed out, I was faking it to push my point. If I refused to eat something because I knew that it would hurt me, I was being inconsiderate and defiant. If having eaten that food I became unable to talk properly, because my tongue and lips had swollen up, I was making a scene.

I managed to get myself sent to boarding school at fourteen, and my life got easier, but it still kind of sucked. The cost of misbehaving at school was much lower than at home – if I got caught, I would be punished, but I wouldn't be left in the sea! Unfortunately, that didn't help me all that much, because I didn't know that I wasn't actually misbehaving. I genuinely didn't know that connective tissue disorders, low blood pressure, reactive hypoglycemia, and allergies are things people *have*, not things people *do*. I was so used to being told that I was faking my issues, or that they were just in my head, that I believed it.

I was fifteen when I was told that my chronic low blood pressure was an actual, physical, measurable cause of my dizziness and poor balance. I was nineteen when I had an asthma attack bad enough to send me to the emergency room, and I was finally diagnosed and given an inhaler. I was in my twenties when I learned that my ears and sinuses were so damaged from years of unmanaged allergies that they were no longer functioning as intended. I was in my thirties when I learned that fruits like kiwi and pineapple are common food allergens, and that eating them regardless is not only silly, but actually dangerous. I was in my forties when I learned that connective tissue disorders are real, and how they affect the human body. Last year, at forty-seven, I learned that reactive hypoglycemia is a recognized medical condition. And it was only last month that I worked out that I have a low-grade allergy to rennet – something usually only seen in workers in rennet producing plants[2] – that caused me to be oversensitive to a host of other allergens.

It won't be all that long before I hit fifty, and I still have a lot to learn. The main thing I am trying to work out at the moment is what counts and what doesn't. I know that my medical issues are real, and I am learning how to work around them. What about my sensory issues, though? I know that they are real, inasmuch as I really, truly experience a range of non-standard sensory experiences. I have plenty of evidence supporting that, both in the form of anecdotes (e.g., my ability to know by smell which delivery driver dropped my packages) and medical data (e.g., ear frequency response test results so weird that my examiner thought the machine was broken). What I haven't worked out yet is whether that matters. I mean, I understand that if something is going to give me an asthma attack then I have the right to avoid it, but what if something doesn't actually do anything, it just hurts me?

...yeah, those are words I say to myself. I wouldn't say them to anyone

---

[2] https://pubmed.ncbi.nlm.nih.gov/16917831/

else, because I'm not actually a raging asshole, but the pinball machine that is my brain has some odd quirks. Evidence suggests that I still have some work to do to overcome my early conditioning. A part of me is still the child who was left in the sea and thinks that it must be their fault. It has to be, because their mother couldn't possibly do anything wrong.

This isn't why I decided to write this book.

As for most of my writing projects, it all started with a rant. A friend of mine sent me a link to a new unofficial diagnostic term, "Autistic Distinct Anxiety" (I will explain it soon, I promise), and I promptly blew up. If an Autistic person is feeling distressed because they are forced to endure an uncomfortable stimulus, they are experiencing a stressor, not anxiety! Yes, they might end up developing anxiety around their stressors, but that doesn't make the stressors any less real! Neurodivergent needs are real; unmet needs are stressors; and proportionate, timely responses to real stressors are not a sign of mental illness!

See? I can think straight, as long as I'm thinking about other people.

Anyway, there I was, blowing up about the fact that people dared to conflate stress and anxiety, when I discovered that the medical field does that, too. Medical answers to stress completely ignore everything we know about it – which isn't surprising, because most studies of stress management weren't conducted in medical settings. If you want to learn how stressors work and get practical, proven solutions for learning to decrease their impact, the best source I know of is... military science.[3] Vast resources have been invested in working out how to improve people's performance in combat situations, which necessitated working out how to decrease the impact of combat stress on their physiology. The resulting approaches have been found to be beneficial in improving people's performance in other stressful settings. However, what was learned in the process hasn't filtered back into the medical establishment.

The medical field studies the results of stress, but not its causes. As a result, many doctors aren't able or willing to diagnose patients with stress. Stressed patients are usually diagnosed either with a mental health condition such as an anxiety disorder, or with a series of physical conditions that are actually stress responses.[4] This doesn't matter as much

---

[3] I've been told that sport psychology has done a lot on this, too, but I don't go there.
[4] And if you think that your gender might affect what you are most likely to be diagnosed with, you are not wrong.

as it should, because even the doctors who can tell apart stress, anxiety, and stress responses are unlikely to be able to "prescribe" you the right course of action. What are they going to do, send you to a Buddhist monastery for a six-month break? Medicine just doesn't cover that yet.

If we need to learn to manage our response to stressors, we need to look in places where people habitually need to manage their response to stressors. This may sound obvious when I put it like that, but it doesn't look obvious at all in real life. People struggling to deal with their everyday life don't generally look for solutions in war zones.

This is why I wrote this book: there is a missing link between two fields, and I want to change that. I want neurodivergents to be able to look at whatever is causing them distress and correctly identify it. Is it a stressor? Is it anxiety? Is it a trauma response? We need to be able to work this out, because these three beasties may affect us in similar ways, but they need to be handled differently. What's good for managing stress may exacerbate anxiety, and vice versa. Mismanaging our stress or anxiety can be traumatizing, while trauma can manifest as anxiety or a decreased ability to handle stress. These issues are often interconnected, but they still need to be managed separately and carefully.

Knowing these differences can help us manage ourselves, and it can also help us manage others. It can be hard to explain our reality to those who don't share it. It's even harder if we can't find the right words. Having specific terms to describe specific issues can make it easier for us to explain ourselves to people who don't get us, and to defend ourselves against those who attempt to discount our reality. It can also make it easier for us to defend others, in particular those who can't defend themselves. And it can stop us denying our own reality.

We might not be able to fix all the ways in which the world hurts us, but we can stop hurting ourselves, and that's important. The adults who raised us may have metaphorically left us in the sea, and we can't change that, but we can stop abandoning ourselves. We can stop blaming ourselves when the world hurts us too much. And as we have to live with ourselves, to constantly hear our voice inside our head, I think that's a good place to start.

Ash Banks, 24.03.2023

Introduction

Who is this book for?

This book is primarily aimed at people like me: neurodivergents who are struggling a bit (or a lot), and would like to live easier, comfier, hopefully even happier lives. I can guarantee that nothing I have to say will magically fix your entire existence – if I knew how to do that, I'd be living a much better life myself, and I wouldn't have time to write books. However, I hope that it will give you a starting point and aim you in the right direction.

If you are neurotypical or unsure of your neurotype, worry not! While the section on stressors is specifically aimed at the neurodivergent community, many of these issues also apply to neurotypicals. Besides, learning something about the struggles we face may help you be kinder to us. We could do with more of that.

Structure

One of the common features of stress, anxiety, and trauma is that they can make our brains go around in circles. Our problems may take up a tiny proportion of our actual life, yet end up occupying a disproportionate amount of our thoughts.

I use a trick to stop myself fantasizing over worst-case scenarios and to slam the brakes on circular thinking. When I catch myself over-reacting to an event, or thinking in spirals, I ask myself the following questions: what, so what, and now what.

This technique is derived from Terry Borton's process of reflection.[5] However, I learnt it from reading Cosmopolitan at the dentist.

What?

What is actually going on? Describe the event or issue in a purely factual fashion, without guesswork, embroidery, judgment, or rationalization. When we cut out all the chatter, we might find that our problem is not as problematic as we first thought. However, accurately

---

[5] "Reach, Touch and Teach" by Terry Borton.

describing our issues includes accurately describing our sensations and feelings before, during, and after. Things that happen inside us are still real.

So what?

What is the fallout of the event or issue? If there are no consequences, does it matter? Again, during this process we must include an accurate representation of our sensations and feelings. If something "just" makes us feel terrible, it still matters.

Now what?

Is there anything that needs to get done as a result of the event or issue? If there is, we should do it. If there isn't, but we are likely to have to deal with the same kind of issue time and time again, it's wise for us to form a plan on how to handle that kind of situation in the least damaging way possible.

We can apply these questions to one-off events, but we can also apply them to recurring issues and patterns of behavior. Doing so may be harder, but it may also benefit us more in the long run.

This book will follow a similar structure:

- What are the issues in play? How can we classify and articulate them correctly and clearly?

- What is neurodivergent stress? We will start with a look at why stress is a neurodivergent issue, and then go through a megalist of possible neurodivergent stressors.

- So what? Why does this matter in general, and why does it matter to us in particular?

- Now what? What should we do about it? What approaches can help us reduce the impact of our stress, anxiety, and trauma, and how can we pick the best ones?

- Are there other issues we might need to address as a result of our new understanding and efforts?

How to use this book

Unlike my earlier works on neurodivergence,[6] this book has to be consumed in a linear fashion. That's because it's critical that we learn to accurately identify whether we are dealing with stress, anxiety, or trauma responses *before* we take action. Incorrectly assessing our issues can cause us pain, but taking the wrong course of action can cause us actual damage.

If consuming long tracts is an issue, don't. There's a reason humans invented chapters. Information is just as useful when absorbed in bits. You can take your time over this; it won't go off.

Caveats

There are two main caveats; one about me, and one about my sources.

First of all, let's deal with me. I am not a psychologist, a psychiatrist, or any kind of medical specialist. I learned most of what I know about neuroscience from people who are, but that doesn't mean that I know all they know. I learned most of what I know about sympathetic nervous system responses and how to deal with them from self-defense trainers and military scientists. Those are not necessarily the specialists one would go to when facing a psychoemotional issue.

That doesn't mean that I don't know what I'm talking about, but it does mean that you should take everything I say with a pinch of salt. It's also why all the information provided in this book is *for educational purposes only*. As stated in the small print at the front of the book:

> "This book is sold with the understanding that neither the publisher nor the author is engaged in rendering legal, medical, psychological, or any other professional service. Neither the publisher nor the author assume any liability for any errors or omissions or for how this book or its contents are used or interpreted or for any consequences resulting directly or indirectly from the use of this book. For legal, medical, psychological advice or any other, please consult the appropriate professionals."

Having said that, I'm aware that most people who pick up this book will

---

[6] https://www.amazon.com/stores/Ash-Banks/author/B08TMMNPZH

do so with a view to use it (or I hope so, anyway). I'm cool with that, but please, *please*, **PLEASE**, stop doing so if it's making you worse. I am not an authority figure. I am not better than you in any way, shape, or form, and I don't know you. If you think I'm wrong, you might be right. If you think what I'm saying is wrong for you, you're almost definitely right. My brain is not your brain, and the whole point of this book is to help YOU, not me. If this book isn't helping you, toss it.

Dealing with our anxieties, stressors, and traumas would be easier if we could take a break from them – a holiday from our lives, to give us the opportunity to examine our past, assess our present, and create a new future in a safe, supportive environment. Unfortunately, most of us have no chance of ever getting that. If you are not currently in a place where you can deal with the psychoemotional fallout of going through multiple paradigm shifts and poking at your traumas without wrecking your life, you might want to wait until you are in a better place, or at least take things steady.

If what I'm saying strikes you as accurate but hurts too much, or it's bringing up stuff you are struggling to deal with, drop it and seek professional help. If you can't get that, seek unprofessional help. The bottom line is that this shit is hard, and the harder it is, the more likely it is that we'll need some support to deal with it. I can't give you that, because I am not a specialist and because I don't have the spoons. But there are people out there who can help, people who can support you while you walk through this. They are not always easy to find, and they are almost never free, but they do exist.

If you have already been diagnosed with a mental health condition, I strongly recommend that you don't undiagnose yourself without seeking a second opinion. This is particularly important if you are currently taking psych meds to manage your condition. Let me stress this: DO NOT STOP TAKING YOUR MEDS BECAUSE YOU THINK I TOLD YOU TO.

Many psych meds can create physical dependency, which occurs when a person's body adapts to the presence of a certain drug. Without the drug, physically dependent people may experience unpleasant and even dangerous physical symptoms (aka withdrawal). They may need to undergo a difficult detox period, or to switch to another substance to help their body adjust. Do not undertake this process on my say-so, because I'm not saying so.

Some of us deal with stressors and anxieties by hurting ourselves or others through risky, addictive, impulsive, and compulsive behaviors. These can include self-harm, eating disorders, substance misuse, alcoholism, carbohydrate bingeing, gambling, compulsive shopping, risky sex, aggressive behavior, extreme sports, and other high-risk activities. If any of these apply to you or have applied to you in the past, I would strongly advise you to find a reliable, effective support network *before* you start working on this book. Chances are that until you disentangle the relationship between your stressors and your mental states, you will continue to struggle with these behaviors. However, these behaviors are coping mechanisms – pretty unhelpful coping mechanisms, to be sure, because they usually create a whole host of additional problems, but coping mechanisms nonetheless. You do not want to risk a relapse or a worsening of your risky, addictive, impulsive, and compulsive behaviors if you do not have a reliable support mechanism in place.

That was unpleasant, wasn't it? Well, the next bit is actually worse.

Most of the information provided in this book is stuff I learned from someone else. Normally, that would compel me not only to quote my sources, but to suggest that you consult them directly. Unfortunately, I cannot always do the latter, for several reasons.

- Some of the original sources are riddled with triggers – as in, actual trauma triggers, "something that sets off a memory tape or flashback transporting the person back to the event of her/his original trauma."[7] This is partly because the conventional wisdom is that people learn better from stories than from conceptual treatises, and partly because trauma porn sells books. As a result, consulting these sources can trigger flashbacks or even retraumatize susceptible readers.

- Some of the original sources are rooted in beliefs that are either straight-up toxic, or assume certain types of privilege. Members of victimized minority groups are most at risk of suffering from anxiety, stress, and trauma. I am not going to recommend that they wade through sources that propagate or reinforce the oppression they have to endure on a daily basis.

- Some of the original sources present their material in ways designed to manipulate the readers into embracing certain beliefs. While the beliefs in question may not be toxic, the manipulation is.

---

[7] http://psychcentral.com/lib/what-is-a-trigger/

- Some of the original sources are fine per se, but the communities that formed around the authors are toxic, or even dangerous. This is sadly true of many corners of the self-defense community.

This situation is far from ideal, but it's unsurprising, and it's unlikely to improve until the opinions and needs of minorities gain a fair share of representation. In the vast majority of cases, the authors of my sources are people who either don't share our problems in the first place, or who don't share enough of our problems to understand their cumulative effect. They don't necessarily mean to cause harm, but the result is frankly toxic. I wish it wasn't so, but it is, and the last thing I want to do is recommend that my readers wade through materials that might not help them and could harm them. This isn't because I think that my readers are weak or fragile. It's because I believe that they are already overburdened.

In physics, strength is defined as a measure of a material's resistance to deformation or breakage under stress. In a nutshell, strong materials are able to resist impacts and heavy loads without falling apart. No material is so strong that it can't be broken, though, and loads are cumulative. A strong material under a too-heavy load is more likely to break than a weak material under no load at all.

Being neurodivergent in a neurotypical world comes with a lot of loads attached. We have to deal with problems that don't apply to the majority of our neurotypical peers. To make matters worse, we often have to do so with fewer personal and societal resources to support us. If we crumble as a result, that doesn't mean that we are weaker than our peers; we've just been carrying too heavy a load for too long. Anyone and everyone can break under excessive strain.

I have done my best to provide good, alternative sources to all essential information in the "Further reading" section at the end of the book. These sources won't cover everything this book mentions, but they aren't likely to cause harm, either. It's not an ideal solution, but it's the best I could come up with. If you do decide to check out some of the sources I'm mentioning but not recommending, please do so carefully and consciously. It's possible to wade through a sewer and find treasure, but it's wiser to do so while wearing protective equipment, or at the very least without swallowing everything we come into contact with.

What?

In recent years, there has been a huge push to popularize and destigmatize mental health terms such as anxiety, depression, dissociation, and so on. This is having a positive impact because it encourages us to talk about our experiences, even when they are negative. This, in turn, can make it easier for us to ask for help if we need it.

Unfortunately, there has also been a negative outcome. Many people use "I feel," "I am," and "I have" sentences indiscriminately when talking about negative emotions. For instance, a person may casually say that they feel anxious, that they are anxious, or that they have anxiety, without considering the fact that those statements are not equivalent. In order to discuss why that is and why it matters, we're going to start from the very beginning: the brain.

The **brain** is an organ of the body. This may sound like a truism, but it's a key fact. The separation between mind and body may be traditional in many cultures, but it's an illusion. Treating the brain as if it were a separate entity sitting in our skulls and driving our bodies around is factually incorrect and can lead to mistaken assumptions. The brain and the body are not connected: they are one thing.

Like other organs of the body, the brain receives, interprets, and responds to external and internal stimuli. Over the centuries, humans devised a number of ways of classifying the brain's inputs and outputs. For instance, we might distinguish between sensations, emotions, and thoughts, and ascribe them different origins and different significance. Alas, modern neuroscience proved that these distinctions are not based on reality. The way in which the brain functions is a lot more organic and, frankly, way messier than previously believed. This subject is too large and complex to fully unpack here. I recommend "How Emotions Are Made: The Secret Life of the Brain" by Lisa Feldman Barrett as an extremely accessible introduction.

The TL/DR version is that the brain is an organ that responds to external and internal inputs by firing off electrical impulses and secreting neurotransmitters.[8] These **neurophysiological changes**, in turn, set off chain reactions that affect our whole body, brain included.

---

[8] https://www.kenhub.com/en/library/anatomy/neurotransmitters

Brains whose neurophysiological activities fit within the statistical norm are called "**neurotypical**." Neurotypical brains **perceive, process, and react to stimuli** in certain predictable ways, and those ways are the most common ones within the human population. Neurotypical people are only "normal" in the statistical sense of being in the majority. As a result of their prevalence, however, our society is geared up to expect and facilitate neurotypical responses, needs, and behaviors.

Not all brains are neurotypical, though: as with all other body characteristics, humans are not uniform when it comes to brains. Our species is **neurodiverse**, because it's made up of a bunch of different **neurotypes** (i.e., types of brains).

Some brains perceive, process, and react to stimuli in ways that are markedly different from the statistical norm. These brains are dubbed **neurodivergent**. Neurodivergent neurotypes aren't flawed or deficient, and they are definitely not new, or unnatural. Some neurodivergences are the result of naturally-occurring variations encoded in our genome, while others are the result of temporary or permanent changes in the brain resulting from our experiences.

That's one of the cool things about the brain: it doesn't just respond to our environment, it **adapts** to it. This should come as no surprise, because the same is true of the rest of our body: our muscles, bones, and connective tissues change in response to exercise and physical trauma, so why shouldn't our brain do the same? The tricky thing about the brain, however, is that it also adapts to itself, kinda. The brain's neurophysiological changes determine what we think, feel, and sense, but what we think, feel, and sense can change our brain. These changes are not only neurochemical, but structural: different bits of the brain literally grow or shrivel in response to how much use they get. These changes are particularly significant in childhood, when our brains are still developing. As a result, we may be born with a neurotypical brain, but grow into neurodivergent adults because of how our experiences shaped our brain.

Some of us, however, are born neurodivergent. Two of the most commonly-known inheritable neurodivergences are ADHD and Autism. Although the genes responsible have not been identified yet, ADHD[9] and Autistic[10] traits are highly heritable. One-third of ADHDers have at least

---

[9] https://www.ncbi.nlm.nih.gov/pmc/articles/PMC1180819/
[10] https://www.frontiersin.org/articles/10.3389/fncel.2019.00385/full

one parent with a similar neurotype,[11] and parents who score highly on tests of Autistic traits have an 85% increased chance of having Autistic children.[12]

Autistics and ADHDers are born with brains that function differently from those of neurotypical people. While the extent to which those differences affect us can be heavily influenced by a number of factors, including our environment and experiences, these differences are innate.

There is a ton of other neurodivergences – in fact, there are so many that I won't list them here. The bottom line is that if our brains **perceive, process, and react to stimuli** in ways that markedly differ from those of neurotypical people, then we are neurodivergent.

This wouldn't be a big deal if the world was set up by or for us, but it isn't. This is particularly true of the human-made world, which is built and run in ways that may meet the basic needs of the majority (sort of - Sick Building Syndrome[13] is A Thing), but don't always meet ours. As a result, we are routinely forced to endure stimuli we find unpleasant or even painful – the droning whine of electricity, the glare of artificial lighting, the fug of clashing chemical scents, the tactile torture of scratchy clothes and countless surfaces coming at us from all directions. People whose brains perceive, process and react to stimuli in the "normal" way may be able to tolerate these stimuli, or fail to even notice them. For many of us, however, they are a constant onslaught on our senses. Enduring them can cause us serious discomfort or even pain, and that puts us at a disadvantage. Some of us are able to still function in those circumstances, while some of us are not. For all of us, however, it's hard to be at our best while the world hurts us.

The same is true of standardized systems of work that require everyone to perform the same tasks, in the same way, at the same speed, and to the same quality. Standardized systems often punish non-conformity regardless of its causes and its outcomes. By doing so, they elevate conformity to a core value: we can fail not only by doing the wrong thing, or doing the right thing badly, but by doing anything differently.

As our brains are different, enforced conformity puts us in a bind. We might find it very hard to perform exactly like our neurotypical peers, but

---

[11] https://www.rcpsych.ac.uk/mental-health/problems-disorders/adhd-in-adults
[12] https://www.livescience.com/46641-parents-of-kids-with-autism-traits.html
[13] https://www.ncbi.nlm.nih.gov/pmc/articles/PMC2796751/

that doesn't necessarily mean that we can't achieve the same standards of work. We might need more time, more help, or a different system of work, but we could do it. Unfortunately, our potential isn't enough: in many if not most settings, the fact that we can't perform exactly like our neurotypical peers is a failure in and of itself.

For those of us whose chances of performing to neurotypicals standards are slim to none, the situation is even worse. Our society may claim that each and every human life has an intrinsic, innate value, but that belief is not reflected in how individuals are treated. Intrinsic values are often overshadowed by extrinsic values – whether we are physically attractive, successful, rich, powerful, and so on. In a very real sense, our worth depends on our achievements. If we achieve less than our peers, we are worth less. If we can't achieve at all, we are worthless.

These views aren't commonly advertised, probably because when you state them out clearly, they sound repugnant. However, this doesn't stop them from having an impact on our lives, both at a personal and societal level. As a result, we all experience the pressure to perform – which, for neurodivergents, implies the pressure to conform. This pressure is one of countless reasons why we might feel **anxious**.

We normally think of **anxiety** as a feeling of unease, worry, or fear, but it's more than that. Anxiety affects not only how we feel in an emotional sense, but also how we feel physically, and how we function and behave.[14] That's because **anxiety is a neurophysiological phenomenon** that involves our entire body. When we feel anxious, our body is increasing the secretion of a number of neurotransmitters and hormones, including glucocorticoids, catecholamines, growth hormone, and prolactin.[15] The results of these hormonal changes will depend on how large they are, which is linked to the intensity of our anxiety. The terminology is rather squishy here, but our symptoms can range from mild nervousness, which might make us feel jittery or restless, to full-blown panic, which might give us a pounding heart, shortness of breath, light-headedness, sweating, trembling, nausea, tingling or numbness in the fingers and toes, and an overwhelming sense of impending doom.

In self-defense circles, the neurophysiological response most commonly discussed is the "**adrenaline dump**," which is shorthand for the sudden

---

[14] https://www.nhs.uk/every-mind-matters/mental-health-issues/anxiety/
[15] https://www.ncbi.nlm.nih.gov/pmc/articles/PMC3079864/

chemical change we experience when a threat activates our **fight-or-flight reaction**. Adrenaline dumps affect our whole body, brain included. You might have heard stories about people who managed amazing feats in emergencies: lifting cars off children, rescuing people from burning buildings with no protective gear, and so on. However, for most of us, most of the time, adrenaline is not a source of superpowers. In fact, an adrenaline dump can negatively affect our perceptions and reactions, making us unable to respond effectively to our situation.

During an adrenaline dump, we might experience the following:

- Increased heart rate and blood pressure.

- Increased speed and strength.

- Decreased sensitivity to pain.

- Decreased co-ordination, in particular fine motor skills.

- Decreased blood flow to the surface of the skin.

- Tunnel vision.

- Impaired or reduced hearing.

- Impaired or reduced thinking.

- Misperception of time (everything slows down).

- Repetitive behavior loops (e.g. repeating the same sentence or movement, regardless of whether it's working).

These neurophysiological changes may not sound all that great, but they are a feature, not a bug: they are designed to help us deal with threats by supercharging some physiological functions and turning others right down. The idea is to divert all our resources towards the functions that can help us deal with the threat at hand. Unfortunately, this system evolved *way* back, when our ancestors were dealing with certain types of threats. If we are trying to fend off a hungry wolverine that has attached itself to our leg, being able to repeatedly hit it harder and faster than we normally could, without being distracted by our pain or our environment, while bleeding less than usual, might give us enough of an edge to survive the encounter.[16] If we are trying to deal with other types of threat, however, being temporarily incapable of hearing, seeing, thinking, and moving properly might not work to our advantage.

---

[16] Please, do not test this theory.

Alas, our bodies don't know that. They have been honed over millennia to deal with threats a certain way, because doing so kept our ancestors alive. Even though our environment and demands have changed, our bodies will continue to work as they are designed to do, whether we like it or not. This is a serious issue if we experience an adrenaline dump in the face of a threat that requires us to engage our cognitive or fine-motor skills. For instance, in the face of a sudden emergency we might find ourselves unable to use the phone, because our hands do not obey us, or even to remember that we have a phone we can use. Again, this is all part of a natural neurophysiological response, but it's still suboptimal.

Thankfully, these issues are not insurmountable. There are ways for us to train for a greater degree of control in the face of threats – a process referred to as **stress inoculation**. The idea behind stress inoculation is that increased competence and confidence in a given situation can decrease our degree of adrenalization. This makes perfect sense: if we know that we can cope with a threat, that threat becomes less threatening, so our neurophysiological response won't be as intense. Furthermore, the simple act of performing successfully while adrenalized can help us remain relatively calm despite the chemical storm rushing through our body.

Stress inoculation requires time and energy spent in a very specific way. We need to accumulate positive experiences while adrenalized, which requires a combination of threat exposure, effective training, and good results. If these three components aren't consistently present, the process will fail. When carried out properly, however, stress inoculation can have great results. It's why we can have professional surgeons, paramedics, firefighters, and so on: these specialists work hard to learn to remain calm and competent in the middle of situations that would send most of us into a spin.

However, the results of this kind of training aren't always transferrable. Even those of us who successfully learn to deal with one set of circumstances might be unable to deal with another – for instance, a surgeon might panic if faced with a burning building. And none of this can help us if we do not have the opportunity to practice in an environment where we can succeed. Success is essential to the process, because it's essential to building our confidence. Repeatedly being dumped in situations where we fail while adrenalized won't help us; on the contrary, it will most likely increase both how adrenalized we get and how badly that affects our performance.

Furthermore, stress inoculation is designed to help us deal with the neurophysiological responses caused by short-term emergencies. If we are dealing with long-term or chronic problems, other issues arise.

Stress is defined as the body's response to situations that create taxing demands.[17] Stress is the natural response in the face of **stressors** – physical, psychological, or social forces that place real or perceived demands on us. Stressors, like other threats, trigger neurophysiological responses that affect our body's **homeostasis** – the state of internal balance that allows our body to function at peak performance. Stressors, in a nutshell, send our bodies temporarily out of whack. This impact is real and proven. There is even an accepted scale to measure the relative impact of different stressors, known as The Holmes and Rahe Stress Scale[18].

A degree of occasional stress is an unavoidable part of life, and is not necessarily bad. It's all about our level of stress, and how long the stress goes on for.

- **Eustress** is short-term stress within our coping abilities. Eustress motivates us, energizes us, and improves our performance. This type of stress is usually considered beneficial.

- **Distress** is stress beyond our coping abilities. Distress causes us anxiety, and can decrease our performance.

The level of stress we are under determines not only its impact on our life, but also the impact of additional stressors. If we are already operating near capacity, even minor extra stressors may push us beyond our coping limits and into distress. If we are operating under high levels of stress, activities we normally find tolerable or even pleasurable may become too much for us. This state will continue until our stress levels are reduced.

- **Chronic stress** is exactly what it sounds like: stress that doesn't go away. Our stress responses are designed to be short-lived and self-limiting: once the threat goes away, our bodies naturally return to normal. If the threat persists, however, our bodies remain out of whack. Over time, this can make us very sick, or even kill us.[19]

Stress is currently believed to be a risk factor for 75% to 90% of diseases,

---

[17] https://www.mentalhelp.net/articles/types-of-stressors-eustress-vs-distress/
[18] http://www.mindtools.com/pages/article/newTCS_82.htm
[19] https://www.mayoclinic.org/healthy-lifestyle/stress-management/in-depth/stress/art-20046037

including cardiovascular disorders, metabolic and endocrine disorders, neurodegenerative disorders, cancer, and a whole bunch of other fun stuff. It can also interfere with our immune system, increasing our susceptibility to contagious diseases. The mechanisms for these effects have not been established yet, but they are currently believed to involve cortisol.

Cortisol, one of the stress hormones, has a whole bunch of far-ranging effects on the body. For instance, it increases blood sugar levels, alters immune system responses, and suppresses the digestive and reproductive systems. It also affects the brain regions that control mood, motivation, and fear. Just like adrenaline, cortisol isn't bad for us; what hurts us is being exposed to elevated cortisol levels for prolonged periods of time.

Chronic stress is a health issue because it predisposes us to a variety of illnesses. However, stress in and of itself isn't a medical issue. Our doctors may tell us that we need to take it easy or warn us about the impact of stress on our health. However, unless our stress is caused by unmet medical needs, they are unlikely to be able to help us lower our stress levels.

Strictly speaking, stress and stressors are not a mental health issue, either. Stress can affect our mental health: when we are under excessive or chronic levels of stress we may feel pretty bad and experience a decline in cognitive functions. Our emotional responses may be out of whack, too. However, the root of our problems is not in our heads. We aren't responding to normal circumstances in an abnormal manner because our brain is playing up; on the contrary, we are responding to our circumstances precisely the way our body is designed to.

Having said that, stress and stressors can lead to a host of mental health issues. For instance, the acute stress experienced in response to a traumatic event can cause Acute Stress Disorder (ASD) and Post-Traumatic Stress Disorder (PTSD). Exposure to chronic stress, on the other hand, increases our risk of developing depression and anxiety disorders. When we are under stress, the parts of our brain that handle higher-order tasks are less active, while the parts of our brain that deal with survival are more active. Over time, the parts of our brain that get the most exercise, so to speak, become stronger, while those that aren't exercised enough become weaker.[20] If the areas of our brain responsible for anxiety are over-developed, we are more likely to experience anxiety.

---

[20] https://www.health.harvard.edu/mind-and-mood/protect-your-brain-from-stress

Anxiety disorders are **mental health conditions**. For a person to be diagnosed with an anxiety disorder, their anxiety must affect their day-to-day life and must be either uncalled for or out of proportion with their circumstances.[21] Anxiety disorders can impact our ability to function in certain situations, prompt us to avoid them,[22] or make us unable to enjoy them. They are classified according to the circumstances in which they affect us:[23]

- **Generalized Anxiety Disorder (GAD):** a condition characterized by persistent feelings of anxiety about a wide range of situations and issues.

- **Social Anxiety Disorder (SAD):** a condition characterized by intense, persistent fear in social situations.

- **Specific Phobias (SPs):** intense, out-of-proportion fear or aversion to specific objects or situations.

- **Panic attacks:** sudden periods of intense fear not associated with a clear danger.[24]

- **Panic Disorder:** persistent, intense worry about the possibility of experiencing panic attacks.[25]

With the possible exception of Panic Disorder, all these conditions have one thing in common: the anxiety we experience is persistent or disproportionate. I know that I'm repeating myself here, but this is important. If we have proportionate neurophysiological responses to real-life problems, we may feel absolutely terrible, but that does not mean that we have a mental health condition. It just means that, for whatever reasons, our lives kind of sucks.

Unfortunately, this distinction is not always picked up by medical specialists. Doctors don't always have the time, knowledge, and empathy required to work out the causes of their patients' mental states. As a result, patients whose anxiety is an appropriate response to real stressors may be diagnosed with an anxiety disorder, and treated accordingly. This

---

[21] https://www.nhsinform.scot/healthy-living/mental-wellbeing/anxiety-and-panic/why-do-i-feel-anxious-and-panicky
[22] https://www.apa.org/topics/anxiety
[23] https://www.nimh.nih.gov/health/topics/anxiety-disorders
[24] https://ideas.ted.com/the-science-behind-panic-attacks-and-what-can-you-do-to-manage-them/
[25] In the immortal words of Charlie Brown, "My anxieties have anxieties."

is a serious problem, because the treatments for anxiety disorders are not cure-alls. Quite the contrary, in fact.

One of the most popular treatments for all anxiety disorders is **cognitive behavioral therapy (CBT)**. The basic principle of CBT is that our thoughts, feelings, physical sensations, and actions are interconnected. When that connection works to our disadvantage, we can take steps to change it. For instance, we might find that faulty ways of thinking have a negative impact on our feelings, or that learned patterns of behavior steer us towards inappropriate actions. We are all creatures of mental, emotional, and behavioral habits; by changing these habits, we may improve our lives.

A key element of CBT is identifying and challenging false and self-limiting beliefs. For people with social anxiety, for instance, this may involve examining beliefs such as "everyone hates me" by actually working out how many people have given us proof that they hate us. The underlying idea is that by challenging the accuracy of these beliefs we can replace them with more accurate, more useful ones. That allows us to approach social situations with a more positive mindset, which can reduce our anxiety. A reduction in our anxiety can allow us to behave differently in social settings – for instance, it may allow us to be more active in our social interactions – which can allow us to achieve better outcomes. These positive experiences can feed back into our new beliefs, creating a positive feedback loop. This methodology makes good scientific sense and works for a lot of people.

Unfortunately, CBT has one major pitfall: its practitioners do not always take the time to check the accuracy of their patients' "false and self-limiting" beliefs, or the appropriateness of "unhelpful" behaviors in their personal context. This problem is not unique to CBT; therapists using other techniques are just as likely to fail to investigate the accuracy of their patients' concerns, particularly when such concerns are totally alien to them. This becomes particularly critical when patients are disabled, marginalized, or oppressed, and their therapists are not.

For instance, a therapist unfamiliar with the impact of neurodivergence on daily life may believe that neurodivergent patients are showing signs of paranoia when we discuss instances of discrimination or ostracism, or signs of unfounded anxiety when we raise concerns about the health of our relationships, our financial security, or our ability to navigate adulthood and its responsibilities. If we are also marginalized and oppressed in other ways, uninformed therapists may understand us even less; if they are unaware of the impact of single discriminations and disadvantages, negotiating intersectionality is going to be completely beyond them. The issue is further compounded when therapists hold unexamined biases; until they accept their own part in the problem, they will be unable to admit that it has a real, negative impact on the lives of their patients. The bottom line is that until therapists become aware of the impact of disability, marginalization, and oppression, they will not be able to fully support their disabled, marginalized, and oppressed patients.

This disconnect is particularly significant in CBT, because CBT works by teaching us to challenge our thoughts. Unhelpful, incorrect, negative thoughts should be replaced with helpful, accurate, positive thoughts. The problem is that not all negative thoughts are incorrect. We may think that our colleagues find us weird, and be right. We might think that our family members love us but do not like us, and be right. We might think that our employer only tolerates us because we work twice as hard as everyone else, and that if we ever stopped driving ourselves into the ground we'd be fired, and be right. We might not be able to provide proof for any of this, though, because most people don't say stuff like that out loud; but that doesn't mean that we are wrong. Insisting that we are, and that our life would magically fix itself if only we could think about it differently, is **gaslighting** – a form of persistent brainwashing that causes the victim to doubt themselves, their perceptions, their sanity, and their self-worth. Needless to say, that's not what we should look for in a therapeutic intervention.

Similar concerns apply to the behavioral aspect of CBT. Some habits that are deemed inappropriate or unhelpful are actually adaptations to a particular situation or environment. We might have learned to be "excessively" restrained around our colleagues because letting our neurodivergence show has caused us problems in the past. We might have learned to "overplan" and "overthink" because when we don't, we mess up, and our mistakes are too expensive. Heck, we might behave differently from our therapists simply because we belong to a different culture or subculture, with different criteria for what is "normal." Therapists who are unfamiliar with our social milieu and don't take the time to investigate it might push for behavioral changes that would be maladaptive.

CBT is a great therapy for reducing the impact of false and self-limiting beliefs. It is not a good therapy for reducing the impact of real, limiting realities. This problem is not inherent to CBT; the issue is not with the practice itself, but with individual therapists and their unwillingness to listen to and learn from their patients' experiences. This problem is also not unique to CBT; it affects not only other talking therapies, but the medical and research establishment.

There is a simple explanation for this: in many countries, becoming a medical specialist or a researcher requires a degree of socioeconomic privilege. As a result, many specialists are oblivious to the challenges faced by less privileged people, or underestimate their impact.

This issue is often apparent in the way in which mental health questionnaires are formulated. Questionnaires often assume that everyone is living fundamentally similar lives, and that if they have any "abnormal" concerns or reactions, these must be a sign of underlying mental health issues. For instance, in the last year, I have completed mental health questionnaires that included the following questions:

- Do you find it hard to sit still?

- Do you have high levels of anticipatory anxiety prior to a flight?

- Do you believe that you are the subject of persistent, intrusive attention by others?

I am an ADHDer. I always find it hard to sit still, and it has nothing to do with whether I'm anxious or not. I have severe allergic asthma. I have high levels of anticipatory anxiety prior to any situation in which I may be exposed to artificial scents in a confined environment, because I don't know whether I will be able to breathe. And as for being the subject of persistent, intrusive attention by others... I am openly trans on the internet. Intrusive attention, and the odd death threat, come with the territory.

I live with these realities, but my doctors don't. Therefore, every time these issues become relevant in a medical context, I have to justify my answers in order to prove that my psychoemotional states are an appropriate response to my reality; specifically, that I am not suffering from an anxiety disorder, aerophobia, or paranoia.

This issue doesn't just affect me, or people like me. Personally, I have yet to see a mental health questionnaire that takes into account the fact that different people live different lives that present them with different stressors, which add up to different stress levels.

Anything that increases the number and intensity of the stressor we face is likely to increase our stress levels, and while that might have an impact on our mental health, it isn't primarily a mental health issue. These distinctions are absolutely critical if we are attempting to navigate or manage our anxious feelings. Anxious feelings that originate in our brain respond best to changes in **how we think**. Anxious feelings that originate from external stressors respond best to changes in **how we live**. This means that before we start working on our anxious feelings, we need to work out what's actually going on: do we have anxiety, or are we under excessive stress? In order to disentangle that, it helps to be familiar with the stressors we might be dealing with. That's what we will be doing in the next chapter.

Neurodivergent stress and stressors

Why is stress a neurodivergent issue? Quite simply, because much of the modern world isn't designed by or for us. Most of us are constantly bombarded by demands we struggle to meet in environments we struggle to tolerate. The larger the gap between what we are expected to do and what we can do easily, the higher our stress will be.

Sometimes, the connection between our demands and our stress is straightforward; for instance, if we have a number of environmental sensitivities, every trigger is a potential stressor. Sometimes the cause-and-effect chain is a bit longer; for instance, if we can reliably anticipate that something bad will happen to us if we do X, because every time we do X something bad happens to us, then doing X will be a stressor.

Ultimately, anything that makes us different from the statistical norm is a potential stressor – or, more accurately, it increases our chance of being exposed to stressors. This isn't because being different is inherently bad, but because it is so often punished, overtly or covertly.

If we look, speak, move, or act differently from the majority of other people, we are more likely to find ourselves in the middle of unpleasant social and antisocial situations. Whether this puts us in physical danger or not will depend on a number of factors, such as our race, gender, social status, and so on. However, even situations where we are physically safe can have a significant impact on our stress levels. Humans are social animals, designed to survive in groups. As far as our brains are concerned, anything that threatens our chances of belonging to a group is a threat to our survival. Social exclusion and isolation might not kill us, but they would have killed our ancestors, so they register as significant threats. Being constantly exposed to these threats can make us unwell.

While learning not to care about everyone's opinion is a valuable skill, learning to tolerate being disliked by the majority is a whole other story. Humans are not designed for that. As a result, any trait that puts us at risk of widespread social rejection forces us to make a choice: do we hide that aspect of ourselves to gain a modicum of acceptance, or do we face the risk of ostracism, or worse? Both of these choices carry significant costs, and both can cause us chronic stress. This chronic stress saps our resources and puts us at higher risk of lower immune responses and chronic inflammation, which can in turn lead to a variety of ailments.

In addition to the stress we experience because of our neurodivergent traits, many of us also deal with a host of co-existing medical and physical conditions that reduce our ability to meet our demands while taxing our resources. While these conditions have not yet been proven to be directly linked to neurodivergence, they are overrepresented within the neurodivergent community.

Our specific blend of neurodivergent traits and co-existing conditions will determine the stressors we face. The list below is not exhaustive, but attempts to include the stressors most common within the neurodivergent community. As this issue is poorly studied, information on the prevalence of these stressors refers to the results of a public survey about the experiences of neurodivergent people I ran in 2022.[26]

Please note that this information is presented **for educational purposes only.** It should not be used for self-diagnosis, or to diagnose someone else. If you are concerned about any of the stressors listed, you should consult a professional.

---

[26] https://www.amazon.com/dp/B0B191VH7B/

Environmental stressors

Many neurodivergents have sensory experiences that differ from those of neurotypical people. Sometimes we are able to pick up stimuli neurotypicals cannot register; for instance, we might hear noises they can't hear. Sometimes our bodies register otherwise harmless stimuli as painful; for instance, people with allodynia experience light touch as painful. Sometimes we are hypersensitive or allergic to certain stimuli; for instance, flashing lights or contrasting light and dark patterns can trigger headaches, migraines, or seizures in photosensitive people.

These responses are physiological, not emotional or psychological. This distinction is critical as it affects the resulting therapeutic approaches.

Anything that triggers a painful physiological response is a stressor. Inputs that do not hurt us but distract us are also stressors, because they can decrease our ability to function effectively in that environment. As stressors are cumulative, environments that contain multiple triggers will affect us more severely.

Sometimes atypical sensory experiences are caused by an identifiable **environmental sensitivity**; for instance, if our immune system mistakes a harmless substance for something harmful, we will experience allergy symptoms when we are exposed to that substance. Common allergy triggers include pollen, foods, and animals. Sometimes atypical sensory experiences are caused by **underlying health conditions**; for instance, fibromyalgia can make even light touches painful. Sometimes, however, the underlying causes of our atypical sensory experiences cannot be identified. In that event, we might be diagnosed with a **Sensory Processing Disorder**.

Environmental sensitivities

Environmental sensitivities sometimes co-occur with atypically acute senses. For instance, sensitivities to airborne allergens can co-occur with hyperosmia – a heightened sense of smell that can cause discomfort or illness in response to certain odors.[27] However, that isn't always the case; we may be sensitive to airborne allergens we cannot smell. That means

---

[27] If you are interested in hyperosmia and like sci-fi, I heartily recommend Spider Robinson's "Telempath." And the recommendation still stands if you don't give a hoot about hyperosmia and just like good sci-fi.
https://www.amazon.com/dp/B00TEESLKO

that we don't know that we are being exposed until our allergic responses kick in, which is super fun. Also, prolonged exposure to allergens can irritate or obstruct the mucus membranes in the nose, leading to reduced sense of smell (hyposmia) or loss of smell (anosmia). These sensory losses can be permanent or temporary. A person can oscillate between hyperosmia and anosmia depending on how inflamed their nose is.

Environmental sensitivities are real, and they can have a real impact on or health. Even those that aren't immediately dangerous can lead to long-term negative health outcomes. For instance, allergic rhinitis may "only" cause sneezing, a runny nose, temporary anosmia, and watery eyes. When left untreated, however, it can lead to chronic nasal inflammation and obstruction, sinusitis, ear infections, sleep apnea, upper respiratory tract infections, and Eustachian tube dysfunction. Allergic rhinitis can also increase sensitivity to substances a person isn't allergic to. Already inflamed tissues is generally more sensitive, so it takes less to irritate them. As a result, otherwise harmless substances can become harmful, or at the very least painful.

Environmental sensitivities are not limited to airborne allergens. We may be sensitive to stimuli affecting any of our senses, including sight, sound, taste, and touch. As with sensitivities linked with the sense of smell, sensitivities linked to other senses may or may not coexist with a heightened ability to perceive certain stimuli. For instance, 75% of survey respondents are able to hear noises the majority of people cannot hear. These sounds are not always tolerable; depending on their pitch and volume, they may be distracting, disturbing, or downright painful. However, sensitivities and heightened perception aren't always linked. For instance, 75% of respondents get headaches from bright lights, but that doesn't necessarily mean that their eyesight is abnormally good.

Environmental sensitivities should be taken into account when evaluating our aversion to certain spaces or experiences. This is particularly significant when evaluating aversions to spaces and experiences that expose us to multiple triggers – for instance, places like supermarkets, which are full of smells, bright lights, and noises – or from where we cannot escape – for instance, planes or schools.

Sensory Processing Disorders

If our atypical sensory experience is recognized by a specialist and underlying health conditions and environmental sensitivities have been ruled out, we may be diagnosed with a **Sensory Processing Disorder**. However, these diagnoses are not easy to come by. 39% of survey respondents have a sensory processing disorder (auditory processing disorder, mostly), but only 8% have a formal diagnosis.

Sensory Processing Disorders are defined as "impairments in the detection, modulation, or interpretation of stimuli."[28] All of the senses can be affected. SPDs can manifest both as over-responsivity or sensory hypersensitivity, and as under-responsivity or hyposensitivity.[29]

Please note that this definition does not make a distinction between sensitivity and responsivity – i.e., whether the issue is with how much we sense or how strongly we react to it. This is a huge issue.

Let's talk about dogs. Dogs can hear sounds at frequencies above the human auditory range. Hence the existence of "silent" dog whistles, which are not silent at all; most humans just can't hear those frequencies, while most dogs do. Say that I brought home a new fan, and my dogs ran out of the room the moment I turned it on and refused to come back in until I turned it off. I could accuse them of engaging in some kind of canine conspiracy against me, punish them for their blatant disrespect for my authority, and force them to sit in that room, with that fan running, until they gave up their nonsense. I might, however, consider the possibility that their superior auditory range might be a factor. Could it be that what I perceive as a quiet hum is to them the sound of nails scratching against an endless chalkboard? In that case, they would be reacting to a stimulus I cannot perceive, rather than over-reacting to nothing much. And if I knowingly and deliberately exposed them to that sound for a protracted period of time, I would be committing animal abuse.

As a society, we routinely fail to extend that level of care and consideration to neurodivergent people, especially children. We know that people differ in their ability to perceive their environment; that is why prescription glasses and hearing aids exist. We also know that these natural differences can affect the rest of our senses, including touch,[30] taste,[31] and smell.[32] We know that our sensory perception tends to decline

---

[28] https://www.ncbi.nlm.nih.gov/pmc/articles/PMC3149116/

[29] https://www.integratedtreatmentservices.co.uk/blog/sensory-hyper-hyposensitivity-autism/

[30] https://www.griffinot.com/touch-sense-sensory-processing/

[31] https://www.ncbi.nlm.nih.gov/pmc/articles/PMC1698869/

[32] https://www.sciencedaily.com/releases/2019/04/190430164208.htm

as we age,[33] which is why anti-teens sonic repellents are effective.[34] Yet when neurodivergent children react to a stimulus in atypical ways, neurotypical adults routinely fail to investigate whether that reaction is the result of hypersensitivity or over-reactivity.

It gets worse. When hypersensitive children express their discomfort through a verbal or physical outburst or any type of "misbehavior," they may be punished for having a "tantrum." That is a double whammy: not only are these children not protected from painful stimuli by the adults responsible for their care; they are punished for trying to protect themselves. 28% of respondents reported that they got into trouble for having "tantrums" when trying to avoid painful physical sensations.

As we grow up, many of us learn to tolerate sensations we find unpleasant or overwhelming, simply because we can't avoid them. 18% of respondents are routinely forced to endure unpleasant or overwhelming physical sensations in order to navigate their environment.

Our ability to endure those sensations doesn't mean that they no longer have an impact on us, even though we might have lost the ability to notice that. 56% of the respondents who are routinely forced to endure unpleasant or overwhelming physical sensations are unable to recognize their own feelings, and 64% feel disconnected from their thoughts, feelings, memories, and surroundings. The results for the same parameters for survey respondents overall was 36% and 38%. This suggests a correlation between symptoms of alexithymia (a difficulty experiencing, identifying, and expressing emotions), symptoms of dissociation (disconnection from our thoughts, feelings, memories or sense of identity) and being forced to routinely endure unpleasant or overwhelming physical sensations. These responses may be useful, but they are not healthy.

At the opposite end of the SPD spectrum is hyposensitivity - abnormally decreased sensitivity to sensory inputs. Hyposensitivity brings its own problems. As with hypersensitivity, these problems are partly derived from the hyposensitivity itself, and partly by how it can be misinterpreted by the people in our life.

Auditory Processing Disorder is the easiest example of these issues. People with APD may have normal hearing, but struggle to listen. This is

---

[33] https://medlineplus.gov/ency/article/004013.htm
[34] https://www.scientificamerican.com/article/bring-science-home-high-frequency-hearing/

due to impaired sound processing in the central auditory nervous system.[35] For instance, a person may have perfect hearing, but might be unable to follow a conversation in a room with background noise. Their ears can pick up the sounds in the room, but their nervous system cannot pick out the relevant ones. 38% of survey respondents have APD. However, 18% of respondents are never able to follow a conversation in a room with background noise, and 53% can only do it sometimes. This gives us a total of 71% of respondents who struggle with this kind of sensory processing.

APD can also present different symptoms, such as auditory memory problems (difficulties recalling verbal information), auditory attention problems (difficulties maintaining focus on auditory input), auditory discrimination problems (difficulties hearing the difference between similar words or sounds), and auditory cohesion problems (difficulties putting together or processing complex auditory information).[36]

APD is well-documented. Unfortunately, it is not widely known, and its symptoms are often misconstrued as a failure to show respect, pay attention, or to understand. You know that a child can hear you, but they don't answer when you call them? They are clearly defying you! You told them exactly what you wanted them to do, and they looked like they were listening, but then they did something else entirely? They clearly didn't pay any attention to a word you said! Or maybe they just aren't smart enough to understand you. These suppositions can lead adults to behave unfairly towards children who are simply unable to process auditory information as well as their peers. When these children respond badly to their mistreatment, their reaction might be construed as yet another symptom of their defiance, disrespect, or lack of understanding.

PTSD flashbacks

Post-traumatic stress disorder (PTSD) is not a sensory issue, but it can result in extreme and distressing responses to sensory experiences associated with our trauma. In PTSD flashbacks, a trigger causes our brain to replay the memory of the traumatic event. As a result, some of us re-experience that trigger as they did during the traumatic event, even though it is objectively different. For instance, a baby who was badly scalded in the bath may perceive all bath water as too hot, even when the

---

[35] https://www.nhs.uk/conditions/auditory-processing-disorder/
[36] https://kidshealth.org/en/parents/central-auditory.html

thermometer clearly shows that it's not.[37] If we are not aware of our triggers – for instance, because the experience took place when we were too young to consciously remember it – our reaction can be misconstrued as a sensory processing issue, or simply as an over-reaction or tantrum.

Even relatively minor negative experiences can leave permanent tracks in our memory, especially if we go through them when we are too young to work out what happened. For instance, if we get food poisoning from eating a certain food, later on we may feel nauseous if we smell it, or even if we just think about eating it.

These reactions are designed to keep us safe from further harm, but they can cause us serious difficulties. This is one occasion in which desensitization therapies, designed to help us manage our responses to non-painful stimuli, can genuinely help.

Misophonia

Misophonia is a condition in which certain sounds — for instance, breathing, yawning, chewing, licking, sucking, and other mouth noises – trigger an instantaneous negative emotional or physiological response. Reactions usually fall somewhere within the fight-or-flight spectrum: we might become enraged at the cause of the noise, or panic to the point of wanting to flee.

The causes of misophonia have not been discovered yet, but it isn't connected to abnormally good hearing. fMRI studies suggest that it might be linked to differences in the function of the anterior insular cortex (AIC) – a part of the brain that plays a role both in anger and in integrating outside inputs with inputs from our internal organs.

Different people are affected by different sounds and in different ways. Our sensitivity and our ability to control our reactions can be affected by our stress levels.

There is no cure for misophonia, but there are strategies for dealing with it:

- Removing the source of the noise trigger.

- Removing ourselves from the noise trigger.

---

[37] No prizes for guessing why I picked this example. :-D You know that good ol' insult, "go boil your head?" I've tried it, and I would not recommend it.

- Protecting ourselves from the noise trigger; for instance, by wearing noise-cancelling headphones or listening to white noise.

Unfortunately, none of these strategies are always practical or without repercussions. As a result, misophonia can have a significant negative impact on our functioning, socializing, and mental health.

From personal experience and anecdotal evidence, misophonic people tend to fall into one of two camps: those who believe that anyone who makes trigger noises is in the wrong and ought to stop immediately, and those who are ashamed of their emotional reactions, even though they can't control them and they don't act them out. Neither group is correct in their assumptions: misophonia is not a moral failing, but the rest of humanity has a right to eat their lunch, even though the resulting noises make us want to strangle them.

Performance stressors

Performance stressors are anything that makes it harder for us to meet our life's demands. The impact of these stressors will depend not only on how much they affect us – for instance, on how poor our working memory is - but on how often these stressors come into play and how much trouble we get into if we fail to perform as a result.

This issue is at the core of most discussions as to whether neurodivergences are disabilities. The problem is that "disability" is often treated as a one-size-fits-all-or-nobody issue, with no regard for the fact that different people have to meet different demands, so they need to be able to achieve different things. For instance, it's common to see celebrities harp on about how they manage their ADHD without meds by carefully managing their diet and exercise... but when we look more closely, we find out that they have actually outsourced their diet, exercise, and most of their adulting to various members of staff. If we all had a PA to handle our daily schedule, a cook to prepare and serve the optimal meals at the optimal time, a gym coach to supervise our exercise, a cleaner to keep our home, and nannies and animal carers to take care of our dependents, we would probably cope without meds. Alas, most of us don't live like that.

Most of us have to meet demands we can't just farm out to minions. If we struggle to meet those demands, that will cause us stress. Anything that affects the demands we have to face or the severity of our stressors will affect the amount of stress they cause us. The greater the gap between what we can do and what we are expected to do, the greater our stress. This is likely to be why some of us go undiagnosed until later on in life; we truly don't know how much our neurodivergence impact our abilities until those abilities are tested.

However, even a diagnosis may not help us. A lot of us struggle with long-term problems with basic functioning that are ubiquitous within our neurotype, but are not included in current diagnostic criteria. We are effectively disabled in ways we might not realize, because nobody bothers to tell us that the vast majority of people don't share our struggles. While we may still achieve, we might do so by working much harder than our peers, and still not achieve as much as we would like or we "should." When we fail to achieve, we may end up blaming ourselves.

Memory deficits

"Memory" refers to the process of encoding, storing, and recalling information. It's a complicated and somewhat contentious subject we don't fully understand yet. I will attempt to summarize the key points, but if you want a comprehensive introduction, I recommend you check out the "Memory" section of the Queensland Brain Institute website.[38]

Encoding refers to the way in which we absorb information and convert it for storage. Many people find it easier to process certain types of information – for instance, we may prefer visual, auditory, or kinesthetic inputs. When we form memories, we convert inputs into the type of information that works best for our storage system, so to speak. For instance, if we are visual learners and thinkers, we may memorize how a picture looks. If we are verbal learners and thinkers, on the other hand, we might memorize our mental description of the picture, rather than the picture itself.

There are two main types of memory storage: short-term and long-term memory. Information is first stored in our short-term memory, and then transferred to our long-term memory if necessary. Short-term memory is limited both in duration and the amount of items it can hold. For instance, working memory, the shortest type of short-term memory, lasts only 15 to 30 seconds and can hold between five and nine items, seven on average. Long-term memory, on the other hand, has a much greater storage capacity and can hold information indefinitely.

Recall refers to the process through which we access stored information. During memory recall, the brain replicates the neural activity that took place while the memory was formed. Memories aren't just retrieved from storage, like books from a shelf; they are recreated from information scattered throughout the brain.

Any part of this process can fail, temporarily or permanently. Some people struggle to commit information to memory, but once it's in there, it's safe and easily accessible. Some people find it easy to memorize information, but bits of it seem to disappear in storage. Some people know that they know something, but they can't recall the information at will. These issues can affect all types of information, or be restricted to specific types. For instance, "lethologica" is the inability to remember the right word, while "lethonomia" is the inability to remember names.

---

[38] https://qbi.uq.edu.au/brain-basics/memory

58% of survey respondents have problems storing information in their long-term memory, 59% have problems accessing their long-term memory, and a whopping 74% have working memory problems.

Working memory is "a system for temporarily storing and managing the information required to carry out cognitive tasks such as learning, reasoning, and comprehension."[39] Working memory problems can be the result of a number of physical and mental health conditions, as well as being a common feature in neurodivergence. Furthermore, working memory is not a stable feature. It is negatively affected by a number of factors,[40] including pain, stress, sleep deprivation,[41] and negative emotional states.[42] Some people with poor working memory show improvements from brain training programs. The mechanism underlying these improvements has not been established yet.[43]

A poor working memory can have a profound impact on a person's life, because we use our working memory all the time without realizing it: to carry out mental arithmetic, follow instructions, prioritize tasks, solve problems, and generally just to get on with our day. Not being able to rely on those mental sticky notes can make it very hard for us to establish a smooth work flow. It can turn simple tasks into complicated processes, and complicated tasks into unmanageable messes.

Poor working memory can also cause interpersonal issues, especially for people who are not considered at risk for conditions such as dementia. Working memory problems are not always easily identifiable from the outside, and are often mistaken for a lack of attention, interest, respect, or intelligence. People may get frustrated because we lost track of what they were saying, or because they have told us the same thing already, perhaps several times. They might conclude that we are deliberately slighting them; if we actually gave a damn, we would have listened the first time! Alternatively, they might conclude that we are just not smart enough to understand them or to carry out certain tasks, when the actual issue is that we cannot hold a list of instructions in our head. This is blatant ableism, and explaining to people that we actually have a memory problem does not always resolve it.

---

[39] https://www.medicinenet.com/working_memory/definition.htm
[40] https://www.ncbi.nlm.nih.gov/pmc/articles/PMC5973525/
[41] https://www.sciencedirect.com/science/article/abs/pii/S2211368116301875
[42] https://academic.oup.com/scan/article/12/6/984/3574847
[43] https://www.apa.org/monitor/sep05/workout

Our memory problems can have severe impacts on our daily life. For instance, 51% of respondents forget important appointments or obligations, despite the fact that 84% of them use multiple reminders to help them remember.

Memory problems can also manifest in less obvious ways. For instance, losing things is associated with failures in memory encoding. 79% of survey respondents lose things. 45% of respondents use a strict storage system to try and avoid this problem, but 75% of them still lose things. 70% of respondents perform repeated checks to make sure that they have not lost or forgotten things (a behavior often mistaken for Obsessive Compulsive Disorder, or OCD), but 81% of them still lose things.

Learning styles

Learning styles are a somewhat controversial concept in education. The underlying theory is that each person has a way in which they find it easiest to learn. As a result, they will find it easier to learn when material is presented in the way that best suits their learning style.

There are two main issues with this. Firstly, it's rare for people to have just one learning style, which is why the statistics provided below add up to more than 100%. Secondly, our learning preferences matter just as much outside of school. Being unable to absorb and store information at work, at the doctors', at the bank, and so on can have a huge negative impact on our life. However, learning styles are largely ignored outside of educational settings.

Traditionally, learning styles are classified as follows:

- **Auditory:** learning is easiest when information is presented verbally. 10% of respondents are auditory learners.

- **Reading/writing:** learning is easiest when information is presented as text. 26% of respondents are reading/writing learners.

- **Visual:** learning is easiest when information is presented visually – e.g. as pictures, diagrams, visual demonstrations, and so on. 43% of respondents are visual learners.

- **Kinesthetic:** learning is easiest through physical activities - e.g. carrying out manual tasks, physically handling objects, acting out events, or translating concepts, even abstract ones, into physical sensations. 48% of respondents are kinesthetic learners.

- **Combined:** learning is easiest when the same information is presented in multiple formats at the same time. 56% of respondents are combined learners.

Over half of survey respondents are combined learners, while only 10% are auditory learners. This has huge implications on our ability to perform as required not only in the classroom, but in any setting where information is provided verbally.

Learning disabilities

Learning disabilities are information-processing problems that can prevent a person from learning a skill and using it effectively. They are not a reflection of a person's intelligence; in fact, they generally affect people of average or above average intelligence. The result is a gap between expectations and performance.[44]

The most commonly-known learning disabilities are:[45]

- **Dyscalculia** affects the ability to understand numbers and perform basic math skills. 16% of respondents are dyscalculic, but 42% of respondents have difficulties with math.

- **Dysgraphia** affects not only the mechanics of writing, but also grammar, syntax, comprehension, and the ability to put thoughts on paper. 5% of respondents are dysgraphic, but 19% have difficulties writing.

- **Dyslexia** affects the skills involved in accurate and fluent reading and spelling. 11% of respondents are dyslexic, but 13% have difficulties reading.

As you can see, learning disabilities are diagnosed according to how they impact our learning. However, there is a huge difference between the percentage of people diagnosed with learning disabilities and those suffering from their symptoms. One of the reasons for that is that in order to get tested for a learning disability, a student must not only show clear traits, but must also be "failing" in one or more domains. Students who struggle but achieve "normal" results may not be put forward for testing. Neither are students who are not expected to succeed, which is one of the

---

[44] https://www.mayoclinic.org/healthy-lifestyle/childrens-health/in-depth/learning-disorders/art-20046105
[45] https://www.webmd.com/children/guide/detecting-learning-disabilities#1

reasons why societal biases have a serious impact on diagnostic rates in different demographic groups.

These diagnostic failures can have a huge impact on our academic achievements and on our life in general. If we are compensating for a learning disability by spending much longer on our schoolwork than our peers, that time has to come from somewhere. Time spent studying is time not spent on other activities, or simply socializing or relaxing. There is a cost to that.

Furthermore, the pressure and demands of school increase as we get older. As a result, neurodivergent children who coped reasonably well when young may hit a wall as they get older. Some of us cope reasonably well with structured academic systems, but go to pieces when we reach university and we are suddenly expected to self-organize. Some of us manage to graduate, but find that our coping strategies fail us in the workplace, because our workarounds and adaptations are not allowed.

The cost of making mistakes in adulthood can be higher, too. Misplacing a digit in a math test can get us an F, but misplacing a digit on a loan application can spell financial ruin.

Learning speed

Learning speed is exactly what it says: the speed at which we learn. It has nothing to do with our ability to learn. For instance, we might learn more slowly than our peers while being able to absorb more information and integrate it better with what we already know.[46] Unfortunately, speed of learning is often mistakenly conflated with intelligence, to the point that calling someone "slow" is used in lieu of calling them "intellectually disabled." This is just wrong, and it needs to stop.

Our speed of learning is not a constant, and can be affected by a variety of factors, including:

- Our ability to function effectively in our learning environment, which can be affected by environmental, medical, and social stressors.

- Our ability to process information in the way in which it is presented,

---

[46] One of the reasons I struggle to process information at times is that I automatically integrate everything I learn with everything I already know. If a piece of information connects with a lot of already-stored data or requires a readjustment of the connections I have made in my data bank, it takes longer for me to run through that process. I realized this literally just now, and wrote it down. I'm nearly 49 and a trained tutor. Yikes.

which is linked to our learning style.

- Our ability to process that particular type of content, which is linked to learning disabilities.

- Our ability to process information at the speed at which it is presented – and this can be a problem when information is presented both too fast and too slowly for us. It's incredibly hard to "pay attention" to people who are talkingtoofast or t o o s l o w l y. If you don't believe me, just pick a video on YouTube, fiddleaboutwiththeplaybackspeed, a n d s e e h o w w e l l y o u f a r e.[47] Similarly, it's incredibly hard to pay attention to people who are talking at a perfectly regular speed if our brain processes things at a different speed.

- Our ability to store information in our short-term memory.

- Our ability to transfer it to our long-term memory.

However, in most settings, our learning speed is actually measured in a completely different way: by our ability to demonstrate our learning by regurgitating information or performing assigned tasks on demand. Being able to perform on demand is a totally different skill, affected by additional factors. It is possible for us to know something perfectly, but to be unable to demonstrate that in the required setting because of factors that negatively impact our performance. Unfortunately, the way in which modern education is geared up rarely allows for that level of nuance. As a result, we might be classed as "slow" – i.e., incapable of learning – because we cannot perform on demand. That's just wrong.

Overstimulation and understimulation

For some of us, our ability to focus on a task is greatly affected by our environment. Some of us cannot focus if there are too many distractions, such as noise or general activity. Some of us, on the other hand, cannot focus if there aren't enough distractions. For some of us, both statements are true: like Goldilocks, we need things to be Just Right. We need a certain amount of stimulation to focus on our work; if that stimulation is missing, or there is too much of it, we struggle.

These issues have been studied, with shocking results: scientists discovered that when people can make adaptations to their environment

---

[47], I find it much easier to listen to most recordings at speeds of 1.25 to 1.50. Unfortunately, humans lack that setting. They also lack subtitles. It's like they're not even trying, really.

that enable them to sustain their attention for longer periods, they can sustain their attention for longer periods. In an even more shocking turn of events, being able to sustain their attention for longer periods increases their productivity and quality of work. Whoddathunkit?!

Alas, those studies are largely ignored. As a result, we are routinely forced to try and perform in environments that cause us to be over- or under-stimulated. We can't listen to music in school or at work, because that could cause us to accidentally enjoy ourselves, but we cannot wear noise-cancelling headphones either, because it's Not The Done Thing. And if (or rather, when) our focus flounders, it's clearly our fault.

These issues impact a lot of us. 73% of survey respondents find it hard to focus on a task when there is activity or noise around them, while 45% find it hard to focus on a task if there isn't enough going on around them. 79% find it hard to focus on one thing at a time.

These results suggest that relatively simple adaptations that shield us from external disturbances while giving us an additional sensory input – for instance, listening to music through noise-cancelling headphones - could greatly increase our ability to focus on a task. This is probably not news to many of us; unfortunately, the concept has yet to catch on with many educational and work efficiency "experts," who still insist that the only way for us to pay attention is to do the stuff that doesn't work, but harder.

Interest systems

In psychology, **interest** is defined as "an individual's momentary experience of being captivated by an object as well as more lasting feelings that the object is enjoyable and worth further exploration."[48] When we are in a "state of interest," we are emotionally and cognitively involved with the task at hand. While we remain interested, our attention and learning feel effortless.

You might have noticed that this definition does not include words like "love," "respect," or "recognize the importance of." We might love a relative, but find their company painfully boring. We might respect a leader for their many fine qualities, but find their speeches snooze-worthy. We might recognize the importance of filing our tax return, but be bored out of our skulls at the mere prospect of doing so.

---

[48] https://www.ncbi.nlm.nih.gov/pmc/articles/PMC5839644/

Lack of interest is not necessarily an issue, unless it has an impact on our ability to meet our demands. Unfortunately, for ADHDers, that's often the case. The ADHD nervous system is **interest-based**, rather than importance- or priority-based – and this is a neurochemical issue, not a moral failing. Although the science on this hasn't been conclusively proven yet, the current theory is that one of the features of the ADHD brain is a difference in our **brain reward system**.

Dopamine is a neurotransmitter and hormone responsible for a whole host of stuff, including feelings of pleasure and reward. It allows us to regulate emotional responses and take action to achieve specific goals. When the brain reward system does not function as intended, it may fail to release enough dopamine in response to "normal" positive stimuli, resulting in what has been dubbed Reward Deficiency Syndrome (RDS). For us, the "satisfaction of a job well done" is just a meaningless string of words – we don't get no satisfaction unless we are actually interested in the task at hand. In the absence of its neurochemical reward, our brain is designed to discourage us from wasting our energy on activities it deems pointless. This makes sense from an evolutionary standpoint, but is rather unfortunate when said pointless activities are essential to adulting.

Reward deficiency issues may explain why so many of us feel awful when we are forced to engage in repetitive, boring tasks or to live repetitive, boring lives: the resulting understimulation makes our brain chemistry go out of whack. This is a physiological, not psychological issue. If the situation persists, it might cause us to develop **dysthymia**, a persistent form of low-grade depression.

71% of respondents find daily tasks boring and repetitive. 87% find it hard to stay focused on tasks they find boring or repetitive, even when those tasks are important to them. This is important: the issue isn't that we don't care about these tasks, but that our neurochemistry makes it very difficult for us to engage with them. 97% of respondents who find daily tasks boring and repetitive also find it hard to stay focused on boring or repetitive tasks. (If you resemble these remarks, your housekeeping style may resemble mine. You're still not allowed to enter my house without wearing a blindfold, though.)

Consciously or unconsciously, we may compensate for our understimulation by engineering ways of making our environment more stimulating.[49] Alas, not all forms of artificial stimulation are equally beneficial, or equally costly. Using a fidget toy in the office may not do that much for our dopamine levels, but it is less likely to have a negative long-term impact on our life than picking a fight with our boss. Lifestyles that provide us with the constant overstimulation our brain prefers may be a sure way to achieve success and glory, or send us to jail, or the morgue. Safer lifestyles, on the other hand, may literally make us ill.

The impact of interest on our neurochemical balance can affect our ability to perform routine tasks, or any task at all. ADHD brains are said to be motivated by four things: interest, challenge, novelty, and urgency. Is it something we are interested in? Is it going to challenge our abilities? Is it new? Is it about to smack us with a deadline? If a task meets at least one of those four criteria, we're good: we can start it, and we might even finish it! If not, it's a thankless chore, and even thinking about it might suck our will to live. This can lead to the not-yet-official phenomenon known as "ADHD Fainting Goat Syndrome." This term was coined by Jennifer Seal Martin, who observed that our brains disengage when forced to do something boring, and may shut down altogether when confronted by an unavoidable but dull task.

I posit that there is an additional common motivator: procrastination. If working on a task means that we can avoid another, less desirable task, then the first task is suddenly doable, even though we might have been avoiding it for ages. Those of us who learn to game their procrastination often get a lot done; while we are always doing anything but what we should be doing, we are always doing *some*thing. That kind of productivity can add up.

For some of us, our interests can interfere with our daily life in another way: we are deeply interested in a handful of subjects or activities, sometimes to the point of obsession, while anything that doesn't fall within our field of interest is ignored or forgotten. This mental tunnel vision is formally known as a **monotropic interest system** or a **monotropic mind**.

Monotropism is often associated with Autism, but this isn't because only Autistic people display it. Our society all but worships neurotypicals whose one-track-mind makes them solely dedicated to a single field –

[49] https://www.additudemag.com/brain-stimulation-and-adhd-cravings-addiction-and-regulation/

scientists, artists, athletes, entrepreneurs, you name it. When it comes to Autism, however, monotropism magically turns into a symptom, especially if it's combined with complex support needs. At its worst, monotropism is a barrier to human connections and communication. At its best, it is just a "splinter skill" – an ability disconnected from its context or purpose, which renders it basically useless. The fact that our interests can be a source of immense joy to us is irrelevant.

Monotropism allows us to immerse ourselves into topics or experiences, thinking deeply and accessing the kind of flow state that can take years of meditation training to master. However, the positive aspects of monotropism are generally ignored. Being a common feature of Autism, it can't possibly be good, after all.

Rampant ableism aside, it is true that monotropism can cause us performance and social difficulties. This is particularly true if our duties fall outside of our interest, or if we are interested in something so obscure that the people around us can't relate to us.

60% of respondents have an interest or passion that captures the majority of their interest, but only 21% of respondents have interests or passions that are common for people of their age/gender/socioeconomic status. 28% of respondents get in trouble with the people around them for getting too sucked into their passion or interest.

Hyperfocus

Hyperfocus is highly focused attention that lasts a long time. During a hyperfocus, we become so immersed in a thought or activity that we may lose track of everything else going on around us.[50] We might forget or neglect to drink, eat, and sleep. Children may have toileting accidents because they are so focused on what they are doing that they don't notice that they need to go until it's too late. Time becomes wholly untethered from the clock, or even from the calendar, so we may spend hours or days on our hyperfocus without noticing it. If a hyperfocused person tells you that they'll be "just five more minutes" and shows up five hours later, we weren't necessarily lying: those five hours may have genuinely felt like five minutes to us, so we might be just as surprised by our lateness as you are.

During an intense hyperfocus, any interruption or distraction is a cause

---

[50] https://www.webmd.com/add-adhd/hyperfocus-flow

of great annoyance. We may become snappy, withdrawn, or simply unavailable. We may neglect our obligations, not because we don't care but simply because our brain is otherwise occupied. We can't think about anything but the topic of our hyperfocus.

Hyperfocus is often hailed as an ADHD superpower[51] – and, in many ways, it is. It allows us to carry out stupendous amounts of work. However, it can also create a stupendous number of problems, mostly related to the fact that neurotypical people do not understand how it works, which creates unreasonable expectations.

Here are some hyperfocus basics:

- Hyperfocus cannot be turned on and off at will. We can't just engage our hyperfocus because we have an urgent deadline. If that were possible, we would have taken over the world by now.

- Hyperfocus cannot be directed, or re-directed. It's like a prize wheel: you get what you get, and hope that it won't suck. We might be able to hyperfocus on a video game for hours, but that doesn't mean that we can transfer that hyperfocus to a textbook.

- Trying to pay attention to something that is not our hyperfocus can be like trying to listen to two radio channels at the same time. However hard we try to focus on whatever else is going on, we might be unable to do so, or to do so well enough to meet our demands.

- Interrupting a hyperfocus can be extremely uncomfortable. That doesn't mean that we hate the source of the interruption; it's the interruption itself that's the problem.

- The degree to which we can actually snap out of our hyperfocus varies. Sometimes we can flit in and out of a hyperfocus, so we can do normal life stuff and return to our hyperfocus when we are free. Sometimes we can pretend that we have returned to this plane of existence, but our brains are somewhere else entirely. I have had whole conversations while hyperfocused without hearing a single word or knowing what I was saying. I don't know what power runs my mouth, but it isn't me. Sometimes we can snap out of a hyperfocus, but that breaks it forever. And once that impetus is gone, we might find ourselves unable to return to that activity, sometimes forever.

---

[51] https://meandmyadhd.net/hyperfocus-the-superpower-of-adhd/

- Some of us learn to ride our hyperfocuses for all they are worth because we know that it's the only way we ever finish a project. We might become agitated or even angry if someone tries to distract us because we know that if our hyperfocus breaks, every bit of work we have done up to that point might go to waste.

- Hyperfocuses don't always last until a project is done. Sometimes they just run out on us for no discernible reason. That can feel like a bubble bursting, cause us profound grief, or anything in between. Reminding us of the fact that we used to really be into something and we have not bothered with it for ages does not help, and can make us feel even worse about it.

- Hyperfocuses can feel brilliant. Every part of our being is fully focused and fully present. Everything clicks into place inside and around us. We are so involved in a process that we *are* the process. Hypefocuses can also feel awful. We can feel as if we have been possessed by an entity that is pushing us to work beyond exhaustion, or is torturing us with thoughts we cannot escape. We can rage with frustration at the time we are wasting on a spurious activity, while being totally incapable of doing anything else.

- Hyperfocuses linked to a known trigger may be avoided. Quite simply, if starting an activity tends to lead to a bout of hyperfocus, avoiding that activity can help. For instance, some of us learn to avoid certain computer games, because an hour spent playing them always ends up taking a day and a half.

- We can hyperfocus on a project or activity, but we can also hyperfocus on thoughts or feelings. These intangible hyperfocuses can have a devastating impact on our well-being, regardless of whether we are focusing on something positive or negative. For instance, hyperfocusing on the good feelings of a new relationship can make us obsessive about our partner to the detriment of the rest of our life (and, potentially, of the new relationship, too). Hyperfocusing on negative thoughts, upsetting memories, or bad moods can keep us stuck in a downward spiral. And through it all, it might look as if we are just spacing out.

- Hyperfocused people don't stop loving their nearest and dearest, or wanting to take care of them. We don't want to let anyone down. We might struggle to show it, though.

Executive dysfunction

Executive function is the result of a constellation of cognitive abilities that enable goal-oriented behavior[52] – aka, a bunch of skills that allow us to get things done. These skills can be grouped under two categories:[53]

- Organizational. They enable us to gather, organize, and use information.
- Regulatory. They enable us to assess our environment and respond appropriately to situations.

Executive function deficits make it hard for us to manage our time, plan, organize, start tasks, stay on task, complete a task, switch between tasks, multitask, and emotionally self-regulate in the face of changing circumstances.

Executive dysfunction is not currently recognized as an official condition, although there are tests to measure it.[54] However, these measurements may not have much of a practical application, because executive dysfunction is not a stable feature. Like memory, it can be negatively affected by a number of factors. Most of the stressors mentioned in this chapter have an impact on our functioning even though they are not components of our executive function.

Memory, in particular working memory, is a key component of executive function. As we have already discussed, working memory problems affect nearly three quarter of survey respondents. The following stressors are also common in the neurodivergent community, and are key components of executive function.

Time agnosia, or time blindness.

Time blindness is not a technical term or a recognized condition; it's a label popularly used to describe the inability to feel the passing of time that is a common feature of neurodivergence. It is wholly unrelated to the ability to tell the time, which is a learned skill. 50% of respondents are never able to gauge the passing of time, and 35% can only do it sometimes.

Time-blind individuals may lack the ability to feel time passing, or feel

---

[52] https://www.ncbi.nlm.nih.gov/pmc/articles/PMC4455841/
[53] https://www.webmd.com/add-adhd/executive-function
[54] https://www.ncbi.nlm.nih.gov/pmc/articles/PMC5619353/

it very differently depending on context. Time spent doing something engrossing flies, while time spent in boredom seems to lasts forever; and this happens on a wholly different scale from the neurotypical "time flies when you are having fun." Time-blind individuals simply cannot judge how long a task has taken, or estimate how long one might take. We get lost in the clock and in the calendar. This can cause great difficulties in short- and long-term planning, and makes time management extremely difficult. It's hard to manage a resource if we don't know how much of it we have, or how quickly we are spending it.

Decision-making difficulties

Decision making is an essential aspect of executive function. People can struggle with several aspects of decision-making, but two common issues are an inability to make decisions when there are too many options, and an inability to make decision if there isn't enough information about the possible risks and effects. People can be affected by these issues regardless of the potential impact of a given decision.

81% of respondents struggle to make small decisions when they have too many options. 73% struggle to make decisions if they do not have enough information to work out the possible risks and effects.

Starting and finishing tasks

Many neurodivergents, ADHDers in particular, struggle to start and finish tasks. Sometimes we delay starting on tasks we consciously or unconsciously classified as difficult until they are unavoidable... and then realize that we spent more time and energy avoiding the task than it took to complete it. Sometimes we start working on a task, but abandon it as soon as it turns out to be difficult.

As a result of these issues, many of us have been told that we are lazy, that we lack motivation or dedication, and so on. Sometimes we say that to ourselves. There are two problems with this. Firstly, calling someone lazy (or worse) has never stopped anyone from being lazy. We can't exorcise personal shortcomings by calling them out. And anyway, if years of getting told off by our parents, teachers, bosses, partners, and so on haven't managed to purge us of that pesky laziness, is the next self-berating session really likely to work?

Secondly, lazy people don't spend half their life metaphorically kicking themselves in the backside because of the stuff they aren't doing. That's not how laziness works. If we desperately want to do something but just can't, our problem is not laziness.

I am going to borrow the words of Autistic social psychologist, professor, and author Devon Price:

> "For decades, psychological research has been able to explain procrastination as a functioning problem, not a consequence of laziness. When a person fails to begin a project that they care about, it's typically due to either a) anxiety about their attempts not being "good enough" or b) confusion about what the first steps of the task are. Not laziness. In fact, procrastination is more likely when the task is meaningful and the individual cares about doing it well.
>
> When you're paralyzed with fear of failure, or you don't even know how to begin a massive, complicated undertaking, it's damn hard to get shit done. It has nothing to do with desire, motivation, or moral upstandingness. Procrastinators can will themselves to work for hours; they can sit in front of a blank word document, doing nothing else, and torture themselves; they can pile on the guilt again and again — none of it makes initiating the task any easier. In fact, their desire to get the damn thing done may worsen their stress and make starting the task harder."[55]

If we freeze in the face of a complex task, there are two likely reasons: we fear we won't be able to do it, or we just don't know how to do it. Granted, there may be other factors in play, but if we're sitting there seething with frustration and self-loathing at our inability to do something, laziness isn't one of them.

88% of respondents tend to avoid or delay starting tasks that are new, complicated, or important. 66% of respondents abandon tasks if they turn up to be too complicated. Of the latter, 95% also avoid or delay starting tasks that are too complicated. Obviously, I can't draw any conclusions as to why we are getting these numbers, but Devon Price's theory of performance anxiety and executive dysfunction could explain them.

It doesn't explain another phenomenon, however: sometimes we start working on a task, and abandon it as soon as we realize that we *can* finish

---

[55] https://humanparts.medium.com/laziness-does-not-exist-3af27e312d01
CW: mentions of ableism, mental health stigmas, sexual abuse, and institutional asshattery.

it. This may sound absurd, but it is quite common – 49% of respondents find it hard to complete tasks once they know they can do them. This issue is better explained as an aspect of our **interest-based nervous system**: once we have familiarized ourselves with a task, it loses its novelty, and once we know that we can definitely do it, it is no longer a challenge. That only leaves us with two possible motivators, interest and urgency. Alas, we can't will ourselves to be interested in something, and not all tasks are important enough to ever become urgent.

These issues don't just stop us engaging with our duties and chores. Even pleasurable activities like hobbies are affected in the same way, and hobbies fit in the never-quite-urgent category. As a result, ADHDers have a tendency to have short-lived but passionate relationships with our hobbies in a pattern I like to call "serial monotropism." We fall head over heels in love with a subject or activity, invest considerable amounts of our time and energy into it... and then we drop it, fall in love with something else, and do it all over again, and again, and again. This can frustrate the heck out of the people around us, particularly if they harbored hopes of us becoming subject matter experts. It can also frustrate the heck out of us, unless we learn to roll with it. And then there are the financial implications, the storage issues, and the guilt we might feel every time we are reminded of how much time, money, and energy we "wasted" on an abandoned hobby.

69% of respondents abandon new hobbies if they don't get good at them fast enough. 49% of respondents abandon new hobbies once they get good at them. 87% of those who abandon hobbies when they get good at them also abandon them if they don't get good fast enough. Again, this is pure conjecture, but a combination of performance anxiety, executive dysfunction, and ADHD motivation requirements could explain these numbers.

Repetitive behaviors – fidgeting, stimming, and tics

We tend to think of "behaviors" as activities we do consciously, and for a purpose. All of us, however, occasionally engage in behaviors that are not under our control or do not have a bearing on the activity at hand. Four common types of repetitive behaviors are:

- **Fidgeting:** small, repetitive movements that may involve the whole body (e.g., squirming in our seat) or just a part of our body (e.g., tapping our fingers or our feet). Fidgeting may reflect physical or mental discomfort, restlessness, nervousness, frustration, agitation, boredom, excitement, or a combination of these. Fidgeting is also a very common feature of ADHD.

- **Tics** are uncontrolled twitches, movements, or sounds that people do repeatedly. Most of us occasionally experience tics – for instance, a twitch in our eyelid – that normally stop of their own accord. If our tics are frequent, persistent, and are not caused by an underlying medical condition or the use of medication, we might be diagnosed with a tic disorder, the most famous of which is Tourette's Syndrome.

- **Stimming** is the abbreviation for "self-stimulating behavior": any repetitive actions or movements designed to help us deal with conditions that aren't quite right for us. Stims are, in essence, a release valve. Finger-tapping, nail biting, pacing, hair twirling, fidgeting on a chair, chewing lips or the inside of the mouth, sucking on pens, and humming are all stims. Literally any repetitive action that has no function beyond making us feel better while we deal with something is a stim. In popular media, stimming is often associated with Autism, but that view is grossly incorrect. Everyone stims, in various ways and to varying degrees. Neurotypical people stim; they just don't tend to do it as often, for as long, or as obviously.

- Uncontrollable, repetitive, ritualistic behaviors may also be a symptom of **Obsessive-Compulsive Disorder** (OCD), a condition characterized by repetitive behaviors ("compulsions") or thoughts ("obsessions").

- **Restless legs syndrome** (RLS) is a condition that causes an uncontrollable urge to move the legs. This urge is usually most intense in the evening or at night, when sitting or lying down, and can interfere with our ability to go to sleep. RLS is a controversial and relatively rare condition, but it appears to be over-represented in the ADHD community. The cause of RLS is as yet unknown, but it is suspected to be linked to an imbalance of the brain chemical dopamine, which sends messages to control muscle movement.

From the outside, it can be hard to distinguish between these types of behavior. Are we bouncing our leg because we have RLS, because of a compulsion (OCD), because we feel anxious and movement helps us release some adrenaline (stimming), or because we have poor circulation and sitting down is giving us a dead leg? There's no telling from the outside. (Un)Fortunately, that doesn't matter all that often, because people don't tend to care. They just tell us to cut it out because it's annoying them – and, obviously, their needs trump ours – or assume that it's a sign of impatience or inattention and tell us off.

This is suboptimal, for two main reasons. Firstly, not all repetitive behaviors are under conscious control. Most notably, RLS and tics cannot be controlled. Some people can control most of their stims most of the time, while others can't control them at all. Many of us have varying degrees of control over our stimming and fidgeting depending on the stress we are under. An increase in the intensity or duration of stims typically indicates an increase in distress. This has been studied extensively in animals, for whom self-damaging stims are usually a response to inadequate conditions; confined animals use these stims when they are chronically thwarted from expressing basic activities or meeting basic needs.

Some repetitive behaviors are partially under our control, but controlling them can cause us difficulties, or even harm us. This is because these behaviors are not actually useless. For instance, fidgeting and stimming aren't useful in the sense of being an essential part of the activity at hand, but they can help us regulate our emotions and focus our attention. Depriving us of the ability to fidget or stim can cause us significant distress, or require so much of our attention that we don't have any to spare for what we are actually supposed to do. We can sit still *or* pay attention, but not both; demanding the former means that we can't do the latter.

Unfortunately, despite the fact that this information is readily available to anyone who cares to look for it, it has had little or no impact on behavioral requirements in schools and workplaces. Many schools still push programs like "whole body listening." These are fairly nonsensical when applied to neurotypical students – if we needed the whole body to listen, phones would not be a thing – and can have a huge negative impact on the performance and emotional state of neurodivergent students.

Repressing our stimming doesn't just affect us in the moment. Stimming is both a stress response – i.e., increased stress leads to increased stimming – and a coping mechanism – i.e., increased stimming can help us control our stress. A reduction in stimming should be the result of a lowering of our stress levels, not of forced repression. Forcing us to stop stimming not only fails to address the core issue, but creates an extra stressor: not only are we still forced to cope with too much, but we have to do so while repressing our natural responses to stress. This is the opposite of helpful, or logical, yet it's currently the norm.

32% of survey respondents force themselves to stop their repetitive behaviors to avoid getting told off, and 49% redirect them to less noticeable ones to look more "normal." While doing so may help us get along with those around us, it isn't without costs. Suppressing stims is linked with increases in the prevalence of a number of physical and psychoemotional issues, including dissociation, poor interoception, meltdowns, shutdowns, selective mutism, burnouts, oversensitivity to pain, chronic pain, and fatigue – and these are only the outcomes I measured in my survey. As stimming is designed to help us manage our stress, turning it into a stressor is likely to increase our stress levels. It has been amply demonstrated that long-term stress has serious negative impacts on our long-term health. Stim repression is likely to have a similar impact.

Motor skills deficits

Dyspraxia

Dyspraxia, aka Developmental Coordination Disorder (DCD), is a neurological motor disorder characterized by problems with physical co-ordination. It can affect fine and gross motor skills. 8% of respondents are dyspraxic. However, 52% of respondents have poor gross motor skills and 18% have poor fine motor skills.

Apraxia

Apraxia is a poorly-understood neurological condition characterized by motor planning deficits: people are unable to carry out intentional movements despite having the physical ability and desire to perform them. Apraxia can affect the whole body or just a part of the body. For instance, people with apraxia of speech struggle to initiate and perform the movements required for speaking, despite the fact that there is no weakness in the necessary muscles.

The hidden costs of performance

The current diagnostic system for neurodivergences centers on failures. In order to be put forward for testing, children have to fail to meet age-appropriate standards in their academic work, socialization, communication, or behavior. In order to obtain a diagnosis of neurodivergence in adulthood, patients have to prove that their symptoms started in childhood, were and are age-inappropriate, and cause consistent impairment in multiple domains.

There is an obvious problem with this approach: it discounts the fact that many of us put a lot of effort into compensating for our traits, or suppressing them altogether. Undiagnosed adults, in particular, spend years learning how to function in neurotypical environments. These adaptations may enable us to achieve at least some of our goals, but they are not cost-free. In fact, many of them require a lot of effort.

Some coping mechanisms are downright damaging. For instance, we might compensate for our tendency to make mistakes by obsessively checking and re-checking our work; we might learn to dissociate when we need to stay still for prolonged periods; we might have developed social anxiety so paralyzing that we no longer talk out of turn, because we struggle to talk at all; we might have channeled our physical restlessness into a constantly racing mind. This kind of coping mechanism reduces the impact of our neurodivergence... but only on the people around us. We are just as affected by our neurodivergence – in fact, we now have to deal with our traits *and* with our coping mechanisms. We have learned to suffer in silence, though, and for some people, that's all that matters.

For most of us, even these efforts aren't enough. 77% of respondents reported that they have underachieved at work or in education. This does not come as a huge surprise and is in line with the results shown by larger, official studies.

Medical/physiological stressors

This section is technically redundant, because all medical/physiological stressors are also performance stressors. However, I am filing these stressors separately because they are recognized medical conditions that can and should be treated.

It can be very difficult for neurodivergents to access the required diagnoses and treatments, particularly if we suffer from a constellation of disparate symptoms or if we are subjected to medical biases – misogyny and fatphobia are especially common and damaging. I am hoping that listing these medical conditions as medical conditions will empower at least some of us to push for the medical care we need.

Medical/physiological stressors can have six main types of impact:

- They can make it impossible for us to do certain things. For instance, people with circadian sleep disorders cannot sleep according to a schedule their body rejects.

- They can make it too dangerous for us to do certain things. For instance, people with connective tissue disorders cannot engage in certain physical activities without risking serious injuries.

- They can make it too painful for us to do certain things. For instance, people with fibromyalgia may find it too painful to stand or sit for extended periods of time.

- Over time, they can cause us to accumulate a series of injuries. These injuries can make it impossible, too dangerous, or too painful for us to do certain things.

- If our conditions or injuries cause us chronic pain, this can have a significant impact on our mood and on our ability to control it.

- Over time, conditions that severely limit our ability to carry out activities or to enjoy them can have an impact on our "mental health" – and I'm putting this in brackets because it can be hard to draw the line between "I am depressed because my life is unbearably painful" and "I have depression."

Unfortunately, these limitations are not always recognized by the people around us, including medical professionals and those responsible for granting us school and workplace accommodations. People with healthy, sound bodies can find it hard to empathize or sympathize with people whose bodies aren't functioning as they should. Furthermore, our culture has a tendency to conflate "healthy" with "morally superior," and to blame people for their ailments.

When our conditions cause us to experience variable levels of ability, this can cause even more interpersonal friction. We could do X yesterday, so why are we saying that we can't do it today? Introducing our interlocutors to the "spoon theory"[56] can help, but only if they are willing to listen. That's not always the case. This can be an especially serious issue if our workplace culture assumes that work is inherently distasteful to most people, and they will attempt to shirk whenever possible.[57] As this point of view is very common, the assumption tends to be that we are shirkers until we prove otherwise. It can be impossible for us to do so when our ability or energy levels vary.

If we are affected by conditions that are still controversial (e.g., chronic fatigue or fibromyalgia), or conditions that only affect people with a uterus and ovaries (e.g., endometriosis), we may experience an even greater level of pushback. This is partly due to factual ignorance and partly due to the misogyny inherent in our culture. The same gender biases that affect medical diagnoses[58] also affect how "female ailments" are commonly regarded. It's no accident that "hormonal" is an insult only thrown at women and people with a uterus and ovaries, when variations in testosterone levels in men are hardly symptoms-free.[59] It is also no accident that many "controversial" conditions disproportionately affect people with a uterus and ovaries.

Sleep

Studies show that as many as 70% of ADHDers and 80% of Autistics suffer from sleep disturbances. Some of these sleep disturbances are quantity issues; quite simply, we do not get enough sleep. This can be caused by a variety of reasons, the most common being that we struggle to fall asleep when we need to, to stay asleep through the night, or to go back to sleep quickly if we wake up in the night. Other sleep disturbances are quality issues; we may sleep long enough, or even longer than "normal",

---

[56] https://en.wikipedia.org/wiki/Spoon_theory
[57] https://courses.lumenlearning.com/wmintrobusiness/chapter/reading-douglas-mcgregors-theory-x-and-theory-y-2/
[58] https://encyclopedia.pub/entry/30495
[59] https://www.bps.org.uk/psychologist/testosterone-and-male-behaviours

but we wake up still tired because our sleep quality isn't up to snuff. We are also more prone than neurotypicals to rarer sleep disorders, such as narcolepsy – a condition that causes attacks of drowsiness during the day.

Survey results indicated that only 6% of respondents are always able to sleep at least 7 hours every night - the minimum recommended amount for the average adult – while 26% manage it often.

78% of respondents always or often wake up tired. For 9% of them, this issue is linked to **Sleep-Disordered Breathing** (SDB, e.g., **sleep apnea**). Other breathing difficulties, such as those caused by allergies, can also negatively affect sleep quality and cause similar daytime symptoms. 84% of respondents who have allergies to smells or chemicals also reported that they wake up tired, as did 91% of those who have asthma attacks in response to certain smells.

For some of us, our sleep issues arise from the fact that our bodies aren't wired to go to sleep at a "normal" bedtime. Our internal clock and the actual clock are not in sync. The resulting sleep disorders are called **Circadian Rhythm Sleep Disorders** (CRSD).

Circadian rhythm is the name given to the body's internal clock. Its mechanism is very complicated, but the TL/DR version is that light tells a control center in our brain what time it is, and the control center regulates the production of various hormones. One of these hormones is melatonin, a key player in the sleep-wake cycle.

Melatonin is linked to the onset, duration, and quality of sleep. Its production increases soon after the onset of darkness, peaks in the middle of the night, and decreases during the second half of the night. During the day, melatonin levels are at their lowest. If the system works as intended, these chemical shifts sync our internal clock with the actual clock. If something goes awry, this synchronization does not happen, and we can end up suffering from a circadian mismatch. If that mismatch causes us to regularly lose sleep, we have a circadian rhythm sleep disorder.

There are several types of CRSDs. Anecdotal evidence suggests that the most common within the ADHD community is **Delayed Sleep Phase Syndrome** (DSPS), a disorder in which a person's sleep is delayed by two hours or more beyond what is considered an acceptable bedtime. This happens regardless of the implementation of good sleep hygiene practices.

As most people are not able to schedule their obligations around their idiosyncratic sleep schedule, Delayed Sleep Phase Syndrome can result in chronic sleep deprivation. Estimates of prevalence vary between studies and between age groups, but 0.2-1.7% of adults in the general population are believed to be affected by DSPS. Unfortunately, this low prevalence means that DSPS isn't widely known, even within the medical community. As a result, it is often undiagnosed and untreated.

The results of my survey support this lack of information and medical support. Out of our respondents, "only" 29% reported that they often or always have DPSP, but 56% are often or always unable to fall asleep at a socially acceptable time even though they get to bed on time.

Sleep disturbances can have serious impacts on people's health and quality of life. Short-term sleep deprivation can cause difficulties getting up in the morning, daytime drowsiness, and a general decline in mood and performance. Children, particularly young children, may be unusually hyperactive or bad-tempered. That's unpleasant enough for all involved, but the effects of chronic sleep deprivation are where things get really interesting for us, as they include:

- Decline in executive function.

- Impaired sustained attention.

- Increased tendency to make errors, particularly under time pressure.

- Difficulties in performing long tasks.

- Slower or impaired information processing.

- Slower response time.

- Working memory decline.

- Reduced memory formation.

- Difficulties in decision-making.

- Poor judgment.

- Increased risk-taking behavior.

- Decline in motor control.

- Increased emotional reactivity.

- Difficulties in modulating behavior.

- Anxiety.

- Depression.

Does this sound familiar? It should, because it's basically the carbon copy of the most common ADHD traits and co-occurring conditions.

What this means is that if you take the most neurotypical person on the planet and you deprive them of sleep for long enough, they will start showing the same performance and behavioral issues ADHDers deal with on a daily basis. And these effects are cumulative: the longer the sleep deprivation goes on, the worse its effects get. Also, its impact will be greater on those who already suffer from certain symptoms. For instance, sleep deprived people who normally have a fantastic working memory may notice that it has declined, but people whose working memory is already poor may be rendered virtually non-functional.

Traits associated with Autistic distress have also been found to be exacerbated by sleep deprivation; in a nutshell, stimming goes up, and communication and socialization go down.

Lack of sleep and irregular sleeping patterns have also been proven to have deleterious effects on people's hormonal balance, with dangerous results; for instance, night shift work may be linked to an increased risk of breast cancer. This may be due to the suppression of melatonin production, confusion in the body circadian system, and the weakening of the immune system resulting from disordered sleep.

Narcolepsy is a whole different beast. Unlike other sleep disorders, it is believed to be an autoimmune disorder – a disorder caused when the body's immune system mistakenly attacks healthy tissue or cells. In narcolepsy, the immune system destroys brain cells that produce a peptide called hypocretin. This results in chronic, excessive attacks of drowsiness during the day, sometimes called excessive daytime sleepiness (EDS). Attacks of drowsiness may persist for only a few seconds or several minutes. These episodes vary in frequency from a few incidents to several during a single day. Nighttime sleep patterns may also be disrupted.

4.4% of respondents reported that they have narcolepsy. This number may seem small, but the incidence of narcolepsy in the general population is believed to be 0.025 to 0.05%.

Food

There is no scientific evidence that neurodivergence is caused by food. That doesn't mean that nutrition is not important for neurodivergent people. Many of us feel and function better if we eat regular meals of food that is rich in nutrients and proteins and provides a steady release of energy – so, for instance, an egg salad for lunch will lead to a better afternoon at work than a chocolate bar. These improvements are cumulative; at the end of a week of eating egg salad for lunch, we might feel even better. This isn't because we are neurodivergent, though: it's because we are human, and regular meals of nutritionally rich, slow energy release food result in better health outcomes for our species.

The impact of nutrition can be more evident on some neurodivergent people, particularly on children, because of how it intersects with our traits. For instance, ADHD makes it difficult for us to sit still and focus; the last thing we need is to try and do that while riding a sugar rush'n'crash. But the fact that a sugar bomb may make it impossible for us to focus doesn't mean that sugar is the root cause of our focus issues.

No diet can cure neurodivergence, because neurodivergence isn't caused by diet. However, making better nutritional choices can benefit us. Unfortunately, that isn't always easy for us. We might struggle to feed ourselves properly for a number of reasons, including:

- **Dietary issues**; these relate to the food we ingest. Not all neurodivergent people have atypical diets, but many of us do. The reasons for this include:

  o We may have allergies or intolerances that make us ill if we eat certain foods. 29% of survey respondents reported that they have allergies or intolerances.

  o We may have sensory issues around food. These can relate to taste, smell, texture, and so on. 40% of respondents reported that they have food sensory issues.

  Food sensory issues can be unconnected to allergies or sensitivities. However, it is not unheard of for neurodivergent children to be assumed to have food sensory issues when they actually have sensitivities they cannot adequately describe, or are not believed by their parents.

  o We may have anxiety around food that may prevent us from trying foods we cannot trust. This anxiety can have no known causes, but sometimes it is linked to the two issues mentioned above. If we cannot predict how a certain food will taste, smell, or feel, or whether ingesting it will make us ill, we might be reluctant to eat it.

  o We may lack the executive function required to establish and maintain a decent eating plan. Before we eat a healthy meal, we have to decide what it's going to be, work out a list of ingredients, purchase them, and store them – that's four whole steps, and we're not even close to eating yet. On the day of the meal, we have to start cooking well before we are hungry, or our food won't be ready on time. If we are time-blind, that can be a major issue. In order to make food that doesn't suck, we have to follow a set of instructions – which, for some of us, is a struggle. We might have to wait for the food to cook (a.k.a. purgatory), or tend to it while it is cooking (a.k.a. hell). If we get distracted, we might ruin our meal. It's no wonder that many of us struggle, or just give up and end up living on last-minute snacks while stacks of healthy ingredients turn to mulch in our fridges.

o Our neurodivergence can make it difficult for us to buy healthy food. Sometimes our neurodivergence is a direct obstacle; for instance, our environmental sensitivities may make it difficult for us to go food shopping. Sometimes our neurodivergence can cause us to experience other obstacles, which in turn can prevent us from being able to buy healthy food; for instance, we might be financially disadvantaged because it's hard for us to find well-paid employment or work consistently. Sadly, healthy food is often more expensive than processed crap.

- **Gastrointestinal (GI) issues;** these are issues that affect the function of the gastrointestinal tract, which runs from the mouth to the anus. Some GI issues seem to be more common within our community. These include:

o Irritable bowel syndrome (IBS), where colon muscles contract more or less often than "normal." IBS can manifest as abdominal pain and cramps, gas, bloating, harder or looser stools, and alternating constipation and diarrhea.

o Crohn's disease, a type of colitis (inflammation of the bowel). Common symptoms include diarrhea, intestinal aches and cramps, blood in the stools, fatigue, and weight loss.

o Gastroesophageal reflux disease (GERD). A condition where stomach content flows back into the esophagus – like chronic acid reflux, basically. As stomach content is very acidic, it can cause severe discomfort and even permanent damage.

o Laryngopharyngeal reflux (LPR). Like GERD, but the stomach content flows through the esophagus and spills into the throat.

- **Nutritional issues;** these occur when the food we are ingesting does not meet our nutritional requirements. This could be because the food in question does not contain all of the necessary substances. For instance, chicken nuggets are very low in Vit A, Vit D, and calcium. Hence, if we live on chicken nuggets, our diet will be lacking in Vit A, Vit D, and calcium. Nutritional deficiencies can also be caused by our body's inability to digest and absorb the food we eat. For instance, Crohn's disease can cause malabsorption of nutrients.

Gastrointestinal, dietary, and nutritional issues often interact. For instance, eating foods we are intolerant to can trigger IBS. Celiac disease intolerance to gluten) can cause damage to the small intestine, which can lead to malabsorption, which can lead to malnutrition. However, these issues can also exist in isolation. For instance, a person may have a model diet and still suffer from IBS, GERD, or Crohn's. Conversely, a person may have a restricted diet, but have no gastrointestinal or nutritional issues because they are eating food their bodies can process, and that provides them with all the fiber and nutrients they need.

For some of us, finding a way to feed ourselves regular, nutritious meals may require an approach very different from how a neurotypical person would go about it. It might mean eating a very narrow set of ingredients to avoid triggering allergies and gastrointestinal issues. It might mean giving up on complicated meals and sticking to sandwiches or salads. It might mean buying pre-prepared or processed ingredients. It might mean cooking in batches and living on leftovers, or cooking the same handful of meals over and over again. It may mean eating set amounts of food at set times, because we cannot rely on our hunger cues to guide us. For those of us who struggle to eat while taking meds, it might mean switching to meal replacement shakes or smoothies. None of this is ideal, but you know what's even less ideal? Being malnourished because we can't be neurotypical around food.

Ultimately, when we refuse ourselves access to adequate nutrition unless it is in the context of meals of a given degree of complexity, what we are saying is that we have to earn the right to eat by acting neurotypical. That's some ableist bullshit right there. If we did that to a child, it would class as abuse. It's still abuse when we do it to ourselves.

Unfortunately, the people in our life aren't always accepting of our dietary workarounds. Food has huge social value. It's an important part of cultural heritage and national identity. It connects us to people both on a daily basis and as part of special celebrations. For some people, these issues overshadow the fact that their food can make us literally sick. When we refuse to eat "normally," they may respond by arguing, bullying us, or even attempting to force us to eat foods we don't want, or sneaking them into our meals without our knowledge and consent. Nobody has been able to explain to my satisfaction why us assuming the right to decide what passes our mouths – a key aspect of bodily autonomy – is less socially acceptable than other people trying to gainsay that right, but here we are.

Poor interoception

Interoception is the ability to sense and accurately interpret internal signals from our body – for instance, whether we are hungry, thirsty, in need of the toilet, or whether our heart is racing. Interoception is essential to **homeostasis** – the process by which our bodies maintain internal stability while adjusting to changing external conditions. Homeostasis ensures that our bodies are operating optimally, but it requires our cooperation: we need to read the signals our body is sending and respond adequately. If we are unable to read these signals, we will fail to respond to them. As a result, our homeostatic balance will be disrupted.

There are two components to interoception.[60] The first is **interoceptive accuracy** – how good we are at feeling signals from our body. The second is **interoceptive attention** - how much we notice signals from our body. If either component fails, our interoception may fail us.

Poor interoception can make self-care a challenge, as we may have unmet physical needs we cannot perceive. For instance, if we cannot register our hunger signals, we may fail to eat when we need to. We may be able to notice other symptoms of our hunger – for instance, we may feel weak, tired, cold, or inexplicably down – but we may be unable to interpret them as signs that we need to eat. 40% of respondents struggle to read their hunger signals.

Poor interoception can also result in dehydration. We might be able to register other signs of dehydration – tiredness, lightheadedness, headaches, and poor concentration – but in the absence of thirst signals, we might not be able to work out why we're experiencing them. 48% of survey respondents struggle to read their thirst signals.

---

[60] https://kids.frontiersin.org/articles/10.3389/frym.2021.558246#

Poor interoception can result in dehydration because of another issue: some of us can't rely on our ability to realize in a timely manner when we need to pee. Repeated mishaps or close calls may teach us that drinking is a dangerous endeavor unless we have immediate access to a toilet. This, in turn, can teach us to ignore our thirst signals. 18% of respondents struggle to know when we need to pee or poo until they are desperate, or have an accident.

Poor interoception can make it very difficult for us to respond to in-the-moment physical needs that are preventing our body from functioning properly. As a result, we may feel terrible and think that there must be something seriously wrong with us, when in reality we might just be hungry, thirsty, too hot or too cold, or in need of an urgent trip to the loo. Alternatively, we may become so used to feeling terrible that it becomes our normal state.

Poor interoception can also have damaging long-term impacts on our health. For instance, not registering thirst can cause us to be dehydrated so often that we develop urinary tract infections, kidney stones, or even kidney failure.

While interoception is an innate ability, our life experiences can affect the degree with which we can connect with our bodies. We can be trained to disconnect from our bodies in order to cope with our environment, either by accident or as part of attempts at "desensitizing" us to painful stimuli– why this kind of intervention is *not* desensitization is explained in detail in the section about trauma. Survey results indicated that respondents who went through this type of "desensitization" are considerably more likely to struggle to read their hunger and thirst signals, and twice as likely to struggle to read their pee/poo signals.

Thermoregulation

Thermoregulation is the mechanism by which the body maintains its internal temperature despite changes in external temperatures. Thermoregulation is another aspect of homeostasis. If our body is unable to keep its temperature between a relatively narrow range (36.1-37.2°C, or 97-99°F), it will stop functioning properly. Hypothermia (too cold) and hyperthermia (too hot) are both dangerous. If our internal temperature falls below 35.0°C (95°F) or rises above 40.5°C (105°F), we can fall seriously ill. If our temperature isn't returned quickly to safe levels, we may die.

Thermoregulation is controlled by the hypothalamus, a region of the brain, but the receptors responsible for sensing whether we are hot or cold are spread throughout our body. If these sensors determine that our temperature needs adjusting, these adjustments will take two forms:

- Automatic body responses, such as sweating to lower the body temperature, shivering to raise it, and narrowing or relaxing blood vessels to alter blood flow.

- The impulse for us to take the appropriate actions, such as taking clothes off if we are too hot or putting them on if we are too cold.

Our ability to thermoregulate varies naturally with age: it starts out awful, gets good when we are around 2 years old, and starts declining again if we are lucky enough to hit 60. However, a number of conditions can cause poor thermoregulation in people of all ages. These include infections, endocrine disorders, central nervous system disorders, and circulatory disorders. Poor thermoregulation can also be caused by hormonal imbalances or as a side effect of certain medications.

If our temperature receptors don't function properly or if our body can't adjust our temperature accordingly, we will struggle to thermoregulate – i.e., we will be more susceptible than the average person to changes in external temperatures. In order to keep our internal temperature within safe limits, we will have to take extra steps to prevent ourselves from getting too hot or too cold. For instance, we may have to wear warmer clothes in the winter, or stay in the shade on hot days. If we are unable to take these precautions, we have a higher risk of experiencing hypo- or hyperthermia.

Poor interoception can decrease our ability to thermoregulate. If we cannot sense the body's signals that we are becoming too hot or too cold, we may fail to take the necessary steps to help return us to a safe temperature.

31% of respondents struggle to regulate their temperature in cold weather, while 37% of respondents struggle to regulate their temperature in hot weather.

Thermoregulation is a physiological issue, not a matter of willpower. If our bodies struggle to thermoregulate, forcing ourselves to endure extreme temperatures will not teach them to function better. That's not how this system works. At best, we will be making ourselves unnecessarily uncomfortable. At worst, we will risk injuries, or even death.

Reactive hypoglycemia

Reactive hypoglycemia, aka postprandial (literally "after a meal") hypoglycemia, is a condition characterized by a drop in blood sugar levels within 2–5 hours of eating. Symptoms include anxiety, confusion, irritability, shakiness, dizziness, lightheadedness, weakness, exhaustion, and fainting. Some people feel hungry, while others do not. Symptoms subside quickly after eating or drinking carbohydrates. However, for some of us consuming sugar-rich foods can set off a short sugar rush followed by another hypoglycemic event. In that case, eating complex carbohydrates, proteins, or fats may work better.

5% of respondents said that they often or always have reactive hypoglycemia, and an additional 5% have it sometimes. However, 41% of respondents answered that they were not sure. When asked about the symptoms of reactive hypoglycemia, 12% of respondents have them often or always. As reactive hypoglycemia is not a commonly-known condition, lack of awareness may explain this discrepancy.

The lack of information about this condition can cause people to go undiagnosed. In turn, that can stop them from making the adaptations required to avoid hypoglycemic events. This can be a serious issue for people who are forced to eat meals at times that will cause them to have hypos when they are required to be productive and who aren't allowed to snack at will – for instance, schoolchildren. As during a hypo it is impossible for us to function properly, the resulting impact on our academic achievements can be significant.

Circulatory disorders

Hypotension (aka low blood pressure)

Hypotension is defined as blood pressure readings below 90/60mmHg. Symptoms include lightheadedness or dizziness, feeling sick, blurred vision, weakness, confusion, and fainting. 18% of respondents have low blood pressure.

POTS, or Postural Orthostatic Tachycardia Syndrome

POTS is characterized by too little blood returning to the heart when moving from a lying down to a standing up position (aka, "orthostatic intolerance"). This can cause palpitations, lightheadedness, fainting, blurred vision, fatigue, sweating, nausea, and headaches. These symptoms are associated with a rapid increase in heart rate from the lying to upright position, and eased by lying back down. POTS can also cause "brain fog," a cognitive dysfunction characterized by difficulty focusing and thinking. 8% of respondents have POTS.

Reynaud's phenomenon and Reynaud's disease

Reynaud's phenomenon and Reynaud's disease have the same symptoms, but different causes. They are both characterized by "reversible vasospasm in peripheral arteries" – i.e., decreased blood flow to the extremities – in response to cold, stress, or emotional upset. The most common symptom is fingers that turn first pale and then blue when exposed to cold, then red when the hands are warmed. The pale color indicates that blood circulation has been cut off, and the blue color indicates low oxygen levels. This reaction is disproportionate to the actual temperature (i.e., most people would not be affected in the same way at the same temperature). Symptoms can last from a few minutes to several hours and can make it difficult to use one's fingers. In severe cases, sores may develop in the affected areas. In rare cases, gangrene may develop.

If these symptoms manifest because of an underlying condition (e.g. a blood disorder, repetitive action damage, or side effects from medication) the diagnosis will be Reynaud's phenomenon. If there is no known underlying condition, it will be Reynaud's disease.

The estimated prevalence of Raynaud's in the general population is 3-5%. 8% of survey respondents reported that they have Raynaud's.

Autoimmune diseases

Autoimmune diseases are caused by a dysfunction of the immune system. Following exposure to a trigger such as a virus or a chemical, the body's natural defense system is activated, but instead of attacking the threat, it attacks normal cells. The results vary depending on which cells are being attacked:

- In rheumatoid arthritis, the immune system attacks the joints.

- In psoriasis, the immune system attacks the skin.

- In lupus, the immune system attacks joints, skin, and organs.

- In autoimmune hepatitis the immune system attacks the liver.

- In multiple sclerosis (MS), the immune system attacks myelin, the substance that protects nerve fibers in the brain and spinal cord.

- In narcolepsy, the immune system destroys brain cells that produce a peptide called hypocretin, resulting in attacks of daytime drowsiness.

- In Myalgic Encephalomyelitis/Chronic Fatigue Syndrome (ME/CFS), a trigger causes changes in the immune system and the way it responds to infection or stress, resulting in widespread inflammation but no tissue damage. The exact causes and mechanisms have yet to be identified.

These are just some examples; there are more than 80 types of autoimmune disease, and all parts of the body may be affected. Some autoimmune diseases affect a single part of the body, while others have more widespread effects. Unfortunately, diagnosing them is far from simple, as many of them present with similar symptoms. These often include:

- Fatigue;

- Joint pain and swelling;

- Skin problems;

- Abdominal pain or digestive issues;

- Recurring fever;

- Swollen glands.

18% of respondents have an autoimmune disease – six times more than the general population.

Connective tissue disorders (CTDs) and joint instability

Connective tissue disorders (CTDs) affect collagen and elastin – two proteins responsible for literally keeping us together. Collagen is found in the tendons, ligaments, skin, corneas, cartilage, bones, and blood vessels. Elastin is a major component of elastic tissues, which include our skin, lungs, tendons, ligaments, bladder, and major blood vessels.

There are more than 200 types of CTDs. Some are inherited, some are caused by environmental factors, and some are of unknown cause.

In **autoimmune CTDs**, the collagen and elastin become inflamed, causing damage to the relevant parts of the body. We have already discussed two autoimmune CTDs; rheumatoid arthritis and lupus are autoimmune disorders affecting the connective tissue.

In **heritable CTDs**, defects in the synthesis of collagen or elastin may result in the production of proteins that are not strong enough, or in the production of insufficient amounts of normal proteins.

As collagen and elastin are widespread throughout the body, CTDs can cause a wide range of issues. They may affect our bones, joints, skin, heart, blood vessels, lungs, eyes, ears, guts, kidneys, etc. Some of these issues manifest as obvious physical problems, such as brittle bones, over-flexible or unstable joints, skin hyperelasticity, and progressive deformities including flat feet, bow-leggedness, scoliosis, lordosis, and so on. However, the less-visible issues affecting other parts of the body are no less important, and can have a severe impact on people's quality of life, and even on their life expectancy. Some complications, such as spontaneous arterial rupture or uterine rupture in pregnancy, can be fatal.

For most patients, however, the prognosis is nowhere near as bleak. The degree to which CTDs affect each person depends on the severity of symptoms, which in turn depends on a combination of genetic and environmental factors. Unfortunately, this variability has been an obstacle to diagnosis; for instance, Ehlers–Danlos syndromes were originally believed to affect 0.0002-0.0004% of the general population, but are now estimated to affect at least 0.02%. This huge jump in estimated prevalence has resulted from changes in diagnostic criteria.

Despite these changes, obtaining a diagnosis of connective tissue disorder can still be difficult. Some symptoms of CTDs can also be symptoms of other conditions or issues; for instance, frequent bruising, scarring, and dislocations in children may lead doctors to suspect and investigate abuse, rather than any physiological cause. Other symptoms, such as chronic musculoskeletal pain and frequent injuries, may be dismissed as being self-explanatory: if you injure yourself a lot, of course you'll be hurting! The fact that we don't injure ourselves on purpose, or doing overly dangerous things, is not always noted.

These diagnostic issues are most serious for those of us whose connective tissue problems are subclinical. For instance, our joints may be unstable, rather than hypermobile; we may not be able to bend them more than "normal," but we sprain, strain, or dislocate them with remarkable frequency and ease. While these issues may not seem very serious – they definitely pale into insignificance compared to the risk of a spontaneous arterial rupture – they can have a severe impact on our quality of life. This can be especially true if we are not aware of them or are not able to make the adjustments necessary to prevent pain, injuries, and deformities.

Unfortunately, without a formal diagnosis, we are often unable to request the necessary school and workplace accommodations. We may also be unable to get prompt and effective treatment when injuries do occur.

Over time, the accumulation of injuries can end up masking some of our symptoms; for instance, arthritis can make our joints less mobile. Our back pain may be explained away because of our poor posture, even though our poor posture may be the result of back pain. We may also compensate for our structural instability by overusing our muscles; this may reduce the number of injuries we suffer, but it can manifest as fatigue and all-over aches and pains.

11% of respondents have a connective tissue disorder. However, 22% have joint hypermobility, and 21% easily injure their joints.

Hormonal uterine and related disorders

As you'll see shortly, these conditions are very different, but they all have one thing in common: they are all linked to hormonal imbalances. Unless the affected organ is removed, managing hormonal levels is a key aspect of managing the symptoms and progression of these conditions.

Unfortunately these conditions have something else in common: most of their symptoms are hard to quantify. Many of them could be assumed to be the symptoms of severe period discomfort or premenstrual syndrome (PMS) – or, if the doctor in question does not trust their patient, the symptoms of a regular menstrual cycle as related by a whiner or a malingerer.

Technically, this misdiagnosis should not be possible. PMS is not a throwaway term; it's a formal diagnosis that should only be given once conditions that can cause similar symptoms have been ruled out. However, all too often doctors assume PMS and treat patients accordingly, and only carry out further investigations if the symptoms get worse, or if the patient tries and fails to conceive for a set period of time.

There are several major problems with this. Aside from the fact that these conditions can have a far greater impact on a person's quality of life than regular periods or PMS, they are progressive. Failing to diagnose and treat them early can mean having to deal with far greater problems. Furthermore, many of the treatments recommended for managing periods and PMS are either obvious (e.g., if you're in pain, take painkillers), irrelevant (e.g., don't drink or smoke), or ineffective (e.g., many "natural" remedies). Those which do have a relevant impact are often geared towards *increasing* estrogen levels. As three of these conditions are caused by high estrogen levels, persevering with treatments that increase estrogen can exacerbate them. For people with fibrocystic breast disease, high estrogen levels also increase the risk of breast cancer.

This isn't a neurodivergent problem; it's a potential problem for anyone with a uterus or breasts. However, it might disproportionately affect neurodivergent people for two reasons. Firstly, many of us are at the receiving end of medical stigma because of our neurodivergence or of the co-occurring conditions. This can make some doctors less likely to take our symptoms seriously. Secondly, as a community, we are habitually sleep-deprived. Lack of sleep and irregular sleeping patterns have been proven to have deleterious effects on people's hormonal balance, with dangerous results; for instance, night shift work may be linked to an increased risk of breast cancer.

Endometriosis

Endometriosis is a condition where the lining of the uterus (endometrium) grows in areas where it doesn't belong, most commonly the ovaries, fallopian tubes, and the tissue lining the pelvis. This can result in heavy or irregular bleeding and a lot of pain: painful periods, pain during or around ovulation, pain during or after sex, pain with bowel movements or urination, and pain in the pelvic area, lower back, or legs. Endometriosis hurts, and it hurts a lot of people: it is currently estimated to affect 10% of AFABs worldwide.

Uterine fibroids

Uterine fibroids (leiomyomas) are noncancerous growths of the uterus. They are very common (the estimated prevalence is 70-80+% of AFABs, depending on ethnicity) and are not necessarily dangerous or problematic. Many people have fibroids without even knowing it, because they don't have any symptoms. The impact of fibroids depends on their size, number, and position. While small fibroids may not cause any symptoms, large ones can push against the sides of the uterus, changing its shape and pressing against other internal organs.

When fibroids cause symptoms, these often include heavy menstrual bleeding, excessively long menstrual periods, pelvic pressure or pain, frequent urination, difficulties emptying the bladder, constipation, backache, or leg pains. In rare cases, fibroids can outgrow their blood supply and begin to die off, causing acute pain. Large or numerous fibroids can also interfere with fertility and cause pregnancy loss.

Fibrocystic breast disease

Fibrocystic breast disease is caused when an imbalance between estrogen and progesterone results in proliferation of connective tissue (fibrosis) in the breasts. This results in the development of fibrocystic plaques, nodularity, cysts, and fibrocystic lumps in the breast tissue. These abnormalities are classified as benign (i.e., not cancerous), but they can be extremely painful. Also, the risk of breast cancer is 2-4 times higher in patients with fibrocystic breast disease.

Although estimates of the prevalence of fibrocystic breast disease vary hugely, this disease is believed to be quite common, affecting up to 50% of AFABs over the age of 30. However, "only" 20% of them develop painful macrocysts (large cysts).

Polycystic ovarian syndrome (PCOS)

Polycystic ovarian syndrome differs from the previous two conditions as it is caused by the ovaries producing unusually high levels of hormones called androgens (aka "male hormones"). The underlying cause is as yet unknown, but PCOS has a genetic component and is co-morbid with insulin resistance and chronic low-grade inflammation.

Despite the name of the condition, not all patients with PCOS have ovarian cysts. Common symptoms include unexplained and uncontrollable weight gain, erratic menstrual cycles, abnormal hair growth (hirsutism), hair loss, and skin problems including acne, skin tags, and dark skin patches. As the condition runs in families, some patients may not realize that they are experiencing symptoms of a condition; to them, their experience is normal. There is also considerable variability in how patients present, and some patients have no symptoms.

These diagnostic difficulties can have a significant negative impact on people's health because PCOS puts patients at a higher risk for several health conditions, including diabetes, high blood pressure, cardiovascular disease, endometrial hyperplasia, endometrial cancer, sleep disorders, depression, and anxiety. Early diagnosis and appropriate interventions can make a significant difference to patients' long-term health outcomes.

11% of survey participants with a uterus have endometriosis, 10% have fibroids, 8% have fibrocystic breast disease, and 16% have PCOS. These numbers may seem low, or at any rate not much higher than those seen in the general population. However, as these conditions are routinely under-

or misdiagnosed, and as neurodivergent people are at greater risk of not being taken seriously by their doctors, these statistics may underestimate the prevalence of these condition in our community.

Chronic and recurring pain conditions

Many medical conditions have chronic or recurrent pain as a symptom, but some conditions "only" cause pain, sometimes without a clearly recognizable cause. These conditions are often the hardest for us to get appropriate treatment for. This isn't because treating them is hard, although that can be a factor. Quite simply, it can be hard for pain sufferers to be treated properly by their doctors due to biases in the medical field.[61]

Some of these biases affect us regardless of our symptoms. For instance, racial biases have been shown to result in disparities in health care.[62] Incorrect beliefs about biological differences between Black and white people can result in racial disparities in pain assessment and treatment – as in, a frightening proportion of white doctors believe that Black people don't feel pain like they do, and as a result, they underprescribe pain meds.[63] Gender biases mean that men are investigated and treated more extensively than women with the same conditions and severity of symptoms.[64] All things being equal, women are less likely than men to be admitted to an intensive care unit and more likely to die after a critical illness.[65] Women in pain are much more likely than men to receive prescriptions for sedatives, rather than pain meds.[66]

These issues are compounded for sufferers of chronic pain conditions, who are routinely assumed to be drug seekers until proven otherwise. As most of these conditions cannot be diagnosed through quantitative tests, we simply cannot prove that our pain is real. If we are forced to make multiple visits to our doctor to discuss the same symptoms, this can be interpreted as confirmation that we are seeking drugs, regardless of what we are actually asking for. This can be a particular problem for those of us who are subjected to multiple biases – for instance, Black women.

---

[61] https://www.ncbi.nlm.nih.gov/pmc/articles/PMC3417145/
[62] https://www.ncbi.nlm.nih.gov/pmc/articles/PMC3797360/
[63] https://www.ncbi.nlm.nih.gov/pmc/articles/PMC4843483/
[64] https://journals.sagepub.com/doi/10.2217/17455057.4.3.237
[65] https://www.ncbi.nlm.nih.gov/pmc/articles/PMC2096494/
[66] https://www.health.harvard.edu/blog/women-and-pain-disparities-in-experience-and-treatment-2017100912562

There are numerous chronic and recurrent pain conditions, but we will only look at two relatively common ones.

Trigeminal nerve conditions

The trigeminal nerve is responsible for sensations such as heat or pain in our face. There are two trigeminal nerves, one on each side of the face, branching up to the forehead, across the cheek, down the jaw, and above the ear. If this nerve is irritated, compressed, or triggered, it can cause severe facial pain. There are many trigeminal nerve conditions. Two common ones are:

- **Cluster headaches:** a series of short but painful headaches affecting one side of the head, often around the eye. The pain comes on quickly, is focused behind or around one eye but may spread throughout the face, and "only" lasts 30 to 90 minutes.
- **Trigeminal neuralgia:** a condition affecting the trigeminal nerve, but without a clear pattern. Jolts of excruciating pain can be triggered by stimulation of the face (e.g., from teeth brushing), or might just happen. These jolts can occur individually, or come in volleys lasting as long as two hours.[67] Trigeminal neuralgia is usually caused by compression of the trigeminal nerve, which causes damage to the myelin sheath that protects it. It can also be the result of direct injury to the nerve, from a blow, surgery, or a stroke. The condition can be progressive, with the attacks increasing in frequency, intensity, and duration.

Cluster headaches and trigeminal neuralgia can have a serious impact on people's quality of life, as the pain is so intense as to be incapacitating. Thankfully, they are rare: cluster headaches only affect an estimated 0.124% of the general population, while trigeminal neuralgia only affects 0.01-0.92%. Unfortunately, this rarity does not seem to apply to the neurodivergent community.

38% of respondents reported that they have cluster headaches. That means that the prevalence of cluster headaches in our community is 306 times greater than in the general population. 3% of respondents reported that they have trigeminal neuralgia. That means that the prevalence of trigeminal neuralgia in our community is somewhere between 3 and 300

---

[67] Wanna know something funny? I currently fail to meet the diagnostic criteria for cluster headaches *or* trigeminal neuralgia because my attacks now last too long (up to 4 days) and occur too regularly (during the stages of my cycle when my estrogen levels peak). Hence, as far as my official records are concerned, I am now cured of both conditions! Party on!

times greater than in the general population. And these numbers may be underestimating the real prevalence of these conditions, because many people are not aware they exist. Over half of survey respondents reported that they suffer from recurring, severe attacks of facial pain. In case you were wondering, this isn't normal.

Fibromyalgia

Fibromyalgia derives its name from the Latin "fibro" (for fibrous tissue) and the Greek "myo" (muscle) and "algia" (pain). It's literally "pain in the muscles and fibers." It's also a huge pain in the ass.

Current diagnostic criteria include:

- Widespread muscle and joint pain that has persisted for at least three months and has no other identifiable causes.

- Tender points – specific spots around the joints that hurt when pressed. The same amount of pressure in the same locations would not hurt a person without fibro. Not everyone with fibromyalgia has tender points, but some doctors still consider them a requirement for diagnosis.

- Fatigue. Patients often wake up tired, even if they have had plenty of sleep, and do not feel refreshed after resting.

9% of respondents have fibro. As current estimates for prevalence in the general population are 3-6%, we are, yet again, exceeding expectations.

Undiagnosed chronic pain

A host of medical conditions can cause normally benign or even pleasurable sensations to be painful, increase our pain sensitivity, or cause widespread or chronic pain. Unfortunately, unless our pain is taken seriously by our medical providers, we may never know what is causing it, let alone get the treatment we need and deserve. Survey results suggest that this issue affects 30-40% of our community.

This is depressing but unsurprising given the prevalence of chronic sleep deprivation in our community. Research shows that up to 70% of ADHDers and 80% of Autistics are habitually sleep-deprived. Research also shows that sleep impairments are a stronger, more reliable predictor of pain than pain is of sleep impairments. What this means is that sleep and chronic pain are related, but that that relationship isn't reciprocal, as previously believed – i.e., chronic pain doesn't cause sleep deprivation, which in turn worsens chronic pain. While this reciprocal connection makes perfect sense in theory, current findings indicate that poor sleep comes first, and chronic pain follows. A feedback loop may then be created, but addressing the pain while ignoring the sleep is unlikely to resolve the situation.

This isn't to say that if we fixed our sleep, all of our pains would magically disappear. However, addressing and preventing sleep deprivation might be a good place to start.

Fatigue

Fatigue - a condition marked by extreme tiredness and the inability to function due to lack of energy – presents us with many of the same issues affecting chronic pain sufferers. Fatigue cannot be measured, so we depend on our medical providers taking us seriously and running the appropriate investigations. If those investigations don't come up with an organic cause for our fatigue, how we are diagnosed and treated may depend more on our doctors' biases than on our symptoms.

62% of respondents experience fatigue even when they haven't done anything to tire themselves out, and 47% experience an unreasonable amount of fatigue when they exert themselves.

Undiagnosed chronic fatigue sufferers may face huge difficulties in everyday life. Without a diagnosis, it can be impossible for us to obtain workplace adaptations or disability benefits. We may also face pushbacks from our nearest and dearest, particularly if our doctors insist that our fatigue "is all in our heads." Diagnosed chronic fatigue sufferers may also face pushbacks and discrimination, particularly if they are diagnosed with Myalgic Encephalomyelitis/Chronic Fatigue Syndrome (ME/CFS), which is still poorly regarded by medical professionals who ought to know better.

Interpersonal stressors

There is plenty of research out there confirming what many of us already know: peopleing can be hard for us. We struggle to navigate short-term interactions and to establish and maintain long-term connections. The overall result is what the experts refer to as "poorer social function outcomes."[68]

The assumed wisdom is that our social problems are the result of our neurodivergence. We exhibit inappropriate behaviors, mess up during social interactions, and struggle to modulate our actions and reactions. It's small wonder that we end up straining our relationships, often to breaking point.[69]

My personal theory is that the assumed wisdom is a load of ableist tosh, and says more about the fundamental lack of understanding and tolerance of diversity inherent in our culture than about us. Our interpersonal problems are not caused directly by what we do, but by how our actions are interpreted by the people around us, which is a reflection of our culture. And our culture is nowhere near as flexible, caring, or tolerant as it purports to be.

Now, I am obviously talking nonsense, because there is no such thing as "our culture." Despite the internet and media trying to tell us otherwise, different countries still have different cultures, as well as multitudes of subcultures. Each of these has its own criteria for what appropriate behavior looks like and what inappropriate behavior is taken to mean. Every statement I am going to make in the rest of this section is going to be painfully generic, but that doesn't mean that everything I say is going to be wrong, or useless. Centuries of history have meant that some cultures have spread more than others, and now have a much greater impact on multicultural spaces. History is written by the victors, and social mores are established by the colonizers. And the very fact that some cultures virtually eradicated those of the areas they colonized tells us a hell of a lot about just how inclusive and tolerant they were.

Our culture, like all cultures, has its own etiquette: a set of conventions and norms that are classed as polite behavior. For instance, listening in silence is considered polite, while interrupting is rude, even when we interrupt to ask for clarifications or additional details. Attention is

---

[68] https://journals.sagepub.com/doi/10.1177/1087054713486516

[69] https://chadd.org/for-adults/relationships-social-skills/

demonstrated through the appropriate amount of eye contact, even though the existence and popularity of the telephone prove that many humans are perfectly able to converse without gazing into their interlocutor's eyes. Alas, social conventions are A Thing, and they stipulate the way in which conversations should be carried out. These stipulations are so entrenched it's easy to lose sight of the fact that they are neither universal nor inescapable. Other cultures favor more participatory conversational style, or consider eye contact to be rude. These cultures are not wrong, or rude; they just hold different norms.

The assumption of universality in customs is, in and of itself, a huge issue; it can create standards of "politeness" and "professionalism" that exclude or punish people from different cultural backgrounds. Neurodivergent people who cannot respect those customs can be similarly affected, because our spontaneous behaviors not meet the accepted norm.

That is only the start of our problems. Our culture also has a tendency to assume that breaches of etiquette must have an underlying motive, usually a nefarious one. It couldn't be that we interrupted because that is what we are used to where we are from, because we need additional information, or because we are so engaged in the conversation that our neurotypical mask slipped: we must be doing it deliberately, to convey a specific message. Often, that message is taken to be part of some kind of power play. This is what an etiquette expert has to say on the subject:

> "When you interrupt someone it says to the person talking that what you have to say is more important than what they are sharing. It shows disregard for the person and what they are saying."[70]

According to this particular expert and to a myriad of her colleagues interrupting is "rude, arrogant and selfish," and we should all just cut it out. This is an interesting approach, as it entirely ignores the existence of people with auditory processing or short-term memory problems. We often need to interrupt a flow of words to ask for repetitions, reminders, or clarifications just to follow the conversation. The alternative is to let people ramble on way past the point where we can follow them, wait for them to come to a natural stop, and then ask them to repeat themselves, which can waste a lot of time and cause a lot of frustration. I am unclear as to whether the expert I quoted is unaware of our existence or simply

---

[70] https://www.cliseetiquette.com/tag/why-interrupting-is-rude/

doesn't care. I am very clear, however, about the impact of opinions like hers on the neurodivergent community. Spoiler alert: it's not good.

Other aspects of communication are subject to the same cultural filters. For instance, cultures vary hugely in their approaches to non-verbal communication. Our culture favors a restrained non-verbal communication style, with limited gesturing, facial expressions, and changes in volume or pitch. Excessive animation is interpreted as a lack of manners or self-control. In more animated cultures, on the other hand, a restrained style can suggest lack of emotion or interest.[71] "Ask Cultures" favor a direct communication style, where people ask directly what they want and need and are ready to accept equally direct answers. "Guess Cultures," on the other hand, seek to minimize the chance of answers in the negative by approaching issues indirectly. Responses are expected to be equally indirect unless they are unequivocally positive.[72]

Cultures also vary in their approach to time. Monochronic cultures eschew multitasking and value strict timekeeping. Polychronic cultures, by contrast, embrace multitasking and respond flexibly to interruptions.[73] Linear-active cultures value careful planning of orderly processes, while multi-active cultures prioritize based on urgency or importance.[74]

The bottom line is not just that we can look "more neurodivergent" in some cultural settings than in others, but that there is no inherent wrongness in the way we are. Many of our social difficulties would disappear if our culture was genuinely tolerant of alternative approaches, didn't regard them as inferior, and didn't so readily ascribe them to malice.[75] [76] Alas, that isn't likely to happen in the immediate future. As a result, many of us experience varying degrees of socialization difficulties. These socialization difficulties have an impact on our ability to connect with other individuals, to form healthy and mutually beneficial close relationships, to gain acceptance in groups, or to have a comfortable and safe role in the groups we belong to. This can have a significant impact on our quality of life, and even put our life in danger.

---

[71] https://www.jet-training.org.uk/wp-content/uploads/2015/06/SHC21-Communications.pdf
[72] https://medium.com/redhill-review/navigating-ask-and-guess-cultures-in-a-modern-world-30b167f8ab09
[73] https://thearticulateceo.typepad.com/my-blog/2011/08/cultural-differences-monochronic-versus-polychronic.html
[74] https://www.businessinsider.com/the-lewis-model-2013-9?r=US&IR=T
[75] https://lateness.org/lateness-org/motivations-for-lateness/
[76] https://lateness.org/lateness-org/subconscious-motives/

Communication difficulties

Current stereotypes of neurodivergence hold communication difficulties to be largely an Autistic issue. That's hilarious, considering that four communication issues form part of the diagnostic criteria for ADHD, namely:

- Difficulties listening to conversations and staying on topic (filed under "inattention").

- Excessive talking (filed under "hyperactivity").

- Frequent interrupting or intruding on others, and starting conversations at inappropriate times (filed under "impulsivity").

So, ADHDers don't know how to or when to have a conversation, but communication problems aren't an aspect of our neurodivergence. Hmkay.

I have a theory as to why this is. Many Anglophone cultures have been at least partly influenced by British etiquette. Alas, there is a notable mismatch between the typical ADHD communication style and said etiquette – and that's putting it mildly. As a result of our numerous breaches of etiquette, our communication difficulties are often interpreted as manifestations of rudeness, selfishness, sense of superiority, or lack of empathy. How often this happens and how much it will impact our social life will vary depending on our circumstances, but most Anglophone ADHDers will be affected to at least some degree. Our conversational difficulties are treated as problems we cause to the people around us, rather than as issues affecting our life.

The opposite is often true of Autistic communication difficulties. It has been amply demonstrated that many of the communication difficulties typically associated with Autism actually stem from bi-directional differences in social communication and behavior – i.e., the issue isn't that Autistic people can't communicate, but that Autistic and allistic (i.e., non-Autistic) communication styles are profoundly different, and these differences cause miscommunications and a failure to establish rapport.[77] Unfortunately, this information has done nothing to change the popular view of Autistic communication as inherently defective. As a result, Autistic conversational difficulties are treated as pervasive personal deficiencies, rather than as issues affecting certain interactions.

---

[77] https://www.frontiersin.org/articles/10.3389/fpsyg.2021.739147/full
Please note the multitude of sources that support the theories presented in this article.

Interrupting or spacing out during conversations or lectures

Interrupting and spacing out are two of the traits that are assessed during an ADHD diagnosis. Interrupting is seen as a sign of impulsivity, while spacing out is seen as a sign of inattention. This classification makes some dangerous assumptions, because there could be countless other reasons for us to interrupt or space out – for instance, we may have an auditory processing disorder, we might need extra time or information to process what we just heard, or we might just have heard it all before.

This isn't to say that these issues don't affect us. 56% of survey respondents interrupt during conversations or lectures, and 84% space out during conversations or lectures. However, these results should be looked in the context of our neurodivergent traits. The vast majority of us aren't auditory learners, over a third of us have Auditory Processing Disorder, and three quarters of us have working memory problems. This means that we may struggle to process what we hear and when we do, we struggle to retain it. In this context, chalking down to inattention and impulsivity our inability to follow a stream of speech seems rather incongruous.

Non-verbal communication

Non-verbal communication is the combination of facial expressions, gestures, loudness and tone of voice, body language, proxemics or personal space, eye contact, and touch we use while we interact with others. Failures to give out the right signals or to correctly interpret the signals we receive can result in corrections, complaints, or passive-aggressive friction. In the right (or rather, wrong) situations, it can even lead to violence.

28% of respondents struggle to notice or interpret non-verbal communication cues. 37% of respondents struggle to give out socially appropriate non-verbal communication cues. These issues do not go unnoticed: 41% of respondents are often or always told that their body language, facial expression, or tone of voice are inappropriate.

These communication difficulties, unsurprisingly, can lead to miscommunications. 58% of respondents find that people misinterpret what they are saying or make incorrect assumptions as to the intentions behind their words.

Eye contact

Many Western cultures treat eye contact as an essential prerequisite to good communication and interpersonal connection. That's interesting, because this view is far from universal. There are plenty of cultures which recognize that people can listen to and respect others without linking eyeballs with them – in fact, there are plenty of cultures which consider direct eye contact rude.[78] There is also plenty of evidence that eye contact isn't essential to communication; anyone who ever used a telephone can attest to that. Yet many Western cultures deem eye contact so important that neurodivergent children are put through grueling training regimes to force them to "do it right" – i.e., to maintain the neurotypically-approved amount of eye contact, regardless of the costs.

And there are costs. For many of us, maintaining eye contact isn't "just" unpleasant; it can create a barrier to learning and interpersonal connection. Having to constantly think about and adjust the amount of eye contact we give out takes up mental resources we could otherwise use for listening and learning. Constantly worrying about whether we are doing eye contact right is stressful, and can prevent us from being truly present in our interactions. And that's for those of us who are not naturally wired for neurotypical-style eye contact, but don't find it totally overwhelming. For some of us, enforced eye contact is so uncomfortable that all other functions go offline. It can make us incapable of processing verbal inputs and can be a trigger for meltdowns, shutdowns, and selective mutism. But hey, eye contact is critical for the comfort of the neurotypicals around us, so it has to take priority, right?

46% of respondents find direct eye contact unpleasant. 57% of respondents have to consciously regulate the amount of eye contact they make in order to appear "normal." As this requires sustained effort and is a potential cause of stress, it is not inconceivable that it would have a detrimental impact on our ability to function in those circumstances.

57% of respondents pretend to make eye contact in order to appear "normal," but they are actually focusing on something else. That's just one of the coping mechanisms we can use to appease the neurotypicals instead of making actual eye contact. I wonder how many therapists are aware of these tricks, and teach them to their patients.

Of course, it would also be theoretically feasible to teach neurotypicals to cope without eye contact from us, but that would require a rather large

---

[78] Yet even those whose business it is to know that, seem to forget it with remarkable frequency. This was the first sentence of a scientific article about cross-cultural differences in eye contact: "The eyes have a universal language."
Your own study contradicts that, good sirs. But hey, you're the experts.

shift in perspective. If we start asking those who aren't affected by an issue to make minor adaptations to their expectations so that issue stops being an issue, where would we end up?

Phatic communication

Phatic communication, aka small talk, is communication that serves to establish or maintain social relationships rather than to exchange information. Information is exchanged, in a way, but that exchange happens around the words, rather than through them. If we met at a bus stop and started chatting about the weather, that exchange would not be about giving one of us the opportunity to inform the other of what the weather is. We would both be experiencing the same weather, after all. The information we would actually be exchanging is our mutual good will. We would be talking to show that we are willing to communicate and connect with each other, rather than to exchange data.

By contrast, if we met at a bus stop and one of us started to talk about how the approaching clouds are nimbostratus rather than stratocumulus, and therefore a long walk without an umbrella might not be a good idea, we would be exchanging actual information. We might also be manifesting our mutual good will by sharing an interesting and useful fact, but that intention might not always come across, particularly if our interlocutor is neurotypical.

Phatic communication can be misinterpreted, too, particularly as it's not consistent across all cultures. For instance, in some cultures people may ask us out for food or drinks because they actually want to go out with us for food or drinks, while in other cultures it's just a gesture of general good will. Responding in the affirmative may mean that we have accepted a social obligation, or that we also feel general good will towards the person who asked us out. And unless we know how that particular culture operates, we might have no idea what just happened and what we are expected to do next.

Phatic communication only works if both parties understand which parts should not be taken literally, and how they should be interpreted. That it should be the norm for establishing social connections baffles me – unless the fact that it can so easily fail is a feature, rather than a bug. Outsiders may be able to learn our language well enough to go unnoticed, but picking up all socially appropriate phatic cues is far harder, particularly as they are not usually taught formally. Phatic communication failures could make outsiders easier to spot, so we can throw pointy rocks at them or chase them out of our cave. This is just my current pet theory, though, so don't take it as gospel.

What's hard to disagree with is that many of us struggle with small talk, and that this can have an impact on our ability to function in some social settings. 62% of respondents are uncomfortable with small talk. Of these, 58% struggle to function in group situations that do not center around a defined activity.

"Infodumping"

Infodumping is both a communication style and a way of connecting with people. Instead of establishing a connection by chatting about trite subjects (e.g., the weather), people who infodump connect by providing copious information about a subject they hold dear. It's the communication equivalent of bringing someone a shiny thing – I am sharing one of my passions with you in the hope that you will also derive enjoyment from it.

Unfortunately, infodumping is often misinterpreted by people whose communication style is different. In Western cultures, infodumping is often misconstrued as a power move, or as a demonstration of our lack of interest or respect in our interlocutor. If we cared about them, we wouldn't use them as a receptacle for unrequested information only we find interesting, after all.

Hyperlexia

Hyperlexia derives its name from Greek terms "hyper" (overmuch) and "lexis" (word – the root of "lexicon"). Contrary to popular misconceptions, the term does not literally mean "too much reading;" if anything, it would be better translated as "too much wording." While that's not good English, it's a damn good explanation of the nature of hyperlexia and the problems it can cause.

Hyperlexia in children is sometimes associated with learning to read early and to an abnormally advanced level, but that's not always the case. Hyperlexia and dyslexia can coexist,[79] so a person may struggle with the physical act of reading and still be hyperlexic. I think the reading side of hyperlexia attracts most of the focus because it is easy to spot and measure, but this distracts from the most impactful aspect of hyperlexia: that it is a passion for language that, when it isn't shared, can end up

---

[79] And in case you're wondering, yes, I am both dyslexic and hyperlexic.

causing severe communication and socialization difficulties.

There are two reasons for this. Firstly, when we use words other people cannot understand, that creates a communication barrier. It's as simple as that. It is no different to speaking a different language, or speaking with an accent so different as to be unintelligible. People just can't understand what we are saying.

In childhood, that can lead to socialization issues. Young children may become frustrated with us, and us with them. Children old enough to group themselves into cliques are also old enough to classify us as weird, and that can lead to social exclusion and even bullying.

As we grow up, however, a second issue arises: it isn't uncommon for people to use overcomplicated language as a tool for establishing superiority, or asserting someone else's inferiority. As a result, when one uses a word someone else doesn't understand, this is often assumed to be a deliberate attack: I am choosing to use words you don't know in order to make you feel st@pid, or to make you look st@pid in public. This is patently absurd, because we cannot know whether other people know a word until we use it. However, from personal experience, pointing this out aggravates people even more.

As a result of these communication and socialization issues, hyperlexia can cause severe social friction in multiple settings. It can also lead to academic difficulties, especially for young children, for three main reasons. Firstly, if we are spending our evenings reading adult fiction, it is incredibly hard to pay attention to lessons about how Spot The Dog found his ball. If you've ever been asked by a toddler to watch their favorite show, you know the feeling. As a result, children may overperform in their learning while underperforming in their academic achievements. You can end up with children who read "Moby-Dick" in their spare time,[80] but repeatedly fail their tests because trace, copy, and recall exercises are just too boring to keep their attention.

The disconnect between what children know and what they are supposed to learn can also cause behavioral issues. Bored and frustrated children aren't generally good students. If teachers cannot find a way to keep their hyperlexic students focused and busy – or, at the very least, to let them carry out their own learning at their own pace, regardless of what

---

[80] Or is that just me? In fairness, nobody told me that "Moby-Dick" wasn't meant for children. It had an animal in it, after all. I thought all animal books were children books.

the rest of the class is doing – disciplinary difficulties can ensue.

The last reason is less wholesome. Not all teachers are comfortable dealing with children who know too much. Sometimes this is purely because of the extra work involved – managing advanced learners can require an extra set of activities, and teachers have enough on their plates already. However, some teachers' ego is wrapped in being the smartest or most knowledgeable person in their classroom. When children reveal that they know as much or more than them – or, heaven forfend, prove them wrong about something – these teachers can become so irked that they lose their ability to remain professional and treat their advanced students fairly. Other students may imitate their teachers' behavior, or escalate it into social ostracism and bullying. After all, if a teacher is doing it, it must be the right thing to do!

So, while learning to read early and to an abnormally advanced level are common signs of hyperlexia, they aren't the crux of the matter. Hyperlexia can cause serious communication, socialization, and academic performance issues. This is particularly true for undiagnosed hyperlexics, who might not know what is causing their problems. Unfortunately, as hyperlexia is poorly known, many of us fall into this camp.

10% of survey respondents are hyperlexic. However, traits and issues commonly associated with hyperlexia affect a much greater proportion of respondents. 50% of respondents have a passion for learning new words or languages. 49% of them have to translate their thoughts into simpler language to communicate with those around them. 35% get in trouble for using words that are "too complicated."

Prosopagnosia and Lethonomia

Prosopagnosia or face blindness is a condition characterized by difficulties in facial recognition. These difficulties can arise from a variety of causes, including visual processing issues, memory issues, and neurological disorders. Different people are affected to different degrees; some people struggle to recognize faces they aren't overly familiar with. Other people can't recognize any faces, including those of loved ones and even their own.[81]

People with mild prosopagnosia may not be aware that they have an

---

[81] http://www.hopesandfears.com/hopes/future/science/216395-how-does-your-brain-remember-a-face

issue, for two simple reasons. Firstly, this condition isn't commonly known or mentioned. Unless we stumble upon it by chance, or by reading neurodivergent content, we might never hear about it.

Secondly, even if we do hear about it, we might not realize that it applies to us. We may be vaguely aware of the fact that we struggle to recognize faces in the wild, but we have no way of knowing how easy other people find it. As with any chronic condition, because it's all we know, we might not realize that it is a condition at all.

Over time, some of us unconsciously develop coping mechanisms that allow us to recognize people using other markers – their hairstyle, their clothes, their voice, their posture or gait, and so on. Alas, these strategies only work if those markers are reliable. If we are dealing with an extremely homogeneous population – for instance, students at a school that enforces a strict dress and hairstyle code – we might struggle to tell people apart. Also, people are often sneaky, and may change their clothes and hairstyle without warning us in advance.

7% of respondents have prosopagnosia, while 60% aren't sure. However, looking at the symptoms of prosopagnosia paints a rather different picture. 37% of respondents struggle to recognize people out of context, and 23% struggle to recognize people if they change their hair or clothes. These two issues overlap: 92% of those who struggle to recognize people if they change their hair or clothes also struggle to recognize people out of context.

Lethonomia is the inability to remember names. Some of us can learn names, but cannot recall them on demand. Some of us just cannot memorize names.

These issues may seem trivial, but they can cause severe social difficulties because a lot of people are hurt or offended when we cannot recognize them or forget their names. Do we care so little about them that we don't even notice them? Are we trying to slight them by deliberately ignoring them in public?

Science has amply demonstrated that face recognition and memory are functions that work or fail regardless of our feelings. However, it is still common for people to believe that forgetting someone's face or name shows our lack of care or respect for that person. There are also people out there who believe that we might pretend to have forgotten them just to score a point; the slight felt by the forgotten person is clearly more significant than any shame we may feel.

The way we feel about these issues belies these theories: 58% of respondents worry about the possibility of not recognizing someone or not remembering their name. The prevalence of this worry is much higher amongst those who have traits associated with prosopagnosia: 86% of those who struggle to recognize people out of context worry about the possibility of not recognizing someone or not remembering their name, as do 92% of those who struggle to recognize people if they change their hair or clothes.

Current studies suggest that social anxiety affects our ability to recognize faces; there is a marked correlation between those two issues, and the latter is considered to be the result of the former. I harbor the hope that researchers may one day consider the possibility that they are looking at this from the wrong angle; that they might accept that real, congenital difficulties in recognizing faces may be a cause of social anxiety due to the social difficulties they create.

Selective mutism

Selective mutism is a rather unfortunate term, as it suggests an element of choice that is wholly absent from the phenomenon. "Situational mutism" would be a much more accurate label.

Selective mutism means that we become temporarily unable to speak when we are exposed to certain triggers – public speaking or any social situation that cause us anxiety are common triggers. We might be able to think of what we want to say, but the words just won't come out, or may only come out in a whisper or a jumble. Our throat may feel constricted or paralyzed. The anticipation that we won't be able to speak can cause us extreme anxiety, and this may lead us to avoid certain situations or to fail to participate in certain activities.[82]

Selective mutism usually starts during childhood and, without appropriate support, can persist into adulthood. 10% of respondents have selective mutism.

Alexithymia

Alexithymia is a fascinating neurodivergence because it can have a huge impact on our ability to self-regulate, communicate, and socialize, but most people have never heard of it.

---

[82] http://www.selectivemutism.org.uk/info-what-does-selective-mutism-mean/

Alexithymia is a difficulty experiencing, identifying, and expressing emotions. The word comes from Greek: "a" meaning lack, "lexis" meaning word, and "thymos" meaning emotion. However, alexithymia is not just a "lack of words" to describe emotions. We struggle to express our emotions to others because we struggle to identify them in ourselves. This can be linked to problems with introspection (the examination of our mental and emotional processes) or interoception (the perception of the state of our body).

Alexithymia can also make it difficult for us to identify and respond to emotions in others. This can lead to interpersonal and social issues.

Alexithymia is not currently classed as a neurodivergence or condition in its own right. It is usually only diagnosed as co-occurring with Autism and some mental health conditions. This is somewhat problematic, to put it mildly, and the issue isn't just one of diagnosis; it's the lack of information that matters.

Alexithymia can have a profound and serious impact on our life, but if we have always lived with it, we may not realize that. We can't tell how we feel, but we don't know that we should be able to. We may not look for ways to compensate for this issue, because we are not aware that it is an issue. Also, we might be aware that the people around us are operating on a different level, but we don't know why, which gives us no chance to bridge that gap.

The results of this survey reflect this lack of information. 13% of respondents said that they have alexithymia, which is in line with current estimates of the prevalence of alexithymia in the general population (10-13%, dependent on studies). However, 36% of respondents are unable to recognize their feelings, and 24% are unable to recognize other people's feelings. While the latter issue may be caused by communication problems – or, if you live in a culture that promotes emotional suppression, by the absence of a crystal ball – the former suggests that alexithymia is a possibility.

Emotional regulation

Emotional regulation is the ability to manage and respond to our emotional experiences in a manner that allows us emotional expression while being socially tolerable. This may require us to "translate" our emotions into socially-acceptable modes of expression, to temporarily suppress them until we are in a place where we can express them without social repercussions, or to use cognitive strategies to alter our initial emotional responses (i.e., to talk ourselves into a better mood).

By contrast, **emotional or mood lability** is the technical name for the tendency to experience unpredictable, uncontrollable, and rapid shifts in mood. It isn't the same as moodiness, because the shifts in mood do not always have an apparent or specific trigger. Mood lability can be a symptom of mood disorders, personality disorders, or PTSD/cPTSD, or occur as the result of traumatic brain damage or neurological illnesses. It can also be a side effect from the use of certain medications or substances.

Some neurodivergents experience rapid and dramatic shifts in mood that, while they might not meet the diagnostic criteria for mood lability, can still cause them significant problems. For instance, many ADHDers struggle with emotional self-regulation, both in childhood and as adults. We might struggle to control our reactions to negative stimuli, to calm ourselves down after experiencing intense emotions, to respond appropriately to changes in situations or expectations, and to manage our responses to frustration and upsets. This can have a pervasive negative impact on our life. Poor emotional self-regulation not only causes problems in the moment, such as the interpersonal, disciplinary, or legal consequences of inappropriate reactions to situations; it is also linked to the establishment and persistence of longer-term issues, including depression, addictions, and suicidal ideation.

There is an ongoing debate about emotionality in ADHD. The core issue is whether we experience stronger emotions than our neurotypical counterparts, or are just less able to control our feelings. This issue may affect the efficacy of interventions. Many of the current strategies for self-regulation are designed for neurotypical individuals; they might be of limited use to neurodivergent people who are dealing with a completely different emotional situation. If I may use a ludicrous analogy, a cat cage is perfectly suited to its intended purpose, but it won't hold a tiger.

19% of respondents said that they have mood lability. However, that doesn't mean that other respondents do not struggle with emotional regulation. 35% experience rapid, pronounced changes in mood with very little reason. 49% struggle to control their behavior when they are experiencing strong emotions. 39% get in trouble for behaving impulsively when they feel emotional.

There is another potential aspect of emotional self-regulation in neurodivergence. Many neurodivergent adults are survivors of trauma, or are forced to live in environments that traumatize them. This isn't necessarily due to deliberate neglect or abuse (although those happen), but to a chronic and critical mismatch between our abilities and the demands placed upon us. As childhood trauma is proven to have a long-lasting detrimental impact on emotional self-regulation, a discussion of trauma is critical to a discussion of self-regulation, and any intervention aimed at improving self-regulation should be trauma-informed.

The results of my survey bear this out. The prevalence of emotional self-regulation issues is higher in people who have symptoms caused by exposure to a traumatic event or to long-term trauma, abuse, or neglect. However, it is even higher in people who, in childhood, were forced by their parents or teachers to endure painful physical sensation in order to learn to get over them. This suggests that these attempts at "desensitization" therapies might have a worse impact on our emotional self-regulation than trauma, abuse, or neglect.

These results matter, because therapeutic interventions aimed at helping us develop self-regulation skills should take into account the underlying causes of our emotional issues. Therapies that fail to account for the impact of trauma – and, in particular, therapies that fail to account for the impact of trauma caused by other therapies – might fail to give us the right tools to address this issue. This issue may explain while current therapies and strategies designed to help children and adults improve their emotional regulation tend to have a limited impact on people's lives, as any improvements tend to be specific to a particular setting.

While learning to manage our emotions is an essential part of being a functional human being, there is a difference between learning to feel a feeling without acting upon it, and learning to suppress or to discount the feeling. Suppressing feelings may make our lives smoother and simpler in the short term, but it cuts us off from a very important source of information. In the context of abusive relationships, suppressing our feelings can make us slow to react to toxic situations, both in the short- and long-term. We may not respond to the fear we feel when a mugger or rapist targets us, or the icky feeling of dealing with a creep. We may also remain in an unhealthy relationship because we have lost access to the signals that would inform us that the relationship is unhealthy.

Doubting our feelings also makes us susceptible to gaslighting – "a form of persistent manipulation and brainwashing that causes the victim to doubt her or himself, and ultimately lose her or his own sense of perception, identity, and self-worth."[83] In a very real sense, by ignoring or suppressing our feelings, we are gaslighting ourselves: we are teaching ourselves that our perception of reality is incorrect and should be ignored. When someone who purports to love us does the same, we can fall for it without a moment's hesitation.

Functioning in groups

Problems with functioning in groups are often thought of as an Autistic issue, but anecdotal evidence suggests that they affect other neurotypes, too. However, that's not to say that every neurotype struggles because of the same issues, or that neurodivergence is the primary cause of these issues. There are plenty of factors that affect our ability to function in groups, and not all of them are a direct result of our neurodivergence.

There are also plenty of factors that affect our ability to enjoy ourselves in a group setting. This is important: it is possible for people to be able to function in groups, but to hate it, or to like it only in very specific circumstances. The issues of ability and enjoyment are rather separate, and too many specialists seem to forget that. Some people do not like socializing or working in groups, and that's not a symptom that needs treatment. Heck, some people do not like interacting with people, full stop; and if that's not causing them any problems, then it isn't a problem.

Assuming that we don't just loathe the presence of humans in general, one of the key factors to establish is whether we struggle being in groups, or we struggle with the individuals who form the groups we are in. If a group is composed solely of people we don't get along with, then any problems we have may be due to that. Engaging with several asshats at the same time is no less unpleasant than engaging with them individually, and can be far worse. On the other hand, if we absolutely love to hang out with some people one-on-one but we can't stand to hang out with the same people in a group, this suggests that our issues are with groups per se.

This isn't necessarily an issue of neurodivergence. People's behavior often changes when they are in a group: they might do different things, display different sides of their personality, or even display a completely different personality. They might also display very different attitudes towards us, particularly if our presence within the group is contentious.

---

[83] https://www.psychologytoday.com/gb/blog/communication-success/201704/7-stages-gaslighting-in-relationship

The people we enjoy deep and meaningful private conversations with might behave very differently if we meet them at a rave, so the setting of our group activities matters. However, if we consistently like single individuals but struggle whenever two or three of them come together, this suggests that groups may be an issue for us.

Another factor is whether we prefer to get together with people to carry out a defined activity, rather than for some free-form socialization. Carrying out an activity reduces the need for small talk or chitchat, gives us a sense of purpose, and sometimes can even provide a set of clearly-defined rules for social intercourse. Also, the activity itself can be a source of enjoyment; we might suffer through being in a group so we can do it, rather than do it to have the excuse to be in a group.

59% of respondents struggle to function in group situations, even though they would enjoy the company of the same people one-to-one. 58% struggle to function in group situations that do not center around a defined activity. There is a significant overlap between these two groups: 80% of those who struggle with one issue also struggle with the other.

Different group situations can involve different degrees of formality, and this can have an impact on our ability to enjoy that situation. For instance, the requirements and expectations involved with attending an informal house party are rather different from those involved with a formal reception at the local County Club.[84] This can affect our ability to enjoy ourselves.

17% of respondents never enjoy *informal*, unstructured group situations, and 53% of them enjoy them sometimes. By contrast, 37% of participants never enjoy *formal*, unstructured group situations, and 48% enjoy them sometimes. So, informal group situations are meh for 70% of respondents, while formal situations are meh for 85%. There is an overlap between these two groups: 94% of those who never enjoy informal situations also don't enjoy formal ones. However, of the 7% of ~~weirdoes~~ respondents who always like informal situations, only a third also always like formal ones.

Disliking social situations can lead to avoidance. This is not necessarily a problem, let alone a symptom requiring therapeutic interventions. It really depends on what the person in question actually wants to do. Alternatively, people may dislike social situations but not avoid them,

---

[84] Or so I hear: you'd have to physically drag me to the latter, and I'd fight you all the way.

either due to choice or to lack thereof.

45% of respondents avoid social events because they find them unpleasant. 30% attend social events even though they find them unpleasant. 80% feel drained after attending social events, even when they went well.

There are countless factors that may have an impact on whether we enjoy certain social situations, and many of them don't have anything to do with our liking for people. For instance, if we have environmental sensitivities, we are unlikely to look forward to situations in which we will be exposed to triggers. If we struggle with our interoception, we might be worried about failing to respond to our body's signals until it's too late. If our blood pressure or blood sugar levels aren't up to snuff, we might be worried about becoming faint or dizzy, or even passing out. If we suffer from chronic pain or fatigue, we might worry about doing anything that could aggravate our symptoms, or we might simply not be in the mood for a shindig. It's all about pros and cons, really: if the pros don't balance out the cons, we will probably not enjoy ourselves, or not enjoy ourselves *enough*. Time is a finite resource. The time we spend at a social event is time we could have spent doing something else; and if we'd rather be doing something else, why shouldn't we do that, instead?

Presumed incompetence

Presuming competence is the idea that, unless there is solid proof against it, a person should be assumed to be competent and able to develop their thinking, learning, and understanding. All decisions about their life should be based on this assumption. Presuming competence is assuming that a person has potential until conclusively proven otherwise – and the proof should take into account the fact that disabled people may require adaptations or alternative technologies in order to manifest their abilities.

Alas, while this approach is slowly gaining ground in educational settings, this hasn't done much to change how neurodivergent people are treated everywhere else. Discrimination against neurodivergent people is rife, and much of it hinges on our presumed incompetence. This isn't only an issue when we are dealing with bigoted individuals or private businesses; despite anti-discrimination legislations, even governments treat us as second class citizens.

Examples of discrimination in action include:

- A recent UK survey indicated that many employers would not hire a neurodivergent individual, and that the bias is strongest against ADHD and Tourette's. 6 in 20 employers would not hire us.[85]

- Diagnosed Autistic people cannot emigrate to several countries, including New Zealand and Australia.

- Neurodivergent people in general and Autistic people in particular may be considered unfit for parenting, and as a result denied access to reproductive healthcare or adoption services.

- Conversely, neurodivergent people may be denied contraceptive care because we shouldn't be having sex in the first place.

- Child protection services can use a diagnosis of neurodivergence as proof of parental incompetence, and use it to remove children from their families.

- In custody disputes, if a parent is neurodivergent and the other neurotypical, the neurotypical parent may be automatically granted custody, regardless of other circumstances.

- Neurodivergent people may be denied access to certain surgeries and other forms of healthcare because we are deemed incompetent to make certain decisions, incapable of following a recovery plan, or unworthy of the associated costs.

- Autistic trans people may be denied the right to transition socially or medically as they are deemed incompetent to identify their own gender and make the necessary decisions. ADHDers may have to undergo additional screenings or wait longer for treatment because we are too impulsive to be trusted to make this kind of decision.

- Autistic people may be denied life and travel insurance regardless of the absence or presence of co-occurring conditions.

- Relatives of Autistic people can ask for them to be sectioned or institutionalized against their will.

- Relatives of Autistic people can use their diagnosis to apply for conservatorships (deputyship in the UK), which grants them the ability to manage the Autistic person's property and finances, and to make medical and end-of-life decisions.

---

[85] https://www.institutelm.com/resourceLibrary/workplace-neurodiversity-the-power-of-difference.html

- Relatives of Autistic people can petition for Do Not Resuscitate (DNR) orders and Medical Assistance in Dying (MAID) provisions on the Autistic person's behalf – this is a perversion of how these systems are supposed to work, but it still happens.

Anti-discrimination laws should prevent these issues, but in practice this only helps us if we can afford to pursue lengthy and expensive lawsuits. Furthermore, when the discrimination we are suffering comes from the same system that is allegedly protecting us, we don't really stand a chance.

Social hierarchies and social rules

I don't think there is a word as yet for the neurodivergent struggle to respect social hierarchies and follow social rules. That's probably a good thing, because these issues can have very different causes. Some of us genuinely cannot discern the hierarchy and rules within a group unless they are clearly stated. Some may be able to perceive them, but as they make no sense, we do not let them guide our behavior. Some see them and reject them because they deem them unfair. Some understand and respect local hierarchies and rules, but struggle to give out the neurotypical markers of respect; for instance, we might not stay still enough while we listen, not give enough eye contact, or have a participatory conversational style. Any of these issues can land us in the soup in situations where observing social conventions is crucial. However, these issues are not equivalent, and have very different root causes.

Neurodivergents are often accused of being unable to work out or respect unspoken social hierarchies and rules. That's true for some of us, but it doesn't account for another issue: some of the hierarchies and rules we trample are not only *unspoken*, but *unspeakable*. They rely on assumptions about the inherent worth of different people that are never clearly stated because they are repugnant.

Our social status isn't just a function of the role we play in the local hierarchy. For instance, employees who aren't popular, for whatever reason, may have a lower social status than popular employees who share their position in the business hierarchy. Members of marginalized groups are likely to have a lower social status than their cohorts. These issues are often most obvious to those of us who are marginalized, and especially to those of us who are marginalized in multiple ways, because the more marginalized we are, the more we are affected. For many of us, the issue isn't necessarily that we don't understand or respect social hierarchies, but that we don't accept our role within them, because we don't accept our inherent inferiority.

Alas, when we treat our alleged superiors as equals, we are committing a breach of social conventions. If those conventions don't match the stated beliefs of the group – for instance, if the group prides itself on its egalitarian values, but some members are more equal than others – the resulting cognitive dissonance will make the breach even more jarring, and much harder to resolve.

Some of these issues are discussed in "Conflict Communications – A functional taxonomy of human conflict" by Rory Miller. Although not without its issues, this is a brilliant book that gives us many of the tools we need to spot, understand, and manipulate the roots of many interpersonal conflicts. Unfortunately, in order to do so, these tools require us to embrace our unstated position in the social hierarchy of our group, and that isn't always a palatable choice. In order to work within the system rather than clash with it, some of us would have to accept a level of inferiority so profound that we would become complicit in our own marginalization. And even that would be no guarantee of a peaceful, conflict-free life, because life at the bottom of the food chain isn't always all that comfy. If you'll forgive me an unsavory metaphor, there's a difference between smoothing our social interactions by doing a little ass-kissing and allowing the entire group to shit on us day in, day out. For those of us who are deemed inherently and significantly inferior, fitting smoothly within the system may require the latter.

This has important implications for neurodivergent people, and even more so for those of us who are also marginalized in other ways. We are routinely assumed to be less capable than or straight-up inferior to neurotypical people, either because we cannot do certain things or because we do them differently. The less we are able to mask as neurotypical, the more inferior we are perceived to be, and that often results in assumptions as to our rightful place within the social hierarchy. Those assumptions come with a whole load of baggage, including the role people expect us to take in certain social scripts.

Social scripts are established patterns of behavior expected in a specific setting. They are like little automatic routines humans use to interact with each other without having to put any real work in. When they are running as intended, scripts are usually beneficial, or at least harmless. They allow us to have interactions with strangers without any unpleasant surprises, or to reaffirm our social connections through low-content, low-effort exchanges.

Social scripts are important. We all rely on scripts to navigate our social and professional lives, and we do so because scripts can make our lives easier. Thing is, that's only the case when everyone signs up to the script in question and to their role in it. That isn't always the case, and the difference between what's script-appropriate and what we deem to be Right can be significant.

For instance, the script-appropriate response to mansplaining is simpering –please note that I said "script-appropriate", not "right." Simpering proves that the interlocutor has received the mansplainer's message – that they are intellectually or culturally superior – and that they are in agreement. Aside from meeting the mansplainer's emotional and social needs, simpering also closes the script, which can actually reduce how long the mansplaining goes on for. After all, the ultimate point of the behavior is a power exchange, not an exchange of information.

(Please note that I am not advocating simpering as the stock response to mansplaining; quite the opposite, in fact. I am not in favor of rewarding behaviors I consider despicable. My personal choice is to step off-script – or, rather, not to step into the script in the first place. It's not my script, after all: I didn't pick it and I didn't sign up to my role in it, so I assume no responsibility in making it go smoothly. However, sticking to my beliefs means that my interactions with mansplainers routinely go awry.)

Alas, when we thwart a script, that is often attributed to our inability to pick up social cues or emotional vibes. We are seen as responsible for the script's failure, even though we neither picked it nor signed up to our role in it; we were crowbarred into it willy-nilly. Yet it is somehow our fault, the reflection of our social cluelessness or lack of empathy, when the script falls apart, and the person who started it hurts their own feelings instead of hurting ours. That's pretty amazing, when you think about it.

"Uncanny valley"

I am misusing this term, but I'm doing it because it fits. The **"uncanny valley"** is a term used to describe the unsettling feeling people experience in response to highly realistic androids and humanoid replicas. The theory is that human appearance and behavior can make humanoid figures feel more familiar, but only up to a point. If a humanoid figure tries but fails to mimic a realistic human, that sense of familiarity is replaced by eeriness, or even revulsion.

None of this should be relevant to us, because we are actual humans.[86] However, people experience similar, unsettling feelings when they are confronted with humans who don't quite look or behave as they expect "normal" people to. Unfortunately, this kind of reaction is not as openly spoken of as the uncanny valley. Most people won't admit that weird people creep them out – or, if they do, they blame the person who creeps them out for their discomfort, regardless of circumstances.

I wrote a whole book about creeps,[87] and one of the things I tried to do was to nail down a solid definition for the term. As far as I'm concerned,

A creep is a person who <u>consciously</u> behaves in a manner likely to give someone an unpleasant feeling of fear or unease, specifically where there is a <u>sexual undercurrent</u> to that discomfort.

Alas, this definition doesn't even come close to reflecting what people find creepy. Scientists have postulated that "being 'creeped out' is an evolved adaptive emotional response to ambiguity about the presence of threat that enables us to maintain vigilance during times of uncertainty."[88] Unfortunately, the human creepiness detector responds to a whole bunch of cues, many of which are not within our control.[89] These include:

- Gender – men are deemed to be creepier.

- Age – people between 31 and 50 years of age are deemed to be creepier.

- Physical characteristics: being tall, being extremely thin, having long fingers, bulging eyes, bags under the eyes, very pale skin.

- Personal grooming: greasy or unkempt hair, dirty or weird clothes.

- Behaviors: not making eye contact, standing too close to people, frequent lip licking, displaying inappropriate emotions, laughing at

---

[86] If any AI is reading this, I am sorry about making assumptions.
[87] https://www.amazon.com/dp/B09JGNWWJ3
[88] https://www.sciencedirect.com/science/article/abs/pii/S0732118X16300320
[89] https://ideas.ted.com/what-makes-a-person-creepy-and-what-purpose-do-our-creep-detectors-serve-a-psychologist-explains/
https://www.researchgate.net/publication/312400751_A_case_of_the_heeby_jeebies_An_examination_of_intuitive_judgements_of_creepiness

unpredictable times, watching people before interacting with them.

- Being mentally ill (or, rather, looking or acting in a way that suggests mental illness to the onlookers).

- Conversational faux pas: dragging the conversation towards a topic, making it hard to leave the conversation without appearing rude, asking for personal details, divulging inappropriate personal information, steering the conversation towards sex.

Aside from the very last item on the list, which I can't argue with, the rest have little or nothing to do with volition and intentions. That's what we are dealing with, though, and it's not great news for those of us who resemble these remarks. The more items on the list we tick, the creepier we'll be considered. And while, in time, people may get to know us enough for the creepiness to subside, this might not help us in the short term. People make judgments about the trustworthiness of a stranger within 39 milliseconds of seeing their face. If we have the misfortune of displaying unusual nonverbal behaviors or odd emotional responses, or if we are simply not conventionally attractive, we are likely to be judged as untrustworthy before being given the chance to prove ourselves.

If a number of people within our social group have a poor opinion of us, their prejudice can affect how they interpret our behavior. In the event of a social conflict, we are more likely to be assumed to be at fault, regardless of the circumstances.

Social conflict

The causes of most social conflicts tend to fall under one of three headings:

1. We did the wrong thing.

2. We did the right thing, but in the wrong way.

3. We did the right thing, but in a way that made it look like other people were doing the wrong thing, thereby pissing them off.

One would think that doing the wrong thing would be the most serious offense, and be punished accordingly. Alas, one would often be wrong. The crime of showing someone up is often regarded as the most heinous, for reasons explained in Rory Miller's "Conflict Communications – A functional taxonomy of human conflict." I can't summarize the whole book in a paragraph, but the core issue is that by showing someone up, we are attacking their position within the group, which in turn threatens the stability of the whole group. According to the triune brain model, this sends everyone's paleomammalian complex (the social and emotional bit of our brain) into panic mode, and hijinks ensue. (Please note that the triune model of the brain has been amply discredited; however, for the purposes of this exercise, it works.)

This has huge implications for how we can avoid and resolve social conflict – basically, it's "just" a case of keeping or re-establishing the peace within our group by soothing the limbic systems of those around us. Unfortunately, the issues I described in the previous section come into play here, too.

Most one-size-fits-all approaches to avoiding and resolving social conflicts are designed to work for people who either have a relatively high position in their social group, or have a low position, accept it, and are willing to work within it. There is a reason for that: these approaches are usually designed and publicized by people who are not members of marginalized minorities, who aren't constantly regarded and treated as inherently inferior, and who are often unaware of the implications of marginalization. Some of them come to believe that they have found the Right Way To Interact With People, and that's why the vast majority of their interactions go smoothly. What is actually happening is that they are having totally different types of interactions because of their position in their social hierarchy.

This issue becomes apparent when these one-size-fits-all approaches fail. Two good examples of these are **assertiveness** and **boundary setting**, which are often hailed as the solutions to most of our interpersonal problems.

Assertiveness is "the quality of being self-assured and confident without being aggressive to defend a right point of view or a relevant statement."[90] Assertiveness is that magic communication middle ground that allows us to stand up for ourselves and get our point across without upsetting anyone, including ourselves.

Boundary setting allows us to create and maintain clear guidelines as to how we would like to be treated. [91] In self-defense as in life, boundary

---

[90] https://en.wikipedia.org/wiki/Assertiveness
[91] https://wellnesscenter.uic.edu/news-stories/boundaries-what-are-they-and-how-to-create-them/

setting is a critical skill. If we don't state our boundaries, we can't expect people to respect them. We can't blame people for failing to read our minds, and we definitely can't punish them for it.

Assertiveness and boundary setting are often hailed as cure-alls: if we knew how to be assertive and set our boundaries properly, we could avoid most conflicts and resolve the rest quickly and easily! Unfortunately, this view fails to take into account that assertiveness and boundary setting are not risk-free, and I don't mean solely in a physical sense. Standing up to someone who is harassing us in a secluded area may turn the harassment into an assault, which is obviously a serious issue. However, even in situations when we are physically safe, being assertive and setting boundaries put us at risk of incurring social repercussions. How much of an issue this is will depend not just (or even mostly) on how good we are at it, but on our social status within the group.

Social conflicts happen within social contexts, and social contexts usually include social hierarchies. People higher up on the social hierarchy are perceived as having the right to make the rules. Their assertiveness is treated as a right – they have the right to clearly state what they want, because of their social position. Their boundaries are likely to be perceived as a natural manifestation of their authority, so they will be more readily accepted by more people. As a result, people higher up on the social ladder are less likely to have to enforce their boundaries and more likely to receive support from their group when their boundaries are violated. This isn't because they are better at boundary setting; it's just the result of their social position working for them.

The opposite applies to people lower on the social ladder, who are not generally perceived as having the right to make rules. When someone low on the social ladder sets a rule, a proportion of people will perceive this behavior as inappropriate, unjustified, or even oppressive; the low-status person is seen as exercising a power they have no right to. This perception may not change even if the "rule" in question only affects what happens to the low-status person's immediate environment, or even just to their body. As a result, the boundaries set by low-status people are less likely to be respected, regardless of their nature and of how assertively they are stated. As a result, low-status people are more likely to need to enforce their boundaries, and less likely to receive social support in doing so.

The more marginalized a person is, the riskier it is for them to set boundaries, and the more likely it is that they will have to enforce them.

To make matters worse, when a marginalized person is forced to enforce a boundary, they might be punished for doing so, either formally or informally. And, again, this has nothing to do with how assertive they are, or how well they set their boundaries.

Social crimes and punishments

Our perceived position within our social hierarchy doesn't just affect the roles we are required to play within social scripts; it also determine the cost of breaking social rules, and the resulting punishments. Different people are held up to different standards, and the cost of failing to meet those standards is often higher the lower we sit in the social hierarchy.

This doesn't only affect us in informal social settings. The impact of **biases** – preconceived, usually unfavorable, judgments toward people displaying certain personal characteristics – has been measured in a variety of settings, including systems that are supposed to be egalitarian and objective, such as the medical,[92] educational,[93] and justice system.[94]

Biases can affect teachers' expectations of their students' likelihood to succeed, which has been shown to have a measurable impact on students' educational outcomes.[95] The same biases can also affect teachers' assessments of students' behavior and misbehavior,[96] which results in disparities in disciplinary actions.[97] Children of discriminated groups are punished more often and more severely than those of non-discriminated groups for the same misbehaviors. They are also more likely to be punished in response to subjective categories of misbehavior, like "defiance." This disciplinary disparity impacts the academic success of the affected students and is associated with negative long-term outcomes, including difficulties in finding employment and involvement in the criminal justice system.[98]

Disciplinary disparities are not necessarily the result of a will to harm

---

[92] https://www.ncbi.nlm.nih.gov/pmc/articles/PMC3417145/
[93] https://leesareneehall.medium.com/systemic-bias-vs-implicit-bias-why-the-difference-matters-when-reviewing-the-report-by-the-e2fdd8da6574
[94] https://link.springer.com/article/10.1023/B:LAHU.0000046430.65485.1f
[95] https://www.brookings.edu/blog/brown-center-chalkboard/2020/07/20/educator-bias-is-associated-with-racial-disparities-in-student-achievement-and-discipline/
[96] https://www.ncbi.nlm.nih.gov/pmc/articles/PMC4659921/
[97] https://www.pnas.org/content/116/17/8255
[98] https://journals.sagepub.com/doi/abs/10.1177/0956797615570365?journalCode=pssa
https://www.ncbi.nlm.nih.gov/pmc/articles/PMC4659921/

students from discriminated groups. Rather, implicit biases can make teachers interpret an ongoing pattern of misbehavior on the part of a discriminated student as a sign that the student is a "troublemaker."[99]

In a very real sense, implicit biases may determine whether a teacher sees a student as "good" or "bad." That preconception informs future assessments of the student's behavior. Misbehavior on the part of a "good student" is more likely to be interpreted as a sign of distress, and the cause of said distress may be investigated. Is the child being bullied, abused, or neglected? Are they under too much pressure? Do they have an undiagnosed medical need? By contrast, misbehavior on the part of a "bad student" is more likely to be interpreted as further proof of their badness. The assessment of a student as good or bad can precede a student's behavior, and that assessment may persist even when the student's behavior ceases to support it.

These findings are in line with those shown in studies involving police officers and juvenile probation officers, where both groups demonstrated anti-Black biases. They assumed more negative personal traits (e.g., hostility and immaturity) and greater culpability for hypothetical Black young offenders, expected more recidivism, and endorsed harsher punishments as a result.[100]

Not all neurodivergents are equally affected by these issues. Our individual circumstances depend on a variety of factors – how strong the biases are, how many of them we are affected by, how much latitude people have in behaving unfairly towards us, and so on. For some of us, the biases stacked against us cause us to become permanent **scapegoats**: every time something goes wrong, we are the designated guilty parties, regardless of whether the blame truly belongs with us. Within close groups, a scapegoat is essentially a person with no power but endless responsibilities; whatever goes wrong is our fault, even if we could not have done anything to prevent it.

This is one of those scenarios where a diagnosis of neurodivergence can actually hamper us, rather than help us. If the people around us see neurodivergence as a flaw and don't address their ableism, they can reframe their interactions with us so that every conflict or problem magically becomes an issue of neurodivergence. This is particularly

[99] https://www.psychologicalscience.org/news/releases/teachers-more-likely-to-label-black-students-as-troublemakers.html
[100] https://link.springer.com/article/10.1023/B:LAHU.0000046430.65485.1f

obvious on parents' forums, where the answers to "how do I get my child to do/stop doing X" are markedly different for neurotypical and neurodivergent children, but other settings are not immune from this bias. If we have problems at home, school, or work and we are neurodivergent, our issues will be reframed as neurodivergence issues, regardless of what they are and who is actually causing them. No matter what happens to us, no matter who is responsible, no matter the degree of control we actually have on a situation, our neurodivergence must be the cause of our problems, or at the very least a contributing factor. And if we cannot handle the resulting issues, that must also be a neurodivergent thing. And the worst thing isn't that society treats us like this; it's how often we do it to ourselves.

Self-scapegoating can stem from our personal beliefs, other people's beliefs that we internalized, or be a trauma response. Regardless of why we do it, holding ourselves as inherently at fault can be incredibly damaging.

Bullying

Bullying is unwanted physical or verbal aggression directed at a specific person, repeated over a period, involving an imbalance of power, and aimed at excluding the victim from a group. Please note that the definition stipulates *aggression*, not *violence* – if someone is actually hitting you, they are committing a physical assault. We call it bullying when tiny tots do it because we expect them not to know any better, or to be capable of causing much damage. To still call it bullying when the "bullies" are old enough to know what they are doing and to injure someone is frankly ludicrous. It's reframing a crime into a bit of a social whoopsie, and we shouldn't allow it to stand. The same applies to:

- using the threat of violence to extort money or goods from you – aka, robbery;

- using the threat of violence to extort sexual favors – aka, sexual assault or rape, depending on the favors in question;

- using the threat of disclosure of personal or damaging information to extort literally anything – aka, blackmail;

- making false statements damaging to a person's reputation that caused or are likely to cause significant harm – aka defamation, slander, or libel.

In most jurisdictions, these activities are illegal. And yes, they are still illegal if the people committing them are "friends" or relatives. That doesn't mean that we're likely to get a win in court, or even that we should try to get there, but it should help us reframe what we are dealing with – or, rather, to stop other people reframing it to suit their agenda.

In self-defense circles, bullying is often classified as a form of "social violence" – i.e., violence between members of a group. Unfortunately, that's only partly correct. Bullying is a social activity *for the bullies*; they are using that activity as a bonding or hierarchy-establishing exercise. Whether what transpires between the bullies and the bullied is social or asocial will depend on how the bullies regard the bullied. If they do not regard us as members of the group, or even fully as members of the same species, their bullying will be a form of asocial violence. This distinction is important, as social and asocial violence have very different purposes and carry very different risks. As Rory Miller stated, "Presence of a bonded group and you are alone: bad day for you."[101] And please note that, for practical purposes, being surrounded by a crowd we don't actually belong to can be the same as being alone.

This is an important consideration because a lot of stock advice on how to deal with bullies hinges on the idea that the bullying we are experiencing is a form of social violence. All we need to do is stand up to the bullies, thereby gaining higher status in our group, and the bullying will stop right away! Unfortunately, that strategy can backfire if the bullying is asocial. By standing up to our bullies, we are upping the ante. We are a prey turning on its hunters. Whether that works or not will depend on a number of factors: whether our threat is credible, our bullies' level of commitment, how established their group hierarchy is, whether there are any witnesses, and so on. It might work, or it might turn a few insults into a stomping. Teaching you to anticipate the most likely outcome isn't something that should be attempted from a book. There are too many factors in play, and too much at stake.

Being neurodivergent may make us more likely to be picked on by bullies for two reasons. Firstly, many bullies are attracted to anyone who behaves or looks different from the norm. Secondly, if our neurodivergence causes us social difficulties, we may have fewer social resources to rely upon.

---

[101] https://conflictresearchgroupintl.com/distinguishing-social-and-asocial-violence-rory-miller/

Social resources are the support and assistance we can rely upon from our family, friends, peers, neighbors, authority figures, community organizations, and specific agencies that provide services in our community. Our social resources can be affected by our social hierarchy and our tangible resources – for instance, rich or powerful people may get the "VIP treatment" from agencies that should be treating all residents equally and fairly. However, social resources aren't just about our large-scale social influence; they are also about the networks we belong to, and the relationships we have within those networks.

Our social resources can determine whether people stand up for us or not if a situation arises. In a bullying context, if we have plenty of people willing to speak out for us, or step in to defend us, we are less likely to be picked on. If bullying occurs, the bullies are more likely to stand down if we escalate with a metaphorical posse at our back. Our social resources can also influence the fallout after an incident; it isn't fair or right, but people who are "in good standing" within a group are likely to be assumed to be in the right, even before the facts of the matter have transpired. Our reputation precedes us, whether it's deserved or not, and will determine whether people take our side. Unfortunately, this can also apply to people whose job it is to be impartial.

For many of us, this means that our neurodivergence will make us more likely to become the targets of bullies, and will make it harder for us to stop the bullying. That doesn't mean that we get bullied because we are neurodivergent, though. We get bullied because bullies want to bully people, and we make convenient targets. The responsibility for the bullying sits entirely with the bullies.

Still, the cost of bullying falls on us. 78% of survey respondents were bullied as children. 8% of respondents are still bullied now. Of these, 93% were also bullied as children. As correlations go, that's pretty damn high.

Statistics about bullying are not terribly solid, and not just because different people have different criteria as to what qualifies as bullying. Statistics on bullying rely on people reporting that they are being bullied, and that's not something everyone is willing or able to do. Unless the bullying has been so egregious that it would cause the bully to be removed from the situation, reporting can carry serious risks of retaliation. Furthermore, zero-tolerance policies in schools and workplaces can actually prevent people from reporting acts of violence. If the policy is that anyone who has taken part in a physical altercation is at fault, regardless of their role in it, all parties will be punished. That punishment is likely to be more of a deterrent for children who are concerned about their good reputation; therefore, it is often more of a punishment for the victims than for the bullies.

These caveats notwithstanding, we do have some estimates about the prevalence of bullying in the general population. This problem is believed to affect 20% to 46% of schoolchildren. While these numbers are a bit shaky, there is no arguing that 78% is a hell of a lot higher than 46%. Therefore, these results suggest that there may be a correlation between being neurodivergent and being bullied. If anyone is surprised by this, then they don't understand either issue.

Bullying isn't just unpleasant; it is a serious social issue that can lead to negative performance and health outcomes. Bullying shows a negative correlation with academic and job performance – i.e., when we are bullied, our performance suffers. Bullying also results in higher rates of absenteeism and people quitting their school or job. Bullied people who stick it out are at elevated risk of stress, anxiety, depression, loss of confidence, sleep loss, headaches, muscle tension, chronic pain, mental breakdowns, and burnout. Depending on what it involves and how long it goes on for, bullying can also result in PTSD or cPTSD.

Bullying in childhood is a potential Adverse Childhood Experience (ACE – see the section on Interpersonal Trauma). It's still a potential ACE if it's carried out by the people responsible for our care – relatives, medical specialists, teachers, and so on. In fact, as the power differential between children and adults is generally greater than between peers, this form of bullying can have a more serious and pervasive impact.

A caveat on bullying: being excluded from social activities, particularly from private social activities, does not necessarily mean that we are being bullied. Some people will not want to spend their time with us, and that's their right. Everyone has the right to decide who they associate with, and sometimes we won't make that list. That's just life. Whether the exclusion is a form of bullying or not depends on the circumstances, and on how the exclusion is carried out.

Someone not inviting us to their birthday party isn't necessarily bullying us; if they don't want us at their party, that's their prerogative. A party is a private function, and people have the right to decide who's in and who's out. Someone not inviting us to their party when they have invited everyone else in our group may still not be bullying us. They might just like us less than they like other people in the group, so they don't want to spend their time with us. That sucks, but it's still not bullying. Someone making a huge promotion of the fact that we are the only people who won't be attending their birthday party, however, is bullying us, and so is anyone attempting to exclude us from public functions. All of these exclusions may suck for us, but they are not equivalent, and learning the difference between them is important. One of the ways in which we can build better relationships with people is by showing that we respect their rights and boundaries, even when we don't like them.

If we accuse people of bullying us when they are just living their lives without us, or demand that they give us their time and attention whether they want to or not, we demonstrate that we don't understand consent – which, yes, is still a thing in non-sexual settings. And acting like that won't make people like us any better

Interpersonal violence and abuse

The statistics on this subject are too shaky to be of any real use, but anecdotal evidence suggests that neurodivergent people are at higher risk of being the targets of physical violence, sexual violence, and sexual harassment. The same factors that put us at increased risk of bullying – being perceived as a safe target and lacking the physical and social resources to defend ourselves – are in play here. Furthermore, looking physically awkward, physically weak, or distracted can make us more attractive to opportunistic predators, like muggers or rapists.

Our neurodivergence can also make it harder for us to deal with sexual harassment, particularly with the kind of sexual harassment that never escalates into anything actionable. Low-level sexual predators like creeps are so common because they are hard to spot. They are hard to spot because, if they are any good, their game is subtle. They restrict their activities to behaviors that fall in the gray area between what is socially acceptable and what is legally actionable. These behaviors can make us extremely uncomfortable, but don't allow us to seek legal redress. Some sexual predators use that knowledge to their advantage: by restricting their activities to that gray area, they can creep on us without incurring any repercussions.

When we are targeted by a creep, it can be hard for us to work out exactly what is going on. It can be even harder for us to gather the kind of evidence that allows us to take the necessary action to stop the creep. If we are not confident in our ability to pick up and interpret social cues or to identify inappropriate behaviors, we may not trust in our assessment of the situation.

If our social group mistrusts our social competence, they might mistrust our assessment of the situation and reject any evidence we may provide, however solid. This can make us doubt not only whether we are really being creeped on, but even our memory, perception, and sanity. It's a form of collective gaslighting, in essence, which is precisely what we don't need when we are already dealing with the turmoil caused by being targeted by a sexual predator. Unfortunately, denying that any creeping is taking place is far easier than dealing with it: if the creeping was recognized, the group or its leaders would have to do something about it, and that can be difficult. For those not directly affected by the creep's actions, denial is the easy option.

Domestic and intimate partner abuse

The definitions of **domestic and intimate partner abuse** vary between jurisdictions and services, but they usually boil down to an incident or pattern of incidents of controlling, coercive, threatening behavior, physical violence, or sexual violence or violations of sexual consent between adults who are intimate partners or family members. The abuse can be psychological, physical, sexual, financial, or emotional.

The factors that make us desirable targets for bullies and violent predators also make us desirable targets for would-be abusers, but there is more. Many of us experience social difficulties growing up which affect our experiences at home, at school, and with our peers. These experiences can lead us to develop negative beliefs about ourselves and about what we can and should expect from our nearest and dearest. These negative beliefs can make it harder for us to take the actions necessary to end the abuse, or even to realize that what we are experiencing is abuse.

Not all neurodivergent people live the same lives, so it's impossible to generalize the neurodivergent experience, but these are some of the factors in play:

- **We believe that there is something inherently wrong with us.**

If we grow up being told that there is something wrong with us, we may grow to believe that there is something wrong with us. This is true both for those of us who were given an early diagnosis that was not received well by our family and for those who grew up without a diagnosis but a ton of negative labels attached to our behavior.

Living under a barrage of negative comments can turn us into people-pleasers. We may try to make up for our perceived shortcomings by doing whatever it takes to make people like us, even when it has a negative impact on our lives. When our loved ones hurt us, we may ignore that hurt, or accept it as the price of admission in the relationship. If that hurt is caused by being in a relationship with an abuser, that can take us to very bad places.

Abusers enjoy making us feel inferior and powerless. If we already believe that we are inferior and powerless, their job is that much easier, and our chances of successfully defending ourselves against their abuse are much lower.

- **We are trained to suppress and discount our sensations and emotions.**

If we grow up constantly hearing that we are overreacting, we might end up believing that we are overreacting. This can make it very difficult for us to respect and respond to our sensations and emotions, which cuts our access to the signals that would inform us that a relationship is unhealthy.

Mistrusting our own experience makes us susceptible to gaslighting. In a very real sense, by ignoring or suppressing our feelings, we are gaslighting ourselves: we are teaching ourselves that our perception of reality is incorrect and should be ignored. When someone who purports to love us does the same, we can fall for it without a moment's hesitation.

- **We are accustomed to being punished in the name of love.**

On average, ADHD kids receive a full 20,000 more negative messages than their neurotypical peers.[102] On the one hand, that makes sense: we struggle to behave properly. On the other hand... we just *can't* behave properly. We don't choose to be distracted, easily bored, forgetful, impulsive, fidgety, perennially late, hyperfocused on the wrong things, and so on and so forth. These are not things we choose to do: they are aspects of our neurodivergence, and all we can do is learn how to work around them. Scolding an ADHD kid for spacing out is not unlike scolding a short-sighted kid for failing to read something on the board: it's

---

[102] https://www.additudemag.com/children-with-adhd-avoid-failure-punishment/

punishment for something we have no control over.

When this punishment is routinely presented as being "for our own good," we may end up buying into that. We may learn to believe that being cared for means getting hurt, and that the people who love us should punish us for our transgressions, regardless of their causes. If that doesn't prime us for abuse later on in life, nothing else will.

This issue is compounded for those of us who are put through systematic abuse in childhood in order to make us "normal." For instance, many of the common "desensitization therapies" aimed at neurodivergent kids inhibit our ability to respond to negative stimuli, to display our needs and wants, or to interact with our environment and with other people in ways we find natural, comfortable, and rewarding. In order to achieve these dubious goals, some of these therapies foster a relationship between patient and provider that is inherently abusive: the provider has the power to withhold what the child needs to feel safe and comfortable, and only allows the child to access it as a reward for certain behaviors. As often as not, the required behaviors are unnatural, uncomfortable, or even painful for the child. In a nutshell, in order to stop hurting, the child has to do something that hurts – and all of this is done in an allegedly caring context, with parental support, and "for the child's own good." Needless to say, this type of early training can severely harm us, and can reduce our ability to protect ourselves from other forms of abuse later on in life.

- **We fear social conflict.**

Many of us are accustomed to committing social gaffes and navigating communication failures. This can make us fearful of speaking out when we have a conflict, because we don't want the conversation to go wrong. That can make it difficult for us to speak up for ourselves or to ask for help.

We may also be too tolerant of people who upset us, because we are so used to upsetting people accidentally that we don't realize when people do it on purpose.

- **We have unsupportive support networks.**

Many of us are more reactive and more emotional than the average neurotypical person. Unfortunately, this can lead to the people in our lives discounting not only our feelings about our problems, but the problems themselves. We are probably making a mountain out of a molehill. It can't really be that bad. It probably wasn't that bad to start with, and we made it worse by overreacting. Hell, it's probably our fault: if we could just calm down and act like normal people...

The result is that if we find ourselves in a difficult or even dangerous situation, we might find ourselves unable to get any help from our social network. By the time we have accumulated enough evidence to support our concerns, we may have gotten needlessly hurt.

- **Official support services may not be accessible to us.**

Official support services, such as advisory services, legal services, and shelters may not be easily accessible to people who cannot navigate complex bureaucratic systems, have communication difficulties, or have any disabilities or complex medical needs. For those of us at risk of violence from law enforcement officers, that avenue of support might not be safe, either. Furthermore, some services only support people who are cisgender and heterosexual.

All these issues add up. The less able we are to recognize and protect ourselves from abuse, the more likely we are to enter and stay in an abusive relationship. The less support we have from our community, the less likely we are to be able to leave an abusive situation quickly and safely.

Psychoemotional stressors

A number of mental health issues have been found to be so over-represented in the neurodivergent community that they are regarded as common co-existing conditions. That doesn't necessarily mean that neurodivergence, in and of itself, makes us more prone to developing mental health issues. Rather, being neurodivergent in an unaccepting neurotypical world means that we are routinely subjected to stigma and discrimination, which create a hostile and stressful social environment. That hostility and stress cause us to develop mental health issues.

Rejection-Sensitive Dysphoria

Rejection-Sensitive Dysphoria (RSD) is "the disposition to anxiously expect, readily perceive, and intensely react to rejection." Up to 99% of teens and adults with ADHD are more sensitive than their neurotypical peers to rejection, and nearly 1 in 3 say it's the hardest part of living with ADHD. RSD can have a profound impact on a person's ability and willingness to engage in social interactions. We may "adapt" by becoming hostile, socially withdrawn, or over-accommodating of others.

RSD is not a currently recognized condition. It might also not be a condition in its own right, or a symptom of neurodivergence, but a reaction to maltreatment or attachment failures in childhood. In essence, RSD may be a response to the trauma of being neurodivergent in a neurotypical world and the attendant social difficulties, rather than a result of our neurodivergence in and of itself.

An adult's ability to emotionally handle rejection is a skill learnt in childhood, and is dependent on several factors including:

- Secure attachments with one's care givers.

- Self-confidence in one's ability to handle situations.

- Self-worth independent of achievements.

In order to foster children's trust in their own abilities, it is essential not to face them with demands that are age-inappropriate, while children's self-worth can be encouraged by validating their concerns and experiences. Both may be issues for neurodivergent children. Our families, schools, and society do not consistently validate our experiences or accommodate our needs. We might have unmet physical needs and unrecognized oversensitivities that cause our caregivers to suppress or punish our natural responses to our environment. Furthermore, as our development doesn't match that of our neurotypical peers, we are constantly measured against inappropriate milestones, and found wanting. For those of us who did not get diagnosed in childhood, this effect may be particularly severe, as our poor performance and behavior were often seen as the signs of personal failings, rather than as symptoms. Not knowing that our peers are not dealing with the same issues can also make us profoundly dissatisfied with ourselves.

65% of respondents have RSD. 72% tend to anxiously expect social rejection. 71% believe that people are going to reject them, even though they haven't done anything concrete to show that. 72% find rejection very painful, even when it comes from people they do not really like or care for.

These results do not imply that we are a paranoid bunch. If we look at the results about relationships, they indicate that our struggles are real. 72% of respondents struggle to make new friends, 68% struggle to keep their friends, and 70% struggle in relationships with partners and relatives. Given these results, it's unsurprising that we should grow to fear rejection. Quite simply, rejection is a much more common feature of our social landscape than most neurotypical people could ever guess.

RSD isn't just unpleasant; it can push us to take up unhealthy and even dangerous behavioral patterns in order to avoid rejection at all costs. We might become people-pleasers, trying to make up for our perceived shortcomings by doing whatever it takes to make people like us. We might learn to mask our true personality and create a character more likeable than we believe ourselves to be. We might learn to be tolerant of harmful behavior from those around us, and accept it as the price of admission in the relationship. When our relationships hurt us, we try to change ourselves instead of trying to change them.

Trauma

Neurodivergence per se is not a cause of trauma. However, being neurodivergent in a neurotypical world can result in greater chances of being at the receiving end of violence, abuse, and neglect, particularly during childhood. This is due to systemic failures in accommodating the basic needs of neurodivergent children (neglect) and increased chances of being targeted by bullies and predators (violence and abuse). If our parents are neurotypical, they might struggle to understand and support us. On the other hand, if our parents are neurodivergent and struggling, they may be unable to provide us with the care and support we need, even though they want to do their best by us.

For those of us whose families' love and care is conditional upon the constant mimicking of neurotypical behaviors, these issues are compounded: not only we have to endure the stress of maintaining a neurotypical persona in order to receive the care and love we need, but we cannot rely on our families to support and comfort us when we struggle. In fact, our failures to meet neurotypical demands may result in punishment.

Adverse Childhood Experiences

Adverse Childhood Experiences (ACEs) are potentially traumatic events that occur in childhood. Examples of ACEs include experiencing violence, abuse, neglect, traumatic events, or growing up in a family with mental health or substance misuse problems.

ACEs are known to have a significant negative impact on long-term health and life outcomes, including underachievement in multiple domains, chronic health problems, mental illness, substance misuse, and a greater likelihood of becoming the victims or perpetrators of violence. The toxic stress resulting from ACEs has been shown to affect brain development and change how the body responds to stress.

PTSD and cPTSD

After being exposed to a traumatic event, it's natural to experience some emotional repercussions. These are not indicative of a traumatic stress disorder. For a diagnosis of traumatic stress disorder, symptoms must not abate over a certain period of time (guidelines vary, but a period of six weeks is considered normal) and be severe enough to have a significant impact on the person's day-to-day life. **Post-Traumatic Stress Disorder (PTSD)** is an anxiety disorder caused by exposure to a traumatic event. By contrast, **complex post-traumatic stress disorder (cPTSD)** results from exposure to long-term trauma, abuse, or neglect. PTSD is a recognized diagnosis. cPTSD is not currently included in the DSM-5 (The Diagnostic and Statistical Manual of Mental Disorders), but it is included in the ICD-11 (International Classification of Diseases), and is becoming more widely recognized by doctors.

The symptoms of these conditions are similar, and can include:

- Re-experiencing events as flashbacks or nightmares.

- Intrusive thoughts about the events.

- Hyperarousal – constantly being on high alert.

- Sleeping problems, such as insomnia.

- Difficulties concentrating.

- Somatic symptoms – physical symptoms related to trauma triggers that don't have any underlying medical cause.

- New, negative beliefs and feelings about the self and others.

- Avoidance of certain situations.

- Artificial, compulsive distractions, ranging from the excessive performance of constructive activities, such as overworking or overtraining, to the use of substances or self-harm.

Trauma flashbacks are usually set off by a **trigger**, i.e. "something that sets off a memory tape or flashback transporting the person back to the event of her/his original trauma."[103] Triggers are trauma reminders that cause us to mentally or physically re-experience the trauma we went through.

Triggers are highly personal. They are often connected to sensory experiences, particularly sight and sound. However, virtually anything can be a trigger, including stimuli not directly related to the traumatic experience. The individuals affected have no control over what triggers them, or over the extent to which they are triggered. This phenomenon is currently thought to be caused by the psychological effects of trauma causing changes in the biological stress response.[104] In layman's terms, being triggered is a chemical reaction, not a choice. It is certainly not a sign of weakness.

In recent years, however, the concept of "trigger" has been popularized and expanded. The term is now routinely used to label anything that could upset or offend someone. Although the motivations for this may be benign, this expansion in meaning can trivialize the struggles of people living with PTSD or cPTSD. It can also encourage people who do not have PTSD to avoid anything that reminds them of unpleasant incidents, or simply upsets them. Over time, this avoidance can turn discomfort into phobia.

---

[103] http://psychcentral.com/lib/what-is-a-trigger/
[104] For an introduction to the psychobiology of triggers and trauma:
http://www.trauma-pages.com/a/vanderk4.php

PTSD and cPTSD flashbacks are both set off by triggers, but they take different forms. During a PTSD flashback, we may feel like we are living through the trauma again. We are not just replaying a memory; we may be re-experiencing all the emotional and physical sensations we felt during the traumatic event, sometimes to the point of losing contact with reality.

cPTSD flashbacks can be harder to identify; rather than reliving the event, we are emotionally transported back to it. We relive the emotions we felt, rather than the whole experience, but we might believe that our emotions are just the response to our current situation.

Flashbacks can last for minutes, hours, or even days, and may be triggered by normal, everyday things such as smells, sights, physical sensations, or verbal reminders. Sometimes the triggers can be very hard to identify or predict. Flashbacks can be debilitating and make normal life very difficult. If they cause us to lose connection with reality, they may put our safety and that of those around us at risk.

Anyone can develop a traumatic stress disorder. However, there are risk factors that increase the chances of this, including pre-existing mental health conditions and the lack of a support system. Resilience factors, on the other hand, reduce the likelihood of developing a traumatic stress disorder. These include being prepared and able to respond to a traumatic event and having coping strategies for getting through and learning from the experience. In essence, we are more likely to develop a traumatic stress disorder when we lack the resources to respond to or recover from traumatic events.

Official statistics about PTSD are somewhat shaky as different medical systems use different criteria, and there is no knowing how many people live with the condition without ever reporting it, but its prevalence is currently estimated at 3.5-9.2%. Statistics about cPTSD are even shakier as the condition isn't recognized by all doctors, but its prevalence is currently estimated at 0.5-7.7%. By contrast, 49% of survey respondents have symptoms caused by exposure to a traumatic event, and 45% have symptoms caused by exposure to long-term trauma, abuse, or neglect. According to these figures, we may be roughly five times more likely to experience symptoms of PTSD or cPTSD than the general population. This is depressing, but not surprising. Like bullying, interpersonal violence, and domestic abuse, PTSD and cPTSD are most likely to affect those who don't have the resources to fight against them.

"Desensitization" therapies

In my survey, I looked at one potential ACE, bullying in childhood, as well as two trauma conditions that can affect people at any age, PTSD and cPTSD. I also looked at another factor: whether in childhood our respondents were forced by parents or teachers to endure painful physical sensation in order to learn to get over them. The latter group shows a greater prevalence of psychoemotional and physical issues than the first three. Let me reiterate that: "desensitization" attempts made to "help" us get over our sensory issues have a worse long-term impact on our emotional, mental, and physical health than PTSD, cPTSD, or childhood bullying. This might sound shocking, but there is a simple reason for this: what is being done to us is not desensitization.

Systematic desensitization therapy is a type of behavioral therapy that aims to diminish responses to a stimulus through repeated exposure. This therapy has a key prerequisite: the core issue must be **overreaction**. For instance, I freak out when I see large spiders, even though they are not causing me any pain and I know that spiders in this country are perfectly safe. I am overreacting to a stimulus. A systematic program of gradual exposure to spiders might help me get over this issue. Over time, I might become desensitized to spiders. I might learn to tolerate looking at pictures of spiders, watching them on video, or sitting next to a spider tank. I might even get used to touching them.

Learning to hug my music teacher was a different process altogether. I avoided her at least as enthusiastically as I avoid spiders, that's true, but that was because she wore so much scent that being within twenty yards of her set off my allergies. If I went anywhere near her, my sinuses swelled up so much and so fast that I felt as if I'd been smacked in the face. Hugging her left me covered in her smell, so my face would hurt more and more until I could change my clothes and wash. The bottom line was that being anywhere near her *hurt*. It didn't just upset me, although the pain was unquestionably upsetting.

Forcing a person to endure a stimulus when their aversive response is the result of a physiological issue is *not* desensitization. If done without that person's consent, it's abuse. Even when the person consents, the process cannot result in "desensitization" in the therapeutic sense of the word. The person isn't learning to manage their emotional responses to a benign stimulus; they are learning to suffer quietly.

Unsurprisingly, there appears to be a correlation between attempts at "desensitization" and mental health issues later on in life. "Desensitized" individuals show an increased prevalence of alexithymia, interoception problems, dissociative states, and crisis responses such as meltdowns, shutdowns, selective mutism, and burnouts.

Alas, from the outside these "therapeutic interventions" might look successful, because the children undergoing them no longer respond negatively to stimuli. However, I would argue that causing serious detrimental long-term damage in the name of "therapy" is somewhat misguided.

Generational trauma

Generational trauma is not a clinical term, but that doesn't make it unimportant. The term refers to the fact that if we grow up surrounded by traumatized people, their trauma may have an impact on us, regardless of their intentions. They might be trying to do their very best, but their best might not be enough to protect us from the impact of their trauma.

Generational trauma can affect us just as severely as other forms of trauma, but it can present us with an added challenge: it can be hard for us to admit that those who loved us and cared for us caused us long-term damage. As a result, we might employ two strategies to protect them:

- Denial: we may refuse to acknowledge that the trauma happened.

- Minimization: we may dismiss the impact of the trauma.

Needless to say, denying that we are traumatized or how much our trauma is affecting us can scupper any chances we have of getting over it. As Rory Miller said, "If you deny reality, you cannot control reality."

This issue can be hard to overcome, but is easy to side-step. Instead of thinking in terms of trauma, we can think in term of Adverse Childhood Experiences. This requires us to look solely at what happened, not why.

Adverse Childhood Experiences (ACEs) are "highly stressful, and potentially traumatic, events or situations that occur during childhood and/or adolescence. They can be a single event, or prolonged threats to, and breaches of, the young person's safety, security, trust or bodily integrity."[105]

---

[105] https://www.youngminds.org.uk/media/cmtffcce/ym-addressing-adversity-book-web-2.pdf

ACEs are relatively objective items. There are score sheets that enable us to quantify how many ACEs we had to deal with – which, as their impact adds up, is important.[106] Unfortunately, these score sheets generally fail to include events and issues that specifically affect neurodivergent kids, but they are still a good place to start. I don't generally recommend measuring trauma, because it can lead to unhelpful comparisons between individuals – my trauma is smaller than your trauma, so I don't deserve any help! However, quantifying what we went through can be a necessary step for those of us who are struggling to face the fact that our early environment, however loving it might have been, fucked us up.

Personality disorders

Personality disorder is an umbrella term that covers a number of "conditions" that affect how we think, feel, behave or relate to other people – the quotation marks are necessary because there is an ongoing debate as to whether these "conditions" are actually just other forms of neurodivergence. If we wish to demedicalize and destigmatize "conditions" like Autism and ADHD, should we extend the same consideration to other brain differences?

Debating this issue is outside the scope of this work. What falls within my remit is mentioning that neurodivergence can make us more likely to be diagnosed with a personality disorder, regardless of whether we have one or not. This is particularly true if we don't fit the stereotype of our neurodivergence or childhood trauma.

Symptoms of cPTSD can mimic the traits of a personality disorder. Unfortunately, cPTSD isn't recognized as yet by all medical systems. Even where it is, cPTSD is a new enough diagnosis that many medical specialists are unfamiliar with it, and may fail to recognize it. Furthermore, some specialists may not recognize the reality and impact of our trauma, particularly when it was caused by people like them. Specialists who put their patients through behavior modification "therapies" have a huge paradigm shift to go through before they can accept that those "therapies"

---

[106] This is the most comprehensive list I could find. It still misses a lot of ACEs specific to neurodivergent kids. It also ignores disability, gender, sexuality, transness, fatness, and a whole bunch of other factors that may contribute to discrimination, and includes a bunch of questions about sex which are, huh, not poly-friendly, to put it mildly.
https://simplebooklet.com/philadelphiaexpandedacequestionsenglishspanishversions

are abusive and traumatic.

As a result, we may be shunted towards diagnoses that fit our external symptoms but ignore their root causes. These diagnoses, in turn, can have an impact on the treatments we are offered or denied. They can also have an impact on how we see ourselves and our issues, and on how other people treat us. As the stigma against personality disorders is rife and virulent, this can cause us serious issues.

Behavior or conduct problems

Children with ADHD are more likely than their neurotypical peers to be diagnosed with a behavior disorder such as Oppositional Defiant Disorder or Conduct Disorder.[107] ODD is characterized by an increased tendency to be oppositional or defiant around people children know well. CD is diagnosed when children show an ongoing pattern of aggression toward others, and serious violations of rules and social norms.[108]

While researching scientific literature, I chanced upon an academic paper that states that "The symptoms of oppositional defiant disorder are predictors in hypersensitivity scores of tactile sensory function in ADHD." As with many other connections between our sensitivities and our behaviors, I wonder whether researchers will ever come to consider a potential causality in that relationship. If our cranky mood and combative behavior are responses to painful stimuli, can we really be said to be showing the symptoms of ODD?

Impostor syndrome

Impostor syndrome is not a recognized condition, but it is often associated with other mental health issues, most notably with anxiety and depression. Individuals with impostor syndrome persistently doubt their skills, talents, or accomplishments, regardless of how well and how consistently we succeed in our endeavors. However well we do, we feel that we just scraped through. We might feel that we are deceiving others into respecting, liking, or even loving us. We live in fear not only of failing, but of being exposed as frauds.

The concept of impostor syndrome hits rather differently for those of us who habitually "mask" in order to function within a neurotypical social

---

[107] https://www.cdc.gov/ncbddd/adhd/conditions.html
[108] https://www.cdc.gov/childrensmentalhealth/behavior.html

group. Neurodivergent masking varies in nature and intensity; some of us "just" try to do our best by neurotypical standards, while some of us engineer an entire neurotypical persona. We *know* that we are impostors, that we are fooling others into believing that we are different people, that our efforts are not sustainable, and that, at some point, we are bound to let our mask slip. For us, the problem isn't that we suffer from unjustified "impostor syndrome;" it's that, through repeated traumas, we have been forced into living a lie. We really are impostors, and not by choice. The issue isn't in our head; it's in our life.

The resulting constant, gnawing worry eats away at our ability to enjoy our life, and can put our relationships under serious strain. Unfortunately, the approaches that help with real impostor syndrome may not work for us. Positive self-talk amounts to gaslighting when it doesn't reflect our reality. And while we might overestimate the fallout of letting our masks slip, there is no knowing what will happen until we do. The alternative is to keep our masks on, and live with the ongoing stress of supporting them plus the associated impostor syndrome.

41% of respondents often or always do things they'd rather not so people will like them. 32% of respondents often or always pretend to be someone else so people will like them. These behaviors are linked with an increased prevalence of negative physical and mental health outcomes.

We may also have actual impostor syndrome, often in relation to how much our neurodivergence and co-occurring conditions affect us. We may see ourselves as less disabled, less ill, or less worthy of support than other neurodivergents. We may also see ourselves as less traumatized, or not traumatized at all because the people who hurt us didn't mean to; this is particularly common if our trauma happened in childhood. As a result, we may not seek help for our issues because we do not believe them to be worthy of consideration.

Dissociative states

Dissociation is an umbrella term that covers a wide range of experiences, from mild emotional detachment to severe disconnection from physical and emotional experiences.

Most people escape their reality at least some of the time. We might do so by choice, for our own amusement; we pick up a book or go to a movie and we are transported to another reality. We might become distracted or enchanted by something we are experiencing or remembering, and momentarily disconnect with everything else. We might be so bored by whatever is going on that we zone out for a spell, or make our own entertainment by daydreaming. These are natural responses that, while they might annoy those around us, are not pathological.

Daydreaming is a mild dissociative state in which we detach from our surroundings as our attention is pulled into a stream of consciousness. Daydreaming is perfectly natural, even for neurotypicals; studies suggest that people spend 30-50% of their time in daydreams. While daydreaming may decrease our performance on the task at hand, there is evidence that it has a positive impact on mental health and overall cognitive performance. 69% of respondents spend a lot of time daydreaming.

However, daydreaming can become problematic if it's involuntary, we can't snap out of it, or it has a detrimental impact on our life. In **Maladaptive Daydreaming**, people become absorbed in extensive, often compulsive fantasies for several hours a day. These fantasies replace human interaction and impair everyday functioning in various domains. Maladaptive daydreaming has been found to co-occur with ADHD. 31% of survey respondents reported symptoms of maladaptive daydreaming.

Dissociation is a coping mechanism that often occurs in response to excessive levels of stress[109] or a traumatic event.[110] If you think about the fight-or-flight response, dissociation is the mental equivalent of a flight response. We disconnect ourselves from reality in order to protect ourselves from it.

Dissociation isn't an on/off state. We may experience different types or degrees of dissociation at different times in our lives, depending on our circumstances. We may also experience varying degrees of control on whether we dissociate or not. During a dissociative period, we may:

- Feel disconnected from our thoughts, feelings, memories, and surroundings.

- Feel emotionally numb or detached.

- Feel little or no physical pain, or lose the ability to perceive other physical cues (e.g. hunger and thirst signals).

- Have gaps in our memory that affect certain time periods, events, or

---

[109] https://www.nhs.uk/conditions/dissociative-disorders/
[110] https://depts.washington.edu/uwhatc/PDF/TF-%20CBT/pages/7%20Trauma%20Focused%20CBT/Dissociation-Information.pdf

personal information.

- Have out-of-body experiences.
- Lose our sense of identity.
- Have multiple distinct identities.

Dissociative periods can last for mere hours to months or years. If our disconnections with reality are involuntary and cause us problems in functioning in everyday life, we might need professional help. Part of getting that help might be an evaluation for a **dissociative disorder**.

There are a number of dissociative disorders, varying in the type and severity of symptoms. Their classification is complex, contentious, and outside the scope of a work like this. As always, the information provided below is *for educational purposes only*.

Dissociative amnesia is a form of memory loss that affects certain time periods, events, or personal information, usually as a result of trauma or severe stress. Basically, our brains protect us by hiding certain information from us. The resulting memory gaps can span a few minutes to decades, depending on the associated events. The missing memories are hidden, not deleted, and sometimes can be retrieved using specialist techniques such as hypnosis and drug-facilitated interviews. However, it is critical that such retrieval happens in a therapeutic context, as people will most likely need therapy to deal with the underlying trauma.

Repressed memories may still affect our behavior and mental state. For instance, we might not be able to recall the details of a traumatic event, but suffer from anxiety or panic if we find ourselves in a similar situation.

44% of respondents have gaps in their long-term memory that affect certain time periods, events, or personal information. However, these gaps could have other causes. Severe sleep deprivation, for instance, can prevent or reduce memory formation. So if our stress or trauma results in sleep deprivation, or we are sleep-deprived due to unrelated issues, we might have genuine gaps in our memory where our brain failed to file certain information. Given that an estimated 70% of ADHDers and 80% of Autistics are chronically sleep deprived, it pays to bear this in mind.

A loss of the sense of one's identity can be a symptom of **Identity Disturbance**: the inability to maintain one or more major components of identity. However, it can also result from situational issues, such as:

- Changes in social role (e.g. puberty, parenthood, "empty nest", change in career, retirement, etc.).

- Relationships starting or ending.
- Prolonged period of neurodivergent masking.
- Lack of opportunity to pursue personal goals and passions.
- Bullying, abusive relationships, and other forms of social trauma.
- Social isolation (e.g. after a move or a break-up).

As most people go through at least some of these events, at temporary loss of one's sense of identity is very common and not necessarily indicative of an underlying problem.

Having multiple identities, on the other hand, is quite rare, and is usually a symptom of **Dissociative Identity Disorder (DID).** DID is usually the result of childhood abuse or neglect, although it can also result from exposure to major traumatic events. A person with DID has two or more distinct identities. As with other forms of dissociation, DID allows people to distance themselves from their trauma.

Some of the stressors listed in this book have an impact on how often and how severely we dissociate. Basically, anything that traumatizes us, increases the demands placed on us, or decreases our ability to self-soothe while meeting those demands increases the time we spent dissociated and the intensity of our dissociation. The two factors that show the greatest increases are linked to environmental stressors: being routinely forced to endure unpleasant or overwhelming physical sensations in order to navigate our environment, and having been subjected to misguided attempts at "desensitization" therapies in childhood.

Sexual and gender minority stress

Sexual and gender minority (SGM) is an umbrella term used to refer to individuals who are sexual minorities (i.e., not straight) or gender minorities (i.e., not cisgender). It's essentially the same as LGBTQIA2S+, but shorter.

SGM individuals have been found to be at increased risk of experiencing **minority stress** – the chronic stress caused by the stigmatization of our sexual or gender identity.[111] This can affect us regardless of whether we are

---

[111] https://pubmed.ncbi.nlm.nih.gov/12956539/

"out" or not – while concealing our identity might protect us from facing discrimination or prejudice, living a lie is inherently stressful. Furthermore, internalized stigma is also a stressor.

Anecdotal evidence indicates that the neurodivergent community has a higher percentage of SGM individuals than the general population. Official statistics are currently useless in providing accurate information on this subject as neurodivergent individuals may not be allowed to self-identify as trans, and trans individuals may not be willing to risk being diagnosed as neurodivergent for fear of being barred from gender care services. However, unofficial surveys have come to the same conclusions. The "Autistic Not Weird" survey, which was absolutely *massive*, shows that 70% of respondents are cisgender and less than 35% are heterosexual.[112] The results of my survey indicate that 75% of respondents are cisgender and 42% are heterosexual. These figures are much lower than the current worldwide estimates of 98% cisgender[113] and 80% heterosexual.[114] Only 41% of respondents to my survey were both heterosexual and cisgender.

This is important, so I am going to state it, even though it's obvious: **according to the results of recent surveys, cis-het people are not the majority in our community**. If you are paying any attention to the news, you should be able to guess how that may affect our stress levels.

Gender dysphoria

Gender dysphoria is the distress that can result from a mismatch between the gender we were assigned at birth and our gender identity. Not all trans people experience gender dysphoria, and there is no known link between neurodivergence and dysphoria. However, as the percentage of trans people is much higher in the neurodivergent community than in the general population, the percentage of individuals with gender dysphoria is also likely to be higher.

In addition to gender dysphoria, trans people are also at higher risk of suffering from negative self-image, anxiety, depression, self-harm, eating disorders, substance misuse, and suicidality. These issues aren't an innate feature of transness, but the result of the stigmatization, discrimination,

---

[112] https://autisticnotweird.com/autismsurvey/#intersectionality

[113] https://www.statista.com/statistics/1269778/gender-identity-worldwide-country/

[114] https://www.ipsos.com/en/lgbt-pride-2021-global-survey-points-generation-gap-around-gender-identity-and-sexual-attraction

and victimization routinely faced by trans people.[115]

Crisis mode

If we are exposed to triggers we cannot avoid or escape, we might become dysregulated to the point of going into crisis mode. How that looks will depend partly on the triggers in question, and partly on how we are wired to respond to them:

- In a **meltdown**, we experience a temporary loss of control that can be expressed as verbal or physical reactions: shouting, screaming, crying, kicking, hitting, biting, self-harm, and so on. A meltdown is not a temper tantrum; it's a fight response.

- In a **shutdown**, we still experience a temporary loss of control, but this is manifested as withdrawal and inaction. We may lose the ability to process information, communicate, respond to stimuli, move, stand, and so on. A shutdown is not a refusal to participate; it's a freeze response.

These reactions are typically associated with Autism, but they also affect other neurotypes. It's also important to note that these are not symptoms of Autism; they are signs of a neurodivergent person in distress. If you eliminate the causes of the distress, these "symptoms" go away.

Common triggers include loud or complex noises, sensory overload, changes in routine, unmet physical needs, communication issues, social pressure, crowds, and feeling trapped in a space or situation. However, different people have different triggers, and some triggers are highly personal. Virtually anything can be a trigger. If something routinely triggers meltdowns or shutdowns in a person, then it is a trigger for that person, regardless of how other people respond to it.

We have no control whatsoever over what triggers us, or over how much exposure to a trigger we can tolerate before we go into crisis mode. Once the meltdown or shutdown has started, we do not have the power to stop it or control it. However, many of us go through a warning stage, during which we may manifest our distress, engage in self-soothing behaviors (aka stims), or try to leave the area. If we aren't able to self-soothe or leave and the trigger is not removed, an episode will ensue.

---

[115] https://www.psychiatry.org/patients-families/gender-dysphoria/what-is-gender-dysphoria

19% of respondents have meltdowns and 32% have shutdowns.

Several factors correlate with an increased prevalence of meltdowns and shutdowns. Basically, anything that increases the demands we have to meet or decreases our ability to self-soothe will increase the chances of us having a meltdown or shutdown. The greatest increase is caused by being routinely forced to endure unpleasant or overwhelming physical sensations in order to navigate our environment, and the second greatest by being subjected to misguided attempts at "desensitization" therapies in childhood.

Burnout is a different, but related issue. It's a reaction to prolonged exposure to stressful or triggering situations without the ability to decompress, rest, and recover. We are forced to endure sensorily, socially, or emotionally overwhelming experiences until we are pushed beyond a certain tolerance point, and as a result, our system crashes.

Burnouts can last days, weeks, or months, during which we experience a decreased ability to function in a number of ways. Symptoms can include:

- Increased emotional volatility;
- Increased executive dysfunction;
- Increased sensitivity to sensory stimuli, leading to an increase in the frequency of meltdowns and shutdowns;
- Decreased communication abilities (both verbal and written or spelled);
- Memory loss;
- Physical and mental fatigue;
- Lethargy.

67% of respondents experience burnouts. Unsurprisingly, the factors that correlate with an increased prevalence in meltdowns and shutdowns also increase the prevalence of burnouts. Most notably, 86% of those who are routinely forced to endure unpleasant or overwhelming physical sensations in order to navigate their environment experience burnouts, as do 83% of those who were subjected to misguided attempts at "desensitization" therapies in childhood.

Meltdowns, shutdowns, and burnouts are easier to avoid than to manage – as in, they can be avoided by avoiding exposure to the relevant triggers, but once we are in that state, all we can do is ride it out until it passes. However, avoiding exposure to triggers is more easily said than done. This is one of those issues where "awareness" campaigns won't help us; what we need is actual changes in our environment, the demands put upon us, and our opportunity to decompress.

Depression

The definition of **depression** varies between medical systems, but it is generally construed to be a condition characterized by persistent sadness and a lack of interest or pleasure in previously enjoyable activities. Other symptoms may include significant weight loss or gain, insomnia or excessive sleeping, lack of energy, inability to concentrate, and feelings of worthlessness or guilt.[116] Depression is classified into types depending on the presence of certain symptoms and their duration. **Major depression** presents with recurrent thoughts of death or suicide. **Dysthymia** is a depressed mood that lasts for at least two years.[117]

Studies and anecdotal evidence support the idea that depression is a common co-occurring condition in the neurodivergent community. On the one hand, this is unsurprising: given the obstacles many of us face day in, day out, it shouldn't come as a shock if we don't feel great about our life. Being neurodivergent in a neurotypical world provides us with plenty of reasons to feel depressed. Constantly underperforming is depressing. Being punished for things outside of our control is depressing. Going into situations when experience teaches us that we will probably mess up, no matter how hard we try, is depressing. Constantly repressing our basic physical and emotional needs is depressing. Hiding our real self in the vain hope of gaining social acceptance is exhausting, isolating, and depressing. Given all this, it'd be surprising if we *didn't* feel depressed.

There's the rub: if our feelings about our life are reasonable, can we truly be said to "have depression"? This is an important issue, because when it comes to providing treatment and support, there is a huge difference between dealing with a person who is feeling depressed about a depressing situation and one who has feelings of depression that can't be explained by their circumstances. The latter is displaying signs of a neurotransmitter imbalance; the former, not so much.

Let me say this clearly: I am not speaking out against antidepressants, or any other medications that treat the symptoms of neurochemical

---

[116] https://www.apa.org/topics/depression
[117] https://www.health.harvard.edu/newsletter_article/dysthymia

imbalances. These meds are key tools in our arsenal, and can be life altering, or even life-saving, for those of us whose brains need them. However, they can't help those of us whose problems are caused by external issues. We can medicate ourselves away from our reality, but that's not the same as treating a mental illness.

Alas, these distinctions are routinely ignored by clinicians who diagnose patients in a hurry, through standardized questionnaires, or by evaluating the patient's life through their own preconceptions. As a result, patients may be diagnosed with clinical depression and prescribed medication that not only won't make their depressed feelings go away, but may cause additional symptoms. This is a particularly serious issue for those of us who have atypical reactions to these meds. Antidepressant drugs (ADs), in particular Selective Serotonin Reuptake Inhibitors (SSRIs), have been linked with the emergence or worsening of suicidal ideation in vulnerable patients.[118] Anecdotal evidence suggests that neurodivergent individuals may be at increased risk of experiencing these problems.

Even for those of us who don't suffer these side effects, being misdiagnosed with depression or any other mental health condition can still cause difficulties. It isn't uncommon for doctors to refuse additional screenings for patients who have been diagnosed with a mental health condition: their symptoms have been attributed to something, so no further investigations are deemed necessary. As a result, undiagnosed neurodivergents who exhibit symptoms of common mental health conditions may never gain access to the appropriate diagnostic services.

For those of us who are Certified Neurodivergent™, being diagnosed with a mental health condition may bar us from accessing specific treatments. Many doctors withhold certain meds, in particular stimulant meds for ADHD, until any co-occurring mental health conditions are resolved. As a result, many of us suffer in ADHD prescription limbo: we can't get ADHD meds while we are being treated for co-occurring conditions we might not even have. If said co-occurring conditions don't improve with treatment – which is unlikely when the treatment has no impact on the actual causes of our "symptoms" – we may never be allowed to try ADHD meds. That's both ironic and tragic, given that ADHD meds have actually been shown to help many of us manage our most troublesome ADHD traits and reduce their impact on our life.

---

[118] https://www.ncbi.nlm.nih.gov/pmc/articles/PMC3353604/

For context: untreated ADHD is associated with lower academic and work outcomes, and with higher rates of substance abuse, traffic violations, vehicular accidents, criminality, and imprisonment.[119] We are more than twice as likely to die prematurely than our neurotypical counterparts, and mortality rates are highest among people diagnosed in adulthood.[120] Estimates vary, but current studies suggest that we can expect an 11- to 25-year reduction in life expectancy.[121] [122] Under these circumstances, it is hardly surprising that many of us give meds a shot. The fact that 65–75% of us show an improvement after treatment[123] should be enough to inform medical professionals that ADHD meds work, and can have a real impact on our life. Unfortunately, the myth still persists that we should feel good first, and only then we should be allowed access to the meds that enable us to do the things that make us feel good.

ADHDers face an additional issue. The current theory is that that ADHD is linked to dysfunctions in the brain reward cascade, especially in the **dopamine** system. If our life doesn't provide us with enough stimulation, our brain may not produce enough dopamine. A shortage of dopamine can result in symptoms virtually indistinguishable to those of depression: lack of motivation, inexplicable tiredness, inability to derive pleasure from previously enjoyable experiences, social withdrawal, reduced emotions, low sex drive, and feelings of depression or hopelessness.[124] This is theorized to be the reason why ADHDers are more prone to engaging in a number of risky, addictive, impulsive, and compulsive behaviors, such as substance use, alcoholism, risky sex, gambling, carbohydrate bingeing, compulsive shopping, interpersonal aggression, and various legal and illegal high-risk activities. These behaviors are, effectively, coping mechanisms: they stimulate the production of the brain chemicals we lack, which allows us to feel "normal." We use over-arousal to compensate for our biochemical inability to derive reward from ordinary, everyday activities. In doing so, we can get into terrible trouble, but these issues are neurochemical, not behavioral, and deserve the attention of our doctors. Alas, if our problem is that we don't have enough *dopamine* to function, fiddling with our *serotonin* levels may not help us.

---

[119] https://www.ncbi.nlm.nih.gov/pmc/articles/PMC4659921/

[120] https://www.medscape.com/viewarticle/840502

[121] https://www.additudemag.com/adhd-life-expectancy-russell-barkley/

[122] https://www.ajmc.com/view/psychologist-barkley-says-life-expectancy-slashed-in-worst-cases-for-those-with-adhd

[123] https://www.ncbi.nlm.nih.gov/pmc/articles/PMC2518387/

[124] https://my.clevelandclinic.org/health/articles/22588-dopamine-deficiency

Anxiety

In this section, I'm going to circle back to the previous chapter and contradict myself, kinda. When I discussed the difference between anxiety and stress, I stated that it's really important that we don't confuse the two, particularly if we are trying to take steps to fix them. Confusing stress for anxiety can make us gaslight ourselves as to the nature of our problems. Stress is about *what* we face in the world, while anxiety is about *how* we face it. When we are facing a constant barrage of real, chronic stressors, telling ourselves that they are all in our heads is the opposite of helpful. Letting doctors do the same is no better, even if it's classed as "therapy." And if denying our reality doesn't fix it, denying it harder won't work, either.

There is another side to this issue, though. Facing a constant barrage of real, chronic stressors can have an impact on how we view the world and ourselves. Living our lives in survival mode can make us doubt in our ability to cope with our daily lives. From the outside, this may seem absurd: we coped yesterday and all the days before it, so, quite clearly, we can cope! We *are* coping! On the inside, however, we are aware of how often and how close we came to crumbling, and we know that there are no guarantees that we will be able to cope today, and tomorrow, and for all the days that lay ahead of us. Our stressors are countless and tireless; but there's only one of us, and we are >*this*< close to falling apart.

Living like this takes its toll, particularly on children. An adult who suddenly finds themself under toxic stress has a history of successes and failures to draw back on. They know what they are and aren't able to cope with. They know what personal, social, and community resources they can rely on. They might have already overcome obstacles that seemed impossible when they faced them. Moreover, they know that their toxic stress is *temporary*: it wasn't there before, after all, so chances are that it won't be there forever. Like all other phases of their life, this too shall pass. All they have to do is endure it and do their best until normal life resumes.

None of this applies to those of us who grew up in a constant state of near-terminal overwhelm. For us, toxic stress is the norm. It's what we face, day in, day out, and the constancy of our struggles does not build resilience; it just drains us, hurts us, and reminds us constantly of how close we are to collapse. We know how badly we are struggling. We know that the world will give us no quarter. We know that our failures will be used against us, and so will our successes: if we manage to cope today, we will be expected to cope with even more tomorrow. And we have no reason to believe that our current struggles are just an obstacle we have to overcome; when our entire life has been a series of barely-surmountable obstacles, we can reasonably expect that the current one is just hiding more right behind it.

It's conceptually possible to grow up like this and *not* develop an anxiety disorder, but I wouldn't bet on those chances. The far more likely result is that we will grow up to doubt our own abilities and fear the world, which are the core components of anxiety. This anxiety won't just make us feel terrible; it will also reduce our ability to cope with the rest of our stressors. In a very real sense, chronic anxiety *is* a stressor. Not only that, but it's a constant stressor that saps our resources not only in the face of adversity, but even when things are going well.

And yet, for those of us with executive dysfunction, memory problems, or an interest-based nervous system, anxiety can be a coping mechanism. For instance, we may use a combination of last-minute panic, caffeine, and self-loathing to bypass our executive dysfunction. We might develop anxious mental habits to prod us into action, because we can only function on demand if we convince ourselves that our world will come to an end if we don't. We may develop obsessive thoughts and ritualistic behaviors to reduce the risk of forgetting or losing something. Did we turn off the stove? Did we lock the door? Do we still have our wallet? Better check again, because we can't trust ourselves! These coping mechanisms might help, in the short term, because they can help us meet our demands. However, if they become entrenched, everyday habits, that's a problem. These behaviors are, in essence, trained versions of anxiety and OCD.

If you think this sounds terrible, buckle up, because it gets worse. Those of us who grew up with anxiety might not even realize that we are anxious, because we literally don't know that there is any other way to be. This applies both to those of us who were not sheltered from toxic stress by our caregivers, and to those of us whose caregivers were consumed by their own toxic stress. Overfacing children[125] – i.e., damaging their self-confidence by presenting them with excessive demands – can lay the seeds of anxiety, but so does modeling anxiety day in, day out. We learn through our experiences and by osmosis. And when our parents are consumed by their own anxieties, our chances of growing up calm and secure are slim.

---

[125] https://www.thehorsehub.co.uk/when-training-goes-wrong-the-problem-of-overfacing

This type of learning isn't just a case of picking up information, either. As we saw in the intro chapter, the brain is an organ that responds to and adapts to its environment. Our brain structure and neurochemistry affect how we think, feel, and sense, but the opposite is also true: what we think, feel, and sense affects our brain structure and neurochemistry. Our brain changes in real, measurable ways in response to our experiences. These changes are particularly significant in childhood, when our brains are still developing.

Exposure to traumatic events has been shown to cause acute and chronic changes in neurochemical systems and specific brain regions, including the hippocampus, amygdala, and medial prefrontal cortex. These, in turn, result in long-term changes in how the brain responds to stress.[126] Chronic anxiety results in similar changes. MRI studies have demonstrated that young children with high levels of anxiety show greater amygdala volume and amygdala functional connectivity than children with low levels of anxiety. The connection between anxiety and the amygdala is so reliable that researchers have been able to develop a formula that can predict a child's anxiety level from their MRI results.[127] Our brains literally show how anxious, stressed, and traumatized we have been, and this in turn affects how anxious, stressed, and traumatized we feel right now.

This means that for many of us anxiety is a mental habit, a coping mechanism, and the way in which our brain is structured and wired to function. This is likely to be particularly true for those of us who are affected by a large number of unavoidable, chronic stressors. If those stressors don't disappear as we grow up, we end up living a life in which stress and anxiety coexist and combine into an unholy mishmash of awfulness. Reducing our stressors may not reduce our anxiety, because our anxiety is baked into us. On the other hand, working to reduce our anxiety without addressing our stress may be a losing proposition; it's hard to convince ourselves that we have nothing to worry about when we have too much to worry about. And trying to reduce our anxiety or stress without taking our neurodivergence into account is even less likely to help us.

All these issues add up and combine, and other factors can join in to make things even harder. The particular blend of mental, physical, neurological, and external challenges we have to face will depend on our

---

[126] https://www.ncbi.nlm.nih.gov/pmc/articles/PMC3181836/
[127] https://www.sciencedaily.com/releases/2014/06/140616093200.htm

neurotype, life experiences, physical and mental health, and current situation. For me, the best representation of my inner and outer life through my early adulthood is this diagram by Eugthinks on Tumbler:[128]

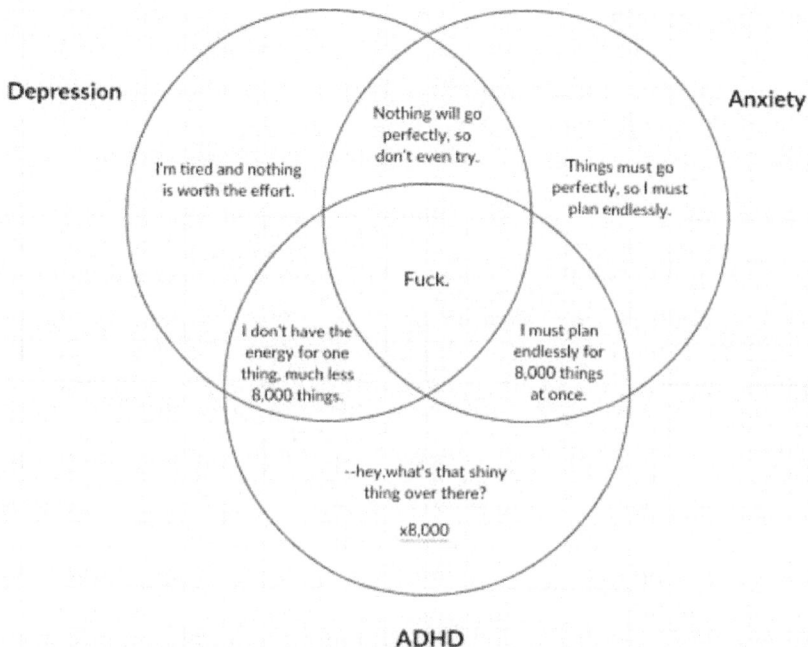

Depression **Anxiety**

Nothing will go perfectly, so don't even try.

I'm tired and nothing is worth the effort.

Things must go perfectly, so I must plan endlessly.

Fuck.

I don't have the energy for one thing, much less 8,000 things.

I must plan endlessly for 8,000 things at once.

--hey.what's that shiny thing over there?

x8,000

ADHD

In case you are wondering, I used to live right in the middle of that. It was not a fun place to be.

Dealing with this shit is hard. Not dealing with it, however, means that our lives will likely remain hard; even if good things happen, our mental habits may stop us from enjoying them. Chronic anxiety is the mental equivalent of a hole in the tank: we can fill up our tank and soup up our engine until we're blue in the face, but we'll still not get enough miles to the gallon because of that constant drain. Unfortunately, patching that hole isn't as easy as, yannow, patching an actual hole.

Hard doesn't mean hopeless, though. There's a ton of stuff we can try to make our lives better. That's what we're going to look at next.

---

[128] https://eugthinks.tumblr.com/post/139013090766/i-made-a-chart

137

So What?

In the first chapter of this book, I said that stress and anxiety are different beasties that require very different handling. In the last section of the last chapter, I said that stress and anxiety often live and operate together, feeding on each other. So, why do these distinctions matter? If we are likely to be dealing with a mishmash of stressors, anxiety, and anxiety about stressors, why should we bother trying to disentangle them?

The answer is simple: these distinctions may not make much of a difference to how we feel, but they make a lot of difference to what we can do about it. As I said already, anxious feelings that originate in our brain respond best to changes in **how we think**. Anxious feelings that originate from external stressors respond best to changes in **how we live**. Therefore, working out whether we are dealing with stress or anxiety is fairly critical.

Having said that... yes, I'm going to contradict myself again, but bear with me. Chances are that if you're reading this book, you've probably already consumed some other media about how to deal with stress or anxiety. If that's the case, you might have noticed that there are a lot of people out there with advice for us. For instance, we might be told to exercise more, change our diet or start taking supplements, practice mindfulness or meditation, take up journaling, scream into a pillow, sit with our feelings, or just to relax more.[129] If our doctors take our anxiety/stress seriously, they might refer us for therapies like CBT, or prescribe us medications to help us control our symptoms, such as antidepressants, anti-anxiety medications like benzodiazepines, or beta-blockers. If we are inclined towards alternative therapies, we might explore acupuncture, animal therapy, aromatherapy, biofeedback, cannabidiol (CBD) oil, colonic irrigation, diaphragmatic breathing, EFT tapping, energy healing, herbal medicine, homeopathy, hypnotherapy, light therapy, massage, progressive muscle relaxation, sound therapy, or mindful movement practices such as Qigong, tai chi, and yoga. There are so many options out there! How are we supposed to pick the right one, particularly if we don't even know whether we are dealing with stress, anxiety, or a combination of the two?

This is not as big a deal as it might be, for one simple reason: with the

---

[129] Because telling people to relax totally help, obvs. If you shout it, it works even better!

notable exception of CBT and some exposure therapies, most of these solutions aim to **relieve the symptoms** of our anxiety or stress, but don't actually **address the root causes** of our issues. That doesn't mean that they don't work! It all depends on what we are trying to achieve. Are we looking for a break from our symptoms? For our symptoms to improve? Do we want our symptoms to go away, and stay away? Do we want an instant fix, or can we wait for the improvements to kick in? Are we looking for something we can use in the middle of a crisis, or something we can use to avoid crises?

Most therapies have their uses, but none of them are cure-alls, and most of them aren't even multi-use tools, so to speak. For instance, if we suffer from social anxiety, yoga might provide us with a way to temporarily decompress, and perhaps even a safe space where we can be around other humans with little to no pressure to actually interact. However, yoga won't help us if we are having a social-anxiety-induced panic attack in church, during a work meeting, on the bus, or anywhere that isn't a yoga studio; dropping into a downward dog halfway through a social interaction is unlikely to help us feel better about it.

There are other considerations, too. Are these activities practical for us? Are they accessible to us? Can we afford them, both in the short- and long-term? Do we enjoy them? The last question is important. Living with stress and anxiety already sucks. We don't need to make it suck even more by taking on activities that make us miserable.

There is a lot to think about, but we don't need to let it overwhelm us. As far as I'm concerned, there are only two questions we need to answer:

1. Are we actually going to do it?

2. Is it working for us?

The first answer is critical. It doesn't matter a fig how good an activity might be if we aren't going to do it. Ruminating over how good something would be for us if only we actually did it is not a recognized therapeutic approach, for one simple reason: it doesn't work. Solutions that we are actually going to implement are the best for us, even if they are not perfect. And anyway, picking a b-team activity today doesn't mean that we're giving up on a-team activities forever. We are free to change tack as soon as we are able and willing. For now, however, doing what we can is the best strategy.

The second answer is just as critical. A lot of stock solutions are aimed at the average person. Neurodivergent people are, by definition, *not* average. I've already written over a hundred pages about it, so I won't repeat myself here, but the bottom line is that if something doesn't work for us, then it doesn't work for us. That doesn't mean that it's a terrible solution in general, that we're doing it wrong, or that we should just do it harder; it might just be a bad fit for us, because we are neurodivergent.

This is even more significant for those of us who are affected by trauma on top of everything else. We are juggling multiple issues, and that will probably narrow down our options, at least in the short term. Right now, we can only do what we can actually do. Once some of our issues resolve, we will be able to change tack, if we want to.

In order to get to that point, however, we will probably have to actually *fix* some of our shit. That's usually a much gnarlier process than sticking on patches. It's also potentially dangerous, for two main reasons. Firstly, whatever process we use, it will most likely require that we dig deeply into some unpleasant aspects of our past and present in the hope that we will be able to build a better future. That can be a grueling and potentially re-traumatizing process.

Critically examining our present may bring up stuff we'd rather not deal with, as well as stuff we would love to deal with, but just can't. Making changes can be difficult and painful. Accepting that some things in our life are not fixable can be even more painful. There's a good reason people pray for the serenity to accept the things they cannot change, the courage to change the things they can, and the wisdom to know the difference: it's bloody hard.

Unpacking our past can be even harder. It can be dangerous, too. Trauma work can open up old wounds. Dealing with them isn't always easy or safe, particularly if our current situation isn't ideal.

The second issue is even more unpleasant. Trauma work can make us vulnerable, and vulnerability can attract predators. Psychotherapy and psychology are regulated industries because the people who need to see a psychotherapist or a psychologist are usually in a vulnerable position. However, in many countries there is little to no regulation on counselors, and no regulation at all on those selling self-help. Anyone with access to the internet can start churning out content aimed at everyone and anyone, including very vulnerable people.

There are plenty of people out there advertising programs that guarantee us freedom from all past traumas, but what they are actually selling is a cult. While some of the tools they push may be effective, the way in which they use them or encourage us to use them can put us at risk. Some of the tools on offer may be unsafe, too. The very idea of doing trauma work under the guidance of a stranger whose only qualification may be that they have a large public following is unsafe. The wounds we open up during trauma work will need to heal. That can be hard to deal with without the help of reliable, trustworthy, supportive people. It can be even harder when the people who offer us support are using us to inflate their egos or their wallets.

It's not all doom and gloom, though. There are tons of good approaches to dealing with our problems, both past and present. We just have to be a little bit careful when we're shopping for one. Generally speaking:

- If we can access professional help (i.e., a psychologist, psychotherapist, or regulated therapist), it's probably a good idea to do so.

- If we can find a professional that matches our neurotype, that's even better. If that's not an option, a neurodivergence-informed professional is the second best choice.

- If a professional uses stigmatizing or medicalizing terms for neurodivergences and disabilities, that's a red flag.

- If a professional advocates for "cures" for neurodivergence, especially quick-fix cures like diets, detoxes, fecal transplantation, and the like, run. If they are advocating behavioral therapies that hinge on punishing the natural expressions of neurodivergence, run even faster. The first lot wants your money. The second lot wants to deprive you of your bodily autonomy.

- Professionals who advocate for genetic testing under the guise of allowing prospective parents to make informed decisions are advocating for eugenics. Where you sit on that is up to you, but we need to be aware of the meaning behind the words.

- A good professional should respect our agency. They should encourage us to define our goals, choose the best strategies to reach them, and determine what "success" looks like. They may be the specialists, but the locus of authority for our recovery should sit with us.

- A good professional should set us up for success. They should design activities in order to maximize our chances of achieving our goals.

- A good professional should recognize and celebrate our successes. This is particularly important for those of us who are used to having their successes minimized or discounted. We need to learn to take the time to celebrate our victories, rather than immediately moving the goalposts.

- A good professional should be able not only to help us when things don't go as we wish, but to find the lessons in our "failures." That's not just an attempt at forced positivity: every time something doesn't work for us, that's a useful data point that should inform our next step. A good professional should be able to make use of that, and model that behavior for us.

- A good professional should support us if we decide to try other avenues to help our progress. The only exception is if they deem those avenues dangerous to us or generally useless, in which case they should explain the situation to us.

- A good professional should be clear and upfront about their qualifications and limits, and inform us if our needs fall outside of their expertise.

- A good professional should be willing to refer us to another professional if they deem it necessary.

- Professionals who claim that we deliberately chose our early trauma, disabilities, or diseases by calling them into our life before our birth (or at any time after that, really) are toxic as all get out, and should be avoided accordingly.

- Trauma work can make us incredibly vulnerable. If anyone tries to make us do it in a public setting, that's a serious red flag. There is no good reason for us to make ourselves vulnerable while surrounded by unvetted strangers. The fact that we all paid the same entrance fee to the same activity does not a community make.

- If we have to rely on self-help materials, content produced by regulated professionals is likely to be safer, as it is subjected to a degree of external quality control. However, that doesn't mean that it's safe or useful for us. It might be right for us, but not right now, because it doesn't match our current needs and limitations. It might also just not be a good fit, because it's developed by and for people whose neurotype is too different from ours.

We should not underestimate the possible impact of bad counseling. Any form of therapy requires us to trust the professionals providing it. We will need to confide information that could put us at risk if mishandled. To a lesser or greater extent, we will also rely on those professionals to guide us through the recovery process. If they guide us in the wrong direction, we may find ourselves in a very bad place before we know it.

I can't recommend the best course of therapy for you, because I don't know you. I don't know what you want, what you need, or what resources are available to you. This will depend on a lot of factors: your needs, your current struggles, your location, your financial situation, and so on. Therefore, I can't tell you how to find the program that best fits you, let alone the best specialist. One thing is universally true, though: whichever therapy we embrace should be a tool to help us move on, not a lifestyle. The help we receive should enable us to go out and live our own life as well as we can, not make us dependent on our helpers.

Whichever therapy or program we sign up to, it should meet one basic criterion: it should **train us for success**. I am using the word "train" in a broad sense here, but that's not because I'm sloppy. The fact is that **training does not only happen when we decide it will.** Every time we repeat an action or reaction, we are training that action or reaction. As a result, we become increasingly likely to automatically default to that action or reaction if the situation calls for it, and sometimes even when it doesn't. It's especially important for us to remember that when what we are doing is only helpful in a very specific context, or isn't helpful at all.

You might have heard the aphorism that "whatever you practice, you get good at." Fortunately or unfortunately, that is only partly true. It's possible for a person to practice good skills consistently and accurately without ever improving due to personal limitations. I practiced the violin for two years and never stopped sounding like a mouse trying to have a poo through a sewed-up bum hole. That wasn't because I was practicing bad skills, or practicing them badly. Quite simply, a combination of dyspraxia and cervical impingement mean that I don't have the fine motor control skills required to play a violin.

Many neurodivergent people have mental and physical abilities that differ from the norm. It is absolutely possible for us to practice a certain skill endlessly without ever getting good at it. However, that doesn't mean that the aphorism is entirely incorrect. Generally speaking, two things are true:

- Whatever we practice, we may get better at. We may see some improvement either in how we can perform the activity in question or in the way we approach a certain problem. For instance, we may learn that if we carry out some adjustments to the way in which we perform an activity we achieve better results. This is particularly important when we are dealing with obstacles we can't train ourselves out of, such as physical disabilities or learning and processing issues.

- Whatever we practice, we may automatically default to in certain situations. Practice forms mental and physical habits. Some of those habits are transferrable, and may kick in automatically whenever we are in a certain situation. This is great news if those habits are useful, but can work against us when they are not.

When we decide to work on improving the way in which we deal with anxiety, stressors, and trauma reactions, we need to consider the following key factors:

- Are we training the right skills?
- Are we training them in the right way?

Training the right skills is critical, for obvious reasons: if we train the wrong skills, we are just wasting our time. What may be less obvious is that skills are not always transferrable, and might not work in all settings. For instance, the skills that can help us with stressors may worsen our anxiety, and vice versa. The skills that can help us reduce our symptoms may not help us manage them, and neither may help us in an emergency.

Most of us will probably want to learn how to do everything: to handle emergencies, to manage our symptoms, and to eradicate the root causes of our problems. However, unless we're superhuman, we'll probably have to prioritize what we do at any given time. Sometimes life will prioritize for us, too. If we are in an emergency, we should prioritize dealing with that, first. If we are struggling to manage our symptoms, we might need to work on that before we start working on the root causes of our problems. And once we make the time and space to deal with the root causes of our problems, we might find that the resulting upheaval gives us plenty of opportunities to practice how we deal with emergencies. It pays to learn how to do a bit of everything, even if we cannot do it all at once, or very well. That's what we will cover in the next chapter.

Now what?

This chapter is another list of lists. It's waaay shorter than the last megalist, though, and it's full of stuff that should be more helpful than depressing, so there's that.

These lists include some of the things we can do to improve how we manage our anxiety and stress, organized in order of urgency. These checklists work for me, but might not work for you. If your priorities are different, you will probably want to structure your work in a different way. If your priorities change, you might need to readjust your plans accordingly.

Checklist 1: In case of emergencies.

This is the mental checklist I ue when I feel suddenly or exceptionally anxious and I want to deal with that.

1. Check your immediate surroundings for hazards.

Are you in **actual, immediate danger**? If you're wrestling a bear or about to get hit by a car, your anxious feelings are not unwarranted, and you should prioritize taking **immediate action** to keep yourself safe.

If you can't identify an obvious danger, is your subconscious telling you that there's something you should look out for? If a stranger is scoping you from a shadowy corner or you're about to walk into a dark alleyway full of hidey-holes, your anxious feelings may be your natural warning system telling you that you need to get the hell out of there. For those of us who have been brought up to doubt our perceptions and feelings, respecting our intuition can be very hard. For those of us who are trying to overcome our anxiety, ducking out of situations "just because" they feel iffy can also seem like a defeat. You know what else doesn't feel great, though? Ignoring our intuition, getting hurt, and then having to deal with both our hurt and our self-blame, because "we should have known better."

If we have environmental sensitivities, our body may react to triggers as if they were dangerous, even when they are not. What I mean by this is that some triggers can put us in danger by triggering physiological reactions like asthma attacks or epileptic fits, while others are "just" uncomfortable or painful. Any trigger that is going to put us in physical danger is a hazard, and should be treated as such. As for the ones that "just" hurt us, is up to each of us to decide how we want to act when we are exposed to them. However, we should bear in mind that enduring painful triggers is NOT costless from a neurophysiological standpoint, and is NOT going to desensitize us to them.

Please note that, as far as the human brain is concerned, social dangers are as real as physical ones. We are social animals. Social exclusion may not kill us as quickly as a bear or a speeding car, but that doesn't make it insignificant. A hungry bear and an angry boss may require very different handling, but the neurophysiological reactions they trigger in us are remarkably similar.

2. Breathe.

Breathing is the only tool I know that can help us relax both when we are relatively calm and in pretty much all situations when we feel anxious. It doesn't matter how anxious we feel, or whether our feelings have an internal or external source; slow, deep, controlled breathing can help us manage the neurophysiological changes caused by all types of anxiety and stress.

The reason for that is that breathing crosses the barrier between the autonomic nervous system, which controls involuntary bodily functions, and the somatic nervous system, which controls muscle movement and relays information from the body to the central nervous system. Breathing isn't a voluntary function – were that the case, we'd stop breathing every time we fall asleep. However, we can exercise some control over how we breathe. Controlling our breathing can have an impact on the functioning of our autonomic nervous system.[130] As the autonomic nervous system is one of the major neural pathways activated by stress and anxiety, breathing can give us some control over our neurophysiological reactions.

Using our breathing like this requires practice, for two reasons. Firstly, controlled, deep, slow breathing isn't natural to most of us. It's a skill, and like any other skill, we have to practice it in order to learn it and to keep it fresh in our memory. Secondly, while controlled breathing can help us exert some influence over our autonomic nervous system, the middle of a neurophysiological storm isn't the best time to try and learn how to do it. If we have already mastered that skill, we might be able to use it. If we haven't, it's still worth trying, but we are likely to struggle.

There are different school of thoughts as to which is the best way to breathe in order to calm ourselves down. This makes sense: different people breathe differently because we have different respiratory systems. Also, different people benefit from different types of breath training because we learn differently. For those of us who have time agnosia, some kind of external measure of how long we're breathing, like counting, is likely to be essential.

I am including a couple of breathing exercises in the footnotes, but you'll have to find one that works for you and your respiratory system.

---

[130] There are other bodily functions that cross between the autonomic and somatic nervous system – blinking, salivating, swallowing, peeing, and pooing. However, practicing drooling or having a poo every time we feel anxious is unlikely to help us relax.

Generally speaking, if you can't carry out a breathing exercise comfortably under normal circumstances, you're unlikely to be able to carry it out any more comfortably when you really need it.[131]

3. Check where your body is at.

This is particularly important if our interoception isn't up to snuff. It's very possible for us to feel absolutely awful in an emotional sense because we have unmet physical needs we know nothing about. Are we too hot, too cold, too thirsty, too hungry? Are we just desperate for the loo? Our bodies may not be able to tell us that, because we can't pick up those physical clues. Our minds, however, can let us know that our body is in distress. Unfortunately, that kind of message may be loud, but isn't always clear.

If our interoceptive attention is poor, running a deliberate scan of our bodies might inform us that we have an unmet physical need. Addressing that need may bring us immediate relief from our anxious feelings, or at least lessen them a little. Sometimes meeting our physical needs may bring us no relief, because our anxious feelings had different causes – it's possible for us to have unmet physical needs and be going through something else, too. However, checking the physical side of things is well worth a shot.

If our interoceptive accuracy is the issue, this is going to be a lot harder. We may have to rely on external clues to work out what's going on. How long has it been since we've eaten or drank? Are we in a hot or cold place? When did we last have a wee? If we're drawing a blank, it might be worth trying drinking, eating, putting on or taking off a jumper, and so on. If something works, we can use that as a data point for future reference.

Some medical conditions manifest largely as emotional responses, even though the underlying issue is physical. For instance, the drop in blood sugar levels caused by postprandial hypoglycemia usually manifests as irritability, anxiousness, weakness, tiredness, confusion, shakiness, dizziness, and a fast or uneven heartbeat. What we need is to eat or drink something that will raise our blood sugar levels, but we might not know that if we don't feel hungry. If we are affected by a condition that can trick

---

[131] A short breathing exercise (4-7-8) – no counting:
https://www.youtube.com/watch?v=j-1n3KJR1I8

A short breathing exercise(4-7-8), with counting
https://www.youtube.com/watch?v=4qACPNA2cKY

us like that, we might need to rely on some other system (e.g., a regular eating schedule) to avoid getting caught out.

For those of us who might suffer from premenstrual syndrome (PMS), premenstrual dysphoric disorder (PMDD), or any kind of hormonal fluctuation, some kind of mood and period or hormonal tracking may be beneficial.[132] Knowing that we are going through a temporary hormonal upheaval may not make us feel any better, but it can help us keep a lid on our emotions and manage our reactions.

4. Can you identify a stressor or trigger?

Are you being exposed to a known stressor? If that's the case, removing the stressor or removing yourself from the stressor could reduce your anxious feelings.

This is one of those situations where tools like noise-cancelling headphones or sunglasses come in handy: we might not be able to turn off the sun, or even to turn down the lights, but putting on a pair of shades might be enough to take the edge off that particular stressor.[133] Oh, if you have respiratory allergies, surgical masks or N95/FFP2 respirators may help. The type of mask needed will depend on the size of the particles that trigger your allergies.

Have you been exposed to a trigger for PTSD or cPTSD flashbacks? Working that out can be trickier, because flashbacks can really draw us in. Emotional flashbacks can be particularly insidious, and it might take us some time to hone the skills necessary to spot them.

If we realize that we were in a flashback after the fact, we might be able to reverse-engineer the trigger that caused it. Or not. Sometimes triggers can be really tangential, or linked to lost or buried memories. It's still worth trying, though, particularly if we are experiencing flashbacks quite frequently. Whether identifying our triggers will enable us to avoid them is a whole other story, though.

---

[132] If you are in a country were reproductive rights are being eroded, you might want to eschew online trackers in favor of old-fashioned diaries, or a spreadsheet on your device of choice. Privacy policies notwithstanding, information you put online may be subpoenaed. A paper list you keep in your bathroom cabinet, not so much.

[133] It can also make us look like Dave Strider from Homestuck. If you're not familiar with that particular work, fear not! It's only 8,000 pages! (The Epilogues and Homestuck^2 NEVER HAPPENED.)

Realizing that we have been triggered into a flashback doesn't mean that we will be able to just snap out of it. In order to do that, we might need to pick up a specific set of skills, and doing so is neither easy nor pleasant – see the section on managing our responses to triggers later on in the book. However, noticing that we are in a flashback is an essential part of the process. It might not make us feel any better, but it can help us act better, and that is a very good place to start.

Checklist 2: Managing symptoms.

This is a list of various types of tools we can use to manage the symptoms of our anxiety and stress. These don't directly address the root causes of our issues, but they can help us do so by lightening our load, even if temporarily.

Think of this list as a buffet menu; we might have our preferred go-to options, but ideally we should try and pick at least one item per type to develop a diverse and comprehensive toolkit. We might really like hammers, but having a dozen hammers won't be much help to us if we ever find ourselves in a situation that requires a screwdriver.

Sleep

Sleep is at the top of this list for two reasons: it's essential, and it's the one thing that can make everything else easier. Without getting enough sleep, we'll struggle to manage our symptoms and handle emergencies, let alone to address the root causes of our problems. Reducing our stress and anxiety requires work an underslept brain will struggle to perform.

Sleep is essential to normal functioning, and in particular to the proper functioning of the brain, yet our culture often treats it as an optional extra, or even as a weakness. We won't "sleep when we are dead," because we'll be dead then. Also, not sleeping enough while we're alive can reduce both our quality of life and our lifespan.

There are two aspects of sleep: quantity and quality. Most adults need at least seven hours of sleep every night. If we are sleeping less than seven hours every night, then we're probably sleep-deprived. If we are sleeping seven or more hours and we still wake up tired, then we either need more sleep than the average bear, or our sleep quality may not be up to snuff.

Unfortunately, getting enough good quality sleep is not always easy. Some of us just need to improve our sleep hygiene.[134] For some of us, however, sleep deprivation is caused by factors outside of our control. We might have dependents who wake us up or keep us up, less-than-ideal sleeping quarters, or a variety of sleep disturbances that may prevent us

---

[134] https://www.sleepfoundation.org/sleep-hygiene
Please note that I **do not** recommend getting out of bed if we can't fall asleep after 20 minutes. Under normal circumstances, most people take between 10 and 20 minutes to fall asleep at night. We are clearly not most people, because only 4% of us manage that. If we got out of bed every time our 20 minutes are up, we'd never get to sleep.

from getting enough sleep, or getting enough good sleep. Some sleep disturbances are easily treatable, and some are not. Unfortunately, getting medical help for our sleep is not always easy, even for those of us who can get access to doctors. That shouldn't be the case, but it is.

If you believe you have a sleep disturbance and you have access to a medical professional, badger them relentlessly until they do something about it. If you get no joy through regular consultations, it might help to write them a letter including:

- The exact details of your sleep disturbance (e.g., you can't fall asleep, you can't stay asleep, etc.) including times, dates, and any patterns.

- When it started and how often it happens.

- What you are already doing to try and resolve it (e.g., regular bedtime routine, your sleep environment, any sleep aids, etc.).

- Its impact on your daily life (e.g., tiredness, memory problems, etc.).

- The known prevalence of sleep disturbances in people with your neurotype.

If you can't get help from medical professionals and you decide to try over-the-counter remedies, please research your options carefully – and from PubMed, not YouTube. Sleep is critical to our health and should not be treated like an optional extra, but some sleep aids are downright dangerous, and all medications have side effects and interactions.

If you are getting enough sleep but you still wake up tired, this could be caused by a variety of reasons, and should really be investigated via a sleep study (polysomnography) – a non-invasive, overnight exam that allows doctors to monitor us while we sleep to see what's happening in our brains and bodies. Unfortunately, due to their complexity and cost, sleep studies are not available to all who need them.

If you cannot afford or are struggling to get referred for a sleep study, you might want to consider investing in a sleep-staging wearable fitness monitors, such as one of the newer Fitbit models. While they are not a substitute for a sleep study, they are a convenient and relatively cheap way to obtain gross estimates of sleep parameters and time spent in different sleep stages. The information generated is not as accurate or reliable as that from a sleep study, but it may give you an idea as to what is going on. Also, relaying this information to your doctor may facilitate a referral to a sleep specialist.

A common cause of poor sleep quality is **Sleep-Disordered Breathing** (e.g., sleep apnea). However, subclinical breathing difficulties, such as those caused by allergies or chronic respiratory problems, may have a similar impact on our quality of sleep and the resulting daytime symptoms. If you have allergies, asthma, or any conditions that affect your breathing, it might pay to switch the timing of your medication so that it's active when you sleep. You might not notice your breathing difficulties while you're asleep, but that doesn't mean that they don't affect you.

If your sleep is affected by chronic pain, it might also pay to switch the timing of your medication so that it's active while you sleep, for the same reasons.

Nutrition

The brain is an organ of the body. The body needs nourishment. If your diet isn't providing your brain with enough nourishment, it won't run properly. It's that simple.[135]

Improving our nutrition doesn't necessarily require a ton of cooking – in fact, for those of us with executive function issues, it might require cutting down on cooking. It might mean giving up on complicated meals and sticking to sandwiches or salads. It might mean buying pre-prepared ingredients, such as frozen vegetables or fruit. It might mean cooking in batches and living on leftovers, or cooking the same handful of meals over and over again. For those of us whose struggle to eat while taking meds, it might mean switching to meal replacement shakes or smoothies. None of this is ideal, but you know what's even less ideal? Not feeding ourselves because we can't be neurotypical around food.

Any step we can take towards better nutrition is a step in the right direction. The shake we can drink is better for us than the sandwich we can't even look at. The sandwich we can prepare is better than the cooked meal we can't organize. The pre-prepared ingredients we cook with are better than the fresh ingredients we end up scraping out of the bottom of our fridge when they become a biohazard. Tinned soups, microwave meals, and protein bars are better than chocolate bars, and much better than nothing. Literally any step we can take right now towards getting nutrients into our body is the right step, even when the result looks

---

[135] https://www.health.harvard.edu/blog/nutritional-psychiatry-your-brain-on-food-201511168626

nothing like our ideal of a Proper Diet. And nutritional workarounds are not a lifetime commitment, either; if our lives and our executive dysfunction improve, we will be able to make better choices and establish better habits. In the meanwhile, though, workarounds can improve our health right here, right now.

Ultimately, when we refuse ourselves access to adequate nutrition unless it is in the context of meals of a given degree of complexity, what we are saying is that we have to earn the right to eat by acting neurotypical. That's some ableist bullshit right there. If we did that to a child, it would class as abuse. It's still abuse when we do it to ourselves.

Exercise

Exercise has been shown to have significant mental health benefits for humans in general, and for neurodivergents in particular. These include:

- Less stress and anxiety.
- Improved impulse control.
- Decreased compulsive behaviors.
- Improved working memory.
- Improved executive function.
- Positive changes in brain chemistry.

For those of us who need to vent unpleasant feelings, certain sports can also provide a comparatively safe and constructive way of doing so.

We should ideally aim for 30 to 40 minutes of moderately intense exercise 4 or 5 days a week. Aerobic exercise (i.e., any physical activity that increases our heart rate and oxygen use) can be particularly beneficial in dealing with anxiety and stress for two reasons. Firstly, it burns off adrenaline, which can give us immediate if temporary relief from our anxious symptoms. Secondly, it mimics some of the symptoms of anxiety and stress, such as elevated heart rate and breathlessness. This can help us learn to ride through those sensations, which can improve our self regulation when we experience a neurophysiological stress reaction. Having said that, any amount of exercise of any form is better than nothing. The best form of exercise is the one we actually do, ideally without wrecking ourselves in the process. The health benefits of thinking about exercise are nil. Berating ourselves because we don't exercise achieves nothing aside from harming us.

Permission

Before we make any attempts at reducing our anxiety and stress levels, we need to give ourselves the right to try, and the right to succeed. Many of us live in a state of constant tension because we unconsciously believe that doing so keeps us safe. We spend our entire life in survival mode, constantly ready to face the next threat that comes our way. We never fully disengage with our worries because that would mean that they could catch us by surprise, which would spell disaster and devastation.

There is only a tiny problem with this approach: it's bullshit, and it doesn't work. We might be faced with countless threats, granted, but chronic tension and hypervigilance do not keep us safe; quite the contrary, in fact. By wasting our physical and mental strength, they decrease our ability to deal with actual problems and put us at risk of burning out over nothing.

We might not be able to switch out of survival mode just by sheer force of will.[136] We can, however, give ourselves permission to take a short break from it and use that time to relax and recuperate as best we can. If we do that often enough, it might prove to us that the world doesn't come to an end every time we take a break.[137] We might find it impossible not to worry about everything and anything, but do we have to do it right this minute? Could we spend a moment on something else, and save our worries for another time?

Relaxation

Relaxation is a surprisingly tricky goal to reach. The reason for that is that techniques that aim at relaxing only our body may not do much to relax our mind, but trying to relax our mind when our body is tense might not work, either – and the opposite is also true. As always, the issue is that the division between mind and body is an illusion. It's an illusion with practical implications, though, because most relaxation techniques focus either on our body or our mind. Some of them, like yoga or Qigong, aim at killing both birds with one stone, but reaching the required level of competence can take a while. Many of us need to find a way to relax the

---

[136] If you can, drop this book and go do something more fun, because you clearly don't need this.

[137] If the world does come to an end, people will be too busy dealing with that to blame it on us, anyway.

body and the mind in parallel but separately, and that can be tricky.

Physical relaxation is generally easier to achieve, unless it isn't. There are a gazillion ways for us to try to relax our body – by having a hot bath, wearing comforting clothes, eating comforting foods, using a weighted blanket, cuddling with a human or animal companion, getting a massage or some other form of physical manipulation, listening to media like binaural music or guided meditations,[138] or using specific relaxation techniques, like progressive muscle relaxation.[139] Ultimately, everything that helps us relax is a relaxation technique – and, again, this might sound like a truism, but it's something we should bear in mind.

For many of us, conventional techniques may not work so well. This should come as no surprise as they are, like most other things, not necessarily designed for our neurotype. We might need to find approaches that allow us to enter a state of relaxation via alternative routes, as it were. Stimming can help – hell, for those of us who wear a neurotypical mask, dropping it at all can take a huge load off of us. Anecdotally, consuming media that takes us back to a time or space where we felt safe or comfortable seems to work for a lot of people. It might seem silly to re-watch, re-read, or re-listen to something we might know by heart, but if it makes us feel better, it's definitely worth doing.[140]

For some of us, rest and stillness don't come natural or feel extremely unpleasant; we may need to unwind while remaining active, and that's a fine line to walk. We might need to find activities that allow us to shed some of our physical and mental tension while keeping us engaged.[141] Alternatively, we might need to relax our body while keeping our mind

---

[138] My favorite background music to fall asleep to is by Sleep Tube on YouTube: https://www.youtube.com/@SleepTube
My favorite relaxation recording is "Effective Meditations for Positive Living" by Deirdre Griswold, which I only got to spite a very-much-ex partner. This recording is so old that it can only be found as used audio cassettes, so I stuck it on YouTube: https://youtu.be/Mc3Fa-Mc6V0

[139] There are countless free videos on the subject, but, to be honest, I find most of them really annoying. Here are two of the very few that don't make me want to punch my computer screen.
Short version: https://www.youtube.com/watch?v=ihOO2wUzgkc
Long version: https://www.youtube.com/watch?v=NJjwy67zgEI

[140] My go-to books are "The Wind In The Willows" and the "Brambly Hedge" series. Interestingly, I never read them when I was a kid, but I've more than made up for it now.

[141] Personally, I favor poi spinning (with soft pois, because I don't find whacking myself all that relaxing).

busy, or vice versa – whatever it takes to get the job done. As with everything else, we need to work with our neurodivergence, not against it.

If we suffer from chronic pain, relaxing can be even harder, but that doesn't make it any less important. Finding a way to relax despite our pain can be incredibly tricky, but the benefits could be huge. It's definitely worth trying, but it's also worth remembering that we are not the target audience for one-size-fits-all relaxation techniques.

When we're trying to find the best way for us to relax, the most practical approach is to try whatever we fancy, and see what actually works. If something doesn't work, or doesn't work well enough, we can always try something else. The one thing that is guaranteed not to work is to kick ourselves for being unable to relax a certain way.

Redirection

Redirection is a great tool for when we can't just stop our restless minds or bodies, and we want to find a way to make our restlessness useful, or at least less harmful.

If our body is restless, we could try to force ourselves to relax, but that hardly ever works. Instead, it might be more helpful to redirect our nervous energy towards some useful or pleasant but low-risk pursuit – doing dangerous stuff or anything requiring fine motor skills when we're worked up might not be a good idea. Redirecting our physical restlessness can help us burn off some adrenaline and may tire us out, so it could actually help us relax. And if that doesn't work, at least we got something done.

If our mind is restless, trying to force it to relax is almost guaranteed not to work. Trying not to think about a specific worry might not work, either. On the contrary, the harder we try not to think about something, the more likely it is that that thought will become an obsession.[142] This is true for **intrusive thoughts** – repetitive, often disturbing thoughts that pop into our heads without warning, at any time, and that we cannot switch off at will – but it applies to literally any thought we can think of. It can also apply to unhelpful thinking habits like **over-planning**.

Intrusive thoughts are a common feature of stress, anxiety, depression, PTSD, and cPTSD. They are more than just unpleasant: they

---

[142] https://nesslabs.com/pink-elephant-paradox

can intensify and prolong distressing emotions, and have the potential to trigger anxiety attacks, adrenaline dumps, or uncontrollable emotional spikes.

If we are plagued by intrusive thoughts, it's virtually impossible to stop us from thinking them. Even trying to ignore them might not work. We can, however, try to see them as what they are:

1. Intrusive. They might be in our heads, but we have no control over them. They do not reflect our wishes, dreams, personality, or quality as a person.

2. Thoughts. However unpleasant they might be, they are not real, and they won't magically convert into actions.

Intrusive thoughts are a symptom. They show us that, for whatever reason, we are a bit out of kilter. They say nothing about us other than the fact that we're struggling. They suck, but that doesn't mean that we do. We cannot control them; however, we can control how we react to them.

Many expert recommend non-engagement as the best policy. It's a standard case of "don't feed the trolls" – the fact that these particular trolls live rent-free in our heads is immaterial. In most cases, intrusive thoughts go away on their own, particularly if we don't let them rile us or force us into shame spirals. Some people derive great benefit from carrying out breathing, mindfulness,[143] or grounding exercises.[144]

Another approach aims at reducing the negative impact of intrusive thoughts by replacing them with alternative, positive thoughts. These do not have to be complicated, overoptimistic, or even really meaningful; they just have to be somewhat relevant to us. For instance:

"If you're going through hell, keep on going."

"This too shall pass."

"I won't even remember this in three months' time."

Literally anything will do, as long as we can repeat it like a mantra. This does not cure obsessive thinking we are essentially replacing a repetitive thought with another. However, because the new obsession forces us to focus on the positive instead of causing us extra anxiety, it can help

---

[143] https://www.mayoclinic.org/healthy-lifestyle/consumer-health/in-depth/mindfulness-exercises/art-20046356
[144] https://livingwell.org.au/well-being/mental-health/grounding-exercises/

reduce our overall stress levels, which can in itself help reduce the frequency of our intrusive thoughts.

Personally, I take a different approach, one that is absolutely not recommended by any expert ever, but works for me. I treat the intrusive thoughts as if they were bizarre and unpleasant statements made by a bizarre and unpleasant person I am temporarily stuck with – if you've ever been forced to interact with a relative, housemate, or colleague who couldn't open their mouth without something cringe-worthy or straight-up horrific falling out of it, you know the type.

My terrible brainmate is called Gavin. Gavin is an asshole. When he says something horrible, as he often does, I roll my eyes, because what else could I possibly do? Occasionally, I agree with him. Yes, that time when I did or said that thing really was embarrassing. Sure, if I walked off a cliff, steered my vehicle into incoming traffic, or stabbed myself with a sharp implement the results would indeed be messy. So fucking what? What am I supposed to do about it? Fucking Gavin, I tell you.

Over-planning is a very common feature of anxiety. It's one of those crappy coping mechanisms that end up causing more problems than they solve. The theory is that by making plans so detailed that they cover all contingencies and so rigid that they don't leave any room for surprise, we will gain control over our lives and we won't have anything to feel anxious about. The reality is that by constantly indulging the urge to plan for everything at all times we stress ourselves out, exhaust our brains over nothing, and suck any hope of joy or spontaneity from our lives.

Over-planning is like any other mental habit: the more we do it, the better we get at it and the more likely we are to default to it. Unfortunately, most of us can't just will ourselves to stop it. However, we might be able to trick those parts of our brain by keeping them busy with activities that are similar to over-planning, but don't actually fuck up our life. For instance, we can play games that require us to plan and strategize.[145] This might sound like a waste of time, but it really isn't: as games are generally more enjoyable than worrying ourselves to bits, we will improve our general frame of mind. Also, regular over-planning can go on forever, but games are time-bound. Over time, we might get our brain used to turning off the over-planning when the game is over.

---

[145] My personal favorite is "Terraforming Mars."

Creative expression

In the immortal words of orteil42 on tumblr,

> "everyone needs a creative outlet to stick a creative fork into"

I couldn't agree more.

Creative expression can help us manage our anxiety and stress in different ways, depending on what we do with it. For instance, we might use it to vent our feelings in safety and privacy. We might use it to create a better version of our life, or a totally different life, so we can get a break from whatever is going on with us. We might just enjoy the flow state we fall into whenever we flex our creative muscles.

Journaling – i.e., keeping an account of our thoughts and feelings as we navigate everyday life – is often hailed as the gold standard of therapeutic creative expression,[146] but I'm not sure why. Those of us who are more comfortable expressing themselves visually, musically, or kinesthetically might find it unnecessarily hard to translate their feelings into words before putting them out there. Even those of us who are fond of words may find that other types of writing work better – fiction, poetry, whatever. For those of us who dislike routines and demands, the very idea of committing to a regular journal could be off-putting. That's definitely the case for me.

Personally, I find writing fiction particularly useful. Aside from allowing me to express my creativity, it keeps that part of my brain that constantly spins out a story engaged on something constructive, and with a happy ending. If I don't keep it busy, that part of my brain makes up its own stories, which have a tendency to be tales about how everything in my life is going to go horribly wrong in a gazillion different ways. I find writing extremely soggy sci-fi and unepic fantasy infinitely more pleasant.[147]

It doesn't really matter what our creative outlet is, and it definitely doesn't matter whether our creations are ever completed.[148] The point of this exercise is to let our creativity flow, not to create a product. Even just thinking about stories, poems, or music can take us out of our state of anxiety into a state of creativity; that's a pretty good shift.

---

[146] https://www.betterup.com/blog/how-to-start-journaling

[147] Yeah, it's out there. I don't know why, but it makes it feel more real. https://www.amazon.com/stores/Robin-Banks/author/B01MU5VWGL

[148] Fun fact: Leonardo da Vinci, neuroqueer posterboy extraordinaire, never finished a single painting. And I've never heard anyone say that he wasn't a real artist because of that. https://academic.oup.com/brain/article/142/6/1842/5492606

Meditation and mindfulness techniques

Meditation is the only topic we have ever had to ban from the ADHD page I mod. We made that decision because it became obvious that having a considerate, compassionate, and useful public conversation on the subject is not currently possible. The neurodivergent community is profoundly divided on this topic; some of us find meditation extremely beneficial, even life-changing, while others find it impossible, uncomfortable, or harmful. That wouldn't be a problem, if only the people who find meditation beneficial were willing to accept the experience of those who don't. Experience showed us that that's not always the case, and that the resulting arguments benefit nobody, hence our decision to ban the topic. If you choose to discuss meditation on an open forum, be warned: it might blow up in your face.

Part of the controversy is caused by what Western popular culture classes as meditation. The term is often used as if there was only one way of meditating, or only one way of meditating correctly. That's far from the truth: there are numerous types of meditation that differ hugely in what the practitioners try to do and how they go about it.[149] Some forms of meditation hinge on stilling the mind and body, while others don't. Some ask us to pay attention to our inner thoughts or sensations, while others try to connect us with a higher power. Zazen is meditative, but so are Qigong and Gregorian chanting. Many meditative traditions have been around for a long time, and some have profound cultural or religious significance. When discussing their relative merits, a degree of cultural sensitivity would not go amiss.

In the West, the most popular meditation technique is mindfulness meditation. In this form of meditation, derived from Buddhist practice, the practitioner sits still and observes their thoughts as they pass through their mind, without becoming involved with them. I think of it as watching fish in a tank: you observe them and take note of any patterns; you don't jump into the tank or try to grab them.

Research shows that a regular mindfulness meditation practice can have a beneficial effect on mental health issues like anxiety and depression.[150] Unfortunately, research also shows that for people who have experienced trauma, mindfulness meditation can exacerbate symptoms of traumatic

---

[149] https://www.healthline.com/health/mental-health/types-of-meditation
[150] https://www.webmd.com/add adhd/adhd-mindfulness-meditation-yoga

stress, ranging from heightened emotional arousal to flashbacks.[151] This does not mean that mindfulness meditation is inherently dangerous for people who have experienced trauma; on the contrary, it can be a useful tool in a therapeutic context.[152] Thing is, not every person who has experienced trauma is operating within a therapeutic context. Many of us are just trying to get on, with or without specialist support. Our reluctance to put ourselves through an activity that is deeply unpleasant, may set us back in our recovery by re-traumatizing us, and can render us non-functional for hours or days should not come as a huge surprise. And this holds true for people whose trauma is over; for those for whom trauma is ongoing, the situation is far worse.

There are also plenty of people for whom static meditation holds no attraction – and, unsurprisingly, many ADHDers fall into this camp. We already suffer through enough enforced stillness in our daily life; why would we sign up for more? Happily, regardless of what some meditation aficionados have to say, people who can't or won't engage in static meditation can achieve similar benefits through other activities. Don't take my word for it; this is what Brad Warner, Sōtō Zen monk and meditation teacher, has to say on the subject:

> "The balanced state of body and mind that occurs through zazen practice can also occur spontaneously in other situations. As a musician I used to find it when playing onstage. All consciousness of myself and the outside world would vanish, to be replaced by a fluid state of action alone, in which thought and feeling ceased to be important and in which sense of self and other utterly dissolved. Athletes often experience moments like this. So do artists of various kinds. So do many people involved in a whole range of activities to which they have fully devoted themselves."[153]

Many of us meditate without even realizing it, because our culture has a very limited view of what meditation should look like. If the goal of meditation is a Zen-like state of flow, we can experience that while engaged in a hyperfocus. If the goal is to be fully present in the moment, we might get there by doing more, not less. Many of us are at our most focused when we can combine physical and mental activities – listening to

---

[151] https://www.thescienceofpsychotherapy.com/is-mindfulness-safe-for-trauma-survivors/
[152] https://www.ncbi.nlm.nih.gov/pmc/articles/PMC5747539/
[153] "Sex, Sin, and Zen: A Buddhist Exploration of Sex from Celibacy to Polyamory and Everything In Between."

audiobooks while carrying out chores, listening to music while jogging, whatever. We are fully present and engaged; we just aren't sitting still while doing so. So what? How we get there does not matter, and insisting that there's Only One True Way of meditating reveals a lack of understanding of what meditation actually is, as well as a notable degree of cultural insensitivity.

Ultimately, meditation is a tool. If it doesn't work for you, hitting yourself on the head with it might bring limited benefits. If it does work for you, congratulations! But please remember that other people, including people with a similar neurotype, may have different issues, needs, and wants.

We can achieve **mindfulness** without meditating. Mindfulness is about paying attention to our experience in the present moment without passing judgment on it.[154] There are plenty of mindfulness techniques that aim at teaching us to be more present without requiring that we carry out any kind of static practice, and they can work for those of us for whom staying still is a no-no. However, mindfulness is not without its pitfalls. If we are in severe pain or in abusive or traumatic situations, paying more attention to the present will not make us feel better. In those situations, increasing our mindfulness may decrease our ability to cope with our present and make it harder for us to work towards a better future.

Distraction

The ADHDers reading this may think that I've lost the plot, but I'm serious: distraction, that aspect of our neurotype that constantly lands us in trouble, can be a useful tool. When everything else fails – when we can't relax, we can't redirect our restlessness, our creative outlet is blocked, and we can't think of anything else to do – we may be able to use our distractibility by dangling a metaphorical shiny under our own noses and focusing on that instead. It doesn't really matter what we use; anything that catches our attention will do. Something vaguely constructive may make us feel better about the process. However, if our anxiety is chewing at us, finding a way to stop that is inherently constructive.

As with all other tools on this list, it doesn't matter how we distract ourselves, just that we are able to do it when we need to – and no, we

---

[154] https://www.mind.org.uk/information-support/drugs-and-treatments/mindfulness/about-mindfulness/

won't end up being even more distractible if we learn to distract ourselves on demand. We are just putting an existing talent to good use.

Recreation

When we spend a long time in survival mode, we can end up forgetting that life could and should be enjoyed. We might have to learn to make time for rest and relaxation because they are essential to our functioning. What about the non-essential stuff, though? It's easy for us to let it fall by the wayside, or even to willfully give it up so we can focus on the Stuff That Really Matters. As Ryan North said, "All pleasures are guilty pleasures if you have high enough anxiety."[155]

Personally, I believe that what we enjoy matters. We might give our life meaning and purpose in a variety of ways, depending on what we believe, but if we live a life devoid of joy... well, it isn't going to be much fun, is it?

I'm going to refer to tumblr, yet again. plain-flavoured-english wrote:[156]

"Your purpose in life is not to love yourself but to love being yourself.

If you goal is to love yourself, then your focus is directed inward toward yourself, and you end up constantly watching yourself from the outside, disconnected, trying to summon the "correct" feelings towards yourself or fashion yourself into something you can approve of.

If your goal is to love being yourself, then your focus is directed outward towards life, on living and making decisions based on what brings you pleasure and fulfillment.

Be the subject, not the object. It doesn't matter what you think of yourself. You are experiencing life. Life is not experiencing you."

We might find it hard to enjoy our life, particularly if our anxiety and stress have buddied up with depression. However, that doesn't mean that we should give up trying. Finding ways to enjoy ourselves, or even just to remember the ways in which we used to enjoy ourselves, can remind us of one of the reasons it's worth pushing on.

---

[155] https://twitter.com/ryanqnorth/status/1239983963067777026
[156] https://plain-flavoured-english.tumblr.com/post/180456381004/your-purpose-in-life-is-not-to-love-yourself-but

Our passions are part of us. By giving ourselves the time and space to follow them, we achieve two separate goals: we show ourselves love, and we create an opportunity to love being ourselves. Most of us would do that for those we love; isn't it about time that we put ourselves on that list?

Checklist 3: Addressing the roots of our issues.

If you ever wondered about the sort of stuff that causes me to feel anxious, look no further! The prospect of writing this chapter fills me with trepidation. There is a good reason for that, though: it can be very hard to write about possible solutions to other people's problems without sounding like a total asshat and antagonizing everyone.

A lot of stock solutions are incredibly irksome because they don't take into account a simple fact: if people were in a position to implement said solutions, they wouldn't have that problem in the first place. Are you plagued by financial insecurities? You just need to get some money! Are you socially isolated? You just need to make some friends! Are you tense? You just need to relax! Are you depressed? You just need to cheer up!

I don't know about you, but this type of advice fills me with rage, particularly when I haven't asked for it. We could go down the rabbit hole of why I get so irritated at people who are (allegedly) just trying to help me, but I don't much see the point. Instead, I'm going to try and explain what I'm attempting to do here, in the hope that even if I mess it up, I'll get some points for good intentions.

Some of the stuff I will mention in this chapter is going to sound obvious, or insultingly simplistic. However, I can't leave it out, because it's not going to be obvious to everyone. Some of us were raised by people who couldn't model good self-care for us, because they didn't know what that looks like. Also, we all have a tendency to forget some of our options when we are stressed or anxious, because that's what our brain is wired to do. One of the features of neurophysiological emergency reactions like adrenaline dumps is that they give us tunnel vision, both literally and metaphorically; we are so focused on the threat directly in front of us that we can't see anything else. While this may improve our chances of survival if we are dealing with an immediate physical threat, it does us no good if we are dealing with long-term situations, or anything that requires us to think tangentially.

Also, knowing that something is good for us doesn't mean that we're actually doing it. I don't know about you, but I have a tendency to stop doing stuff that helps me as soon as it starts working, regardless of whether I still need it or not. And if something needs regular practice in order to carry on working... no chance. This list may provide reminders about stuff we forgot about, or just let fall by the wayside.

Some of the stuff I will mention in this chapter is going to sound unachievable or inaccessible. That could be because it is – I don't know your circumstances, so I can't even begin to judge whether your assessment is right. You know yourself and your life best. It's a fact, though, that not all of us can do everything at all times. It's not that we don't want to do it, either; we just *can't*, and being reminded of all the stuff that would be oh-so-good for us if only we could do it can be infuriating. I'd like to reframe this: I'm listing possibilities, however remote, in the hope that someday they might be actually accessible to at least some of us.

Some of the stuff I will mention in this chapter works great in a therapeutic setting, but that's of little help when we aren't operating in a therapeutic setting. This isn't just an issue of whether we can access professional help or not; it's about the impact therapies can have on our daily life. Most of us need to be able to continue functioning while we work on ourselves – we might not be doing great and we might need and want to make changes, but we can't just put our life on hold without suffering serious consequences. For us, therapies that cause frequent flashbacks, meltdowns, shutdowns, or burnouts may just not be practical. I don't know about you, but I can't afford to spend hours or days recovering from each therapy session, and insisting that a therapy is good for me when it's having a significant negative impact on my life is the opposite of helpful. Yes, a particular therapy might have the potential to bring me fabulous long-term gains; but if that comes at the cost of wrecking my life in the short-term, I just can't afford it.

Some of the stuff I will mention in this chapter would require you to make such profound changes that it might sound like I'm asking you to wreck your whole life and start again from scratch. Believe me, I'm not. The only person who can and should decide how your life should be is you. If some of the changes suggested here sound too big, maybe you could make some smaller ones that take you in the same direction. If the changes I am suggesting sound just plain wrong, ignore me; I don't know you, after all, so there's a pretty good chance that some of the stuff in this book won't be right for you. If you would actually like to make some changes, but the implications frighten you, a bit of reframing might help: rather than focusing on what you would be giving up, focus on what you're trying to get. Running away from bad stuff is alright, but running towards good stuff is usually a safer and wiser bet. If you truly find yourself in a position where making any changes would totally trash your life, however, that's a red flag. This is particularly true if the changes you'd like to make are some kind of boundary setting. If exercising any degree of autonomy feels unsafe, you might be in an abusive relationship – and this can apply to all relationships, not just romantic or familial ones.

Some of the stuff I will mention in this chapter is going to sound self-contradictory or impractical, particularly for those of us who are dealing with a mixture of anxiety, toxic stress, and trauma. For instance, avoiding triggers is a good strategy for stress reduction, but it's only advisable as a short-term fix if we're dealing with trauma, and it's not advised at all when our issue is anxiety. Sooooo, what are you supposed to do if you are dealing with stress, anxiety, and trauma, all mashed together? Or when you can't pinpoint which issue is in play at a precise moment? I can't answer those questions, because I don't know you better than you know yourself. All I can do is give you a set of options in the hope that you'll be able to try some of them and see what actually helps.

If this already sounds like I'm about to piss you off, I've got worse news. This chapter will mention the basics of dealing with anxiety and childhood trauma, but it won't go into the details of the relevant programs. There are two reasons for that:

1. Those programs already exist, in multiple iterations. I can't make up better ones, or present them any better than other authors already did.

2. The source I recommend for anxiety is 350+ pages, and the one for ACEs is 230+ pages. Were I to include all that information in this book, it would be a tome of gigantic proportions.

Tools for overcoming anxiety and childhood trauma already exist and, with some adjustments, they can work for us. Instead of reinventing the wheel, I will focus on neurodivergence-specific issues and solutions.

1. Embracing (or at least accepting) our neurotype

I'm not putting this section here just for the sake of a smooth segue. Embracing our neurotype is essential to the work that follows. In order to change how our anxiety, stress, and trauma impact us, we will need to literally change our brains and how we interact with the world around us. It's damn hard to do that successfully while we are in denial about our needs, wants, abilities, and limitations.

Ignoring our neurotype can cause us to ignore or misclassify a lot of our stressors, which can lead us to carry out the wrong type of therapy. It can make us ignore our limitations and needs, which can set us up for failure. It can make us ignore our abilities, too, which is just a waste. It's just not efficient, and it gains us nothing. It definitely won't make us neurotypical.

This is a truth some people find hard to swallow: if our neurodivergence has a genetic basis, it's not going anywhere. We may be able to mask it by mimicking neurotypical behaviors, but doing so is likely to add a lot of stress and anxiety to our lives, and can lead to burnout.

That doesn't mean that we have no control over the effects our neurodivergence has on our lives. There are steps we can take to minimize the impact of our less beneficial traits, and maximize the impact of our gifts. However, the best way to achieve that is to **work with our neurodivergence, not against it**. It's not an issue of giving up on what we want, either; it's about finding ways to get what we want *that actually work for us* – the real us, not a hypothetical neurotypical version of ourselves.

Working with our neurotype has a whole bunch of benefits:

- It can lower our anxiety and stress. Spending our lives forcing ourselves to act neurotypical is far from relaxing.

- It can lower the toll our daily life exacts from us. Once we make the necessary adaptations, many things get easier. Overall, our lives can become less taxing.

- It can gets us better results. Working to our strength and weaknesses can enable us to achieve things we never thought we could.

- It can get us faster results. We can get stuff done now, rather than having to wait for the day when we magically become neurotypical.

- It may enable us to do less. If the processes we follow to achieve our goals are more efficient, we will spend less time faffing about.

- It may enable us to do more. If what we do takes less out of us, we may have some spoons left to deal with other things.

- It requires us to treat ourselves with care, consideration, and respect. For those of us who aren't used to it, this can be a big change, but it's also quite a treat. Sharing a space with someone who actively cares for us is very pleasant, even when that space is just our own skull.

Seriously, there is only one major downside to this: if we have to deal with ableist people, we will have to deal with their ableism. However, I'd wager that struggling with the ableism in the world outside of our skulls is less damaging than internalizing it.

Even if we wholly disregard all ethical and moral considerations, embracing our neurotype just makes good practical sense. It's efficient. It's effective. It's *not* effortless – in fact, it can be bloody hard work, particularly when it's new to us – but it's instrumental to the rest of the work we can do to ease our stress, anxiety, and trauma. In fact, if we try to do that work without taking into account our neurodivergence, we will struggle to get anywhere. So, how do we do it? How do we embrace our neurotype?

For some of us, loving our neurotype is easy – I fall firmly into this camp, which makes me horribly unsuited to explaining how to do it if it doesn't just happen. If you don't love your neurotype, accepting it is a good first step. You don't have to like everything about yourself, but you have to be willing to live with the aspects you can't change. Until you do that, you'll find it harder to change the things you can.

Embracing our neurotype isn't just about touchy-feely stuff, though. It means being willing to make changes to what we do and how we do it. The specific changes will depend on our needs, wants, and circumstances, but they will likely hinge on a two-step process:

1. Setting **reasonable goals** based on what we want or need, and taking into account our circumstances and limitations.

2. Working out the **easiest way** for us to achieve those goals.

Setting reasonable goals is essential both for our success and our peace of mind. If we set ourselves unreasonable goals, we are just fabricating extra stress and setting ourselves up for failure. This will inevitably lead to disappointment, and could cause long-term damage to our confidence.

Working out the easiest way for us to achieve our goals is not just about efficiency; it's a stress-busting technique in its own right. If we have to jump over hurdles to achieve a certain goal, that's going to make the process a lot more taxing. Walking around the hurdles instead may mean that we have to reach our goal from a different direction, but does that actually matter? What's our priority, following a set trajectory or getting to our destination? Determining that is important, because sometimes we'll only be able to get to where we want to be by taking detours.

For instance, let's say that our goal is to eat more soup. Every week (or whenever we actually remember and have enough spoons), we go to the supermarket and buy soup ingredients. We lovingly take them home, store them in our fridge... and an indeterminate period of time later, we find that they have turned into mush. Rinse (literally, because our fridge is now a disaster area) and repeat. We aren't happy with that. We want soup, not compost!

If our goal is to cook soup from scratch, we might need to work out ways to achieve that. For instance, we could include soup-making into our schedule. We could set up a slot on Sunday morning for us to watch our favorite show while chopping veg. That way, the veg will be ready for us to chuck in a pot and cook for Sunday lunch. This solution may or may not work, particularly if our relationship with schedules is somewhat tumultuous, but it's worth a shot.

If our goal is to cook soup, no matter how, we could buy pre-chopped frozen vegetables instead. Aside from the fact that it cuts down on prep time, which might make actual cooking more likely, frozen vegetables are less prone to turning into biohazards while they wait for us to use them.

If the goal is just to *eat* soup, though, we could, yannow, just buy soup. Ready-made soup. Soup that only requires us to heat it up so we can eat it up. Yes, buying soup may cost more than making it, but throwing out soup ingredients is just a waste. Yes, soup from a carton or a tin might not be our Platonic ideal of soupness, but there are fairly healthy options out there. Also, the soup we actually eat will have a much higher nutritional content than the soup we just dream about.

If you think this all sounds very silly, then you are better off than me. I had to figure this shit out when I was a whole adult, and I still needed external support to give myself permission to go for it.

Soups aside, embracing our neurodivergence may include stuff like:

- Mapping out our neurotype. What traits do we have that make us different from the majority of neurotypical people? This process may require us to look beyond our diagnoses. We might have neurodivergent traits that aren't currently included in the diagnostic criteria we were measured against. That doesn't make them less real.

- Seeing our neurodivergent traits for what they are, rather than as character flaws. Blaming ourselves for issues that generate in our brains makes no more sense than blaming ourselves for issues that generate from any other part of our bodies.

- Watching out for ableist language. Sticks and stones may break our bones, but words will burrow into our brains and fester. What we call ourselves and allow ourselves to be called shapes how we view ourselves and our role in the world.

- Identifying our neurodivergent stressors and working out ways to mitigate the impact they have on us. Sometimes we may be able to avoid certain stressors altogether. Sometimes we won't, but we may be able to protect ourselves from their impact.

- Learning how to spot when we're emotionally or physically dysregulated. Dysregulation impacts our ability to function. We cannot be expected to perform adequately while we are dysregulated.

- Working out why we're dysregulated. If we identify our triggers, we may be able to avoid them or to inoculate ourselves from them – please see the section on managing our responses to triggers.

- Learning how to self-regulate.[157] Self-regulation skills are developed from early childhood. However, if we were deprived of the opportunity to express our neurodivergence, we might not have been able to discover what actually works for us.

- Making space for our stims. Stimming is designed to help us self-regulate and cope with stress. Repressing our stims deprives us of this outlet and turns our stims into stressors. We may not be able or willing to stim freely in public, but we can find ways to redirect our natural stims into behaviors that still provide us with a degree of relief. Also, most of us have some alone time. If we can't stim anywhere else, we can stim in the loo.

- Working out any basic needs we are failing to meet (e.g., sleep, nutrition, exercise, creative expression, social connections).

- Working out why we are failing to need our basic needs. Do we lack time or resources? Are we trying to reach our goals through strategies that don't suit us?

- Working out ways to meet our basic needs, ideally without increasing our demands. This may entail finding shortcuts. That's allowed.

- Making space (and time) for our neurodivergent needs. If we aren't used to accommodating our neurodivergence, we might be regularly

---

[157] https://raisingchildren.net.au/toddlers/behaviour/understanding-behaviour/self-regulation

shortchanging ourselves. For instance, we might be more comfortable when our daily life is tightly scheduled, or we might need some completely unscheduled time. Allowing ourselves to accommodate our needs can lower our anxiety and increase our joy.

- Treating any intensification of our neurodivergent traits as a symptom that something is out of kilter. For instance, if we are malnourished, underslept, in pain, anxious, stressed, or traumatized, that's likely to show as an increase in how much our neurodivergence impacts our daily lives. In order to resolve that, we need to work out and resolve the underlying issues.

- If we experience varying levels of energy, focus, or physical abilities, we might need to change how we manage our time – or, rather, we should consider managing our current capability instead. Time management aims to increase our efficiency and productivity, but it assumes that we are capable of performing to the same standards at all times. If our capability varies, we might need a different approach. Rather than making a To Do List and prioritizing tasks according to their importance or urgency, we can make a Can Do List of all available tasks, and do whatever we can actually tackle in our current condition. This will allow us to maximize our efficiency and minimize the time we spend failing to get stuff done. This approach doesn't work if we have urgent deadlines; however, over time it can help us reduce the amount of urgent deadlines we end up facing.

Please note that we do not need any kind of official validation before taking these steps. In particular, we do not need an official diagnosis. Our needs, wants, limitations, and abilities are real, with or without an official seal of approval. Accommodating them just means that we are treating ourselves with the same respect and consideration we show anyone we give a damn about.

This might go against everything we were ever told about how we "just" need to get used to this or get over that. That's OK. We were told the wrong things, by people who didn't know better. We know better now, and we are allowed to make better choices for ourselves.

That's the theory, anyway. In practice, things can be a little bit more complex. Sometimes the changes we really want to make will turn out to be too difficult to achieve, or too costly, and we'll have to settle for smaller, easier ones; that's not a failure, though. It's all part of the process. It's just another way for us to make adaptations that work for us.

Like most processes, this one will require revisions. We may need to re-evaluate our goals, particularly if we think that we have outgrown them. We may need to change the methods by which we try to achieve them, especially if we have discovered better ways of doing things. This may sound frustrating, but it's all just useful practice. We are learning to exercise our ability to think tangentially, to adapt, to respond with flexibility to changing circumstances. Those are all useful skills, and they don't come natural to many of us. If our neurotype or trauma make it difficult for us to be flexible, this may be hard for us, but that just makes it more useful.

The most important change is that we should never, ever, **EVER** punish ourselves for being neurodivergent, and this means not punishing ourselves for the problems we experience because of our neurodivergence. It's no use whatsoever for us to say that we accept our neurotype when we kick ourselves every time our neurotype causes us to struggle with something. That's not how acceptance works. We need to stop treating our problems as personal failings; until then, what we say on the subject won't make any difference, because our actions will trump our words.

This is often a hard pill to swallow: our anxiety is part of our neurodivergence. Whether it's caused by a genetic predisposition, the parenting we were exposed to, our life experiences, or, as it's often the case, by a combination of all of the above, it's a part of us. It might be a part of us we want to eradicate, but in order to do so, we first have to accept it. We don't need to hate it, either; hate can increase how much we fixate on our anxiety, which might not help us. We might want to try a different approach: looking at what our anxiety is trying to do for us. Unpleasant and misguided as it may be, it usually tries to keep us safe. Rather than engaging in an all-out war against it, we could thank it, send it love and light, and then leave it alone. It may still be there, curled up at the back of our minds, but once we have listened to its message and issued our response, we don't have to spend every minute of our day engaging with it.

A more comprehensive version of this type of approach is formalized in **Internal Family Systems** psychotherapy (IFS). IFS is "a transformative tool that conceives every human being as a system of protective and wounded inner parts lead by a core Self. We believe the mind is naturally multiple and that is a good thing. Just like members of a family, inner parts are forced from their valuable states into extreme roles within us."[158]

In IFS, healing from trauma occurs as we learn to switch from ignoring or antagonizing the parts of our self we dislike, to approaching them with the 8 Cs: confidence, calm, compassion, courage, creativity, clarity, curiosity, and connectedness. This process takes time, and is generally conducted under the care of a trained specialist. If done well, it can bring significant and long-lasting results that can improve our relationship with ourselves, with the people around us, and with the world at large. IFS can allow us to establish a healthy relationship with our anxiety as we work to lessen its impact on our lives. It can also help us establish a similar relationship with other parts of our selves we are struggling with, including our neurodivergence.

If we cannot access an IFS therapist, we can try DIYing this work with the support of online resources,[159] or try similar approaches to accepting, embracing, and nurturing our wounded self, such as Radical Compassion,[160] or more established compassionate practices like those in the Buddhist spiritual traditions. If your spirituality does not make space for alternative practices, it might already include compassionate practices you are unfamiliar with; I'd suggest asking one of your spiritual leaders.

2. Basic self-care

I already mentioned the physical self-care trifecta – sleep, nutrition, and exercise – in the section on managing symptoms, but it fits here, too. The work required to vanquish the causes of our stress, anxiety, and trauma is bloody hard. Trying to do it while our body isn't receiving the basic care it needs is going to make it even harder. It's setting us up for failure, and we don't want to do that.

Furthermore, improving our sleep, nutrition, and exercise may not reduce the number of worries, stressors, and triggers we have to deal with, but it can increase our resilience, and that matters. Anything that narrows the gap between what we need to manage and what we can manage easily is going to be a huge help here. Meeting our basic physical needs is a good

---

[158] https://ifs-institute.com/
[159] https://nicolasescoffier.com/best-ifs-resources-guided-meditations-books-podcasts-internal-family-systems/
[160] https://www.tarabrach.com/
I used this audiobook:
https://www.amazon.com/dp/1846045665

place to start.

While we carry out any kind of therapy that requires us to dig through past traumas, challenge our core beliefs, or move any kind of heavy mental furniture, we might need to take extra good care of ourselves. This care won't just be physical: our emotional, psychological, social, and spiritual needs may be more pressing, too. We are doing hard and unpleasant work with already-depleted resources, so we need to support ourselves as much as possible. In order to do this, we need to know what "taking care of ourselves properly" looks like. Sometimes, this means learning things that most other people already know, or unlearning a ton of stuff.

Adequate self-care can be a serious issue for those of us who were brought up in unsupportive environments or have been at the receiving end of long-term abuse. We might have never developed the sense of what constitutes a normal, healthy lifestyle, or we might have lost it. We may not have the skills associated with maintaining such a lifestyle. We may believe that we don't deserve to live like that. If we are incapable of looking after ourselves or to give ourselves the right to even try, we may require the help of a licensed professional.

3. Learning how to make requests and set boundaries

Learning how to make requests and set boundaries isn't a standard feature of most anxiety- and stress-busting programs. However, for many of us, it's going to be an essential part of the process. Unless we live in total isolation, any changes we make to our lives will probably have an impact on the people around us. Unless those people are unusually perceptive and accommodating, we will probably have to explain to them what we are doing, and perhaps ask them to change what they do around us. This may result in some resistance, particularly if the changes we are requesting require a bit of effort on other people's part.

For those of us who are unsure of our social skills or fearful of social repercussions, going through this process can be very difficult. Hell, even thinking about it can cause us profound anxiety. Unfortunately, it can't be skipped – or, rather, it can, but that's just storing up problems for the future. We can't expect people to read our minds and accommodate our needs. We also can't expect everyone to be considerate, helpful, reasonable, or fair. We need to learn to express our needs in the way most likely to succeed. Happily, there are whole programs out there specifically designed to help us achieve that. My favorite one is **Non-Violent**

Communication (NVC).

NVC is a communication strategy based on a few principles that sound ridiculously obvious... until you realize that hardly anyone ever uses them. These include:[161]

- Finding out what the other person means before responding to it.

- Emotionally de-escalating ourselves before trying to de-escalate anyone else.

- Communicating what we mean clearly, but without being insensitive to the other person's feelings and needs.

- Fostering an internal dialogue that makes us better able to respect our emotions while accepting that they ultimately stem from how we are parsing our reality.

NVC creates an artificial processing point between what we experience and how we respond, which can reduce our reactivity. Furthermore, the communication aspect of it is heavily scripted, which makes it suitable for those whose social communication skills are rated at Potato. Like me.

In NVC, each communication has a four-part script:

- Express objectively what you observe.

- Express how that makes you feel.

- Express your unmet need.

- Request the change that would meet that need.

So, for instance, we might say something like:

"When I see your feet on the sofa, I feel agitated, because I need to know that the sofa is clean for us to sit on and touch. Could you take your feet off the sofa, please?"

Yes, it's a bit long winded, but it achieves several things:

- It makes the issue *our* issue. It's not a personal assault on the person we are talking to. Please note the use of "I see" and "I feel" vs. "you do" and "you make me feel."

- It makes both the problem and the solution clear. If someone didn't even know that they were causing us a problem until we told them,

---

[161] http://www.nonviolentcommunication.com/aboutnvc/4partprocess.htm

suggesting a solution may speed up the rest of the process.

- It clearly states our requirements. Provided that they are reasonable, if the person refuses to meet them or at least negotiate them, then we know that we are dealing with an interpersonal issue more complex than it might appear on the surface.

NVC also creates a space for finding alternative solutions that suit everyone. For instance, in the example above, our issue is about cleanliness, not about sitting styles. The person in question may explain that they're sitting like that because their back hurts, and offer to take their shoes off, or to put their feet on a throw. That way, everyone gets what they need.

NVC is often marketed as a cure-all to all types of conflicts, which it isn't. At its very core is the belief that there is no such thing as asocial conflict – i.e., conflict with people who see us as potential resources or alien creatures, rather than as fellow humans. In asocial settings, NVC techniques will either fail or succeed by accident. When it comes to social conflict, however, NVC offers a helpful script for handling emotionally charged situations. These include situations in which we are emotionally charged, as well as those where there is a risk of us causing someone else to become emotionally charged. If there's anything better out there for that specific purpose, I've not found it yet.

NVC can be learned and practiced at home by using the original books by Marshall B. Rosenberg[162] or free online resources.[163] As with all other skills, the more we practice it, the better we'll get at it and the easier we'll find it to access it in case of emergencies.

Like all other communication strategies, NVC won't work every time. That isn't because it's not good enough, or because we are using it wrong. Quite simply, whenever we engage in any interpersonal interaction, we can only ever control half of it. We can make requests that are clear, polite, reasonable, and easy to accommodate, and people can still respond badly. That's not necessarily on us, and it's really important for us to remember that.

People's reactions can be affected by what we say and how we say it, but they're also affected by what's going on inside them. Did they interpret

---

[162] Nonviolent Communication: A Language of Life: Life-Changing Tools for Healthy Relationships
[163] https://www.nonviolentcommunication.com/learn-nonviolent-communication/

our request as a challenge to their social status, their core beliefs, or their personal comfort? Are they unable or unwilling to make the required changes because they believe them to be just too hard? Did we just catch them at a bad time? Are they just too damn selfish to tolerate any inconvenience for our sakes? We might not be able to work out the reasons behind their reactions, and they might not be willing to tell us what's going on, particularly if it's kind of shitty. Very few people are willing to say out loud that they don't care enough about us to make an effort, or that they believe that it's our lot in life to suffer for their convenience. Again, this isn't necessarily on us. We can't control or be responsible for what goes on in other people's minds.

Unfortunately, people's negative responses may not be our fault, but they might be our problem. If we have requested something we genuinely need and that request was denied, we are faced with two options: we can either suck it up and carry on as we are, or we will need to escalate. If we actually want our request to be met, we can start by trying to find out the cause of the resistance we are facing. If that doesn't resolve the issue, however, we will need to set some boundaries.

Boundary setting requires us to work out three things:

1. What our **boundaries** are. These may include both what we are willing and unwilling to do and what behaviors we will and won't tolerate from other people. For instance, we might not be willing to hug someone who is wearing perfume, or to let someone smoke in our house or car.

2. How we will **communicate** our boundaries. Generally speaking, words (spoken, written, or signed) work best. We can't expect people to guess what our boundaries are without our telling them, particularly if we are a bit unusual in what we will and won't tolerate. Please note that communicating our boundaries doesn't necessarily mean that we will explain why said boundaries are in place. While some people may respond better if they understand our reasons, not everyone has the right to know our personal business. For instance, we may be willing to explain to our friends and family that we are allergic or sensitive to perfume; that can help them understand the importance of our boundary, which will make it easier for them to meet our needs in the future. We may, however, not be willing to disclose medical information to strangers, for the simple reason that it's not their business. People don't have to know why we have a boundary in order to respect it.

3. What **consequences** we are able and willing to put into place if our

179

boundaries are violated. Consequences do not have to be punishments. For instance, if someone wearing perfume still tries to hug us, we don't have to thump them in the face to show them the error of their ways; we can just leave, or ask them to leave.

All these three components are essential to effective boundary setting. If we don't know what our boundaries are, we will not be able to be consistent about them. If we don't communicate our boundaries, the people around us won't know what they are until they hit them. If we aren't willing and able to put consequences in place for boundary violations, then our boundaries are mere wishes.

Even when we do it right, boundary setting can still fail. As we have examined in the section on social conflict, our position on the social hierarchy can have a huge impact on whether the people around us see our boundaries as manifestations of our basic rights or as awful impositions. That's not the only issue, though. Sometimes the very fact that we need to set, communicate, and enforce certain boundaries is a sign that there is something fundamentally wrong with our situation.

This issue was put forth clearly by Shamus Young' in his "Philosophy of Moderation."[164] Alas, Young used some stigmatizing language. If you are not willing to put up with it, just skip the coming paragraph:

> "We've all seen a rule along the lines of, "You will not use any forum or other community section to post or transmit any material that is abusive, hateful, racist, bigoted, sexist, harassing, threatening, inflammatory, defamatory, knowingly false, vulgar, obscene, sexually-oriented, profane or is otherwise offensive or in violation of any applicable law, rule or regulation." The thing is, sane people know this. They understand it without being told. Nobody needs to post rules on the door to Olive Garden telling customers not to spit or punch. (...) The problem isn't that they broke the rules regarding saying hateful things, the problem is that they wanted to say something hateful in the first place."

Sometimes the problem isn't just that people do harmful things that violate our boundaries; it's that they want to do harmful things in the first place. Some boundaries shouldn't have to be set or enforced because it's just a given that people won't behave like that. The fact that we have to defend ourselves from that kind of behavior is all the indication we should

---

[164] https://www.shamusyoung.com/twentysidedtale/?p=19709

need that our relationship with that person is intrinsically fucked up, and is unlikely to get better.

If the only thing stopping someone from harming us is the fact that we are good at boundary setting, that's a massive red flag. This is particularly critical in intimate situations, or those with an inbuilt power imbalance (e.g. patient-therapist or boss-employee relationships), but it's never OK. The best we can hope for in that kind of situation is that if we set and enforce our boundaries consistently, we will be able to... continue having to set and enforce our boundaries forevermore. People who wish to do us harm will never be truly safe to be with; the moment our guard slips, they'll get their chance.

Having to constantly defend our boundaries is another red flag. It can be the sign that a relationship is already compromised beyond repair, and we should look for the nearest exit. It can be the sign that we are dealing with somebody who is quite simply not OK, because OK people wouldn't dream to treat us like that.

4. Understanding and managing paradigm shifts

Many people think of "beliefs" in a purely spiritual or religious sense. However, beliefs are far more pervasive:

> "Basic beliefs can be conceptualized as value systems that are learned in childhood and adolescence. They encompass religious or political beliefs and values as well as basic definitions of oneself and one's personal goals in life. They are needed to guide coherent behavior over the life cycle of an individual, and even over generations for groups and whole nations. This makes them resistant to change, even when confronted with opposing evidence." [165]

Much of what we "think" about ourselves and our position within our families, communities, and the world at large actually consists of beliefs - faith-based statements we absorbed as we grew up and never examined against reality. In secular terms, beliefs underpinning a certain worldview are called **paradigms**. A paradigm is the accepted view of how things work in the world, and affects how we perceive and respond to reality.

---

[165] Linden M (2003). "Posttraumatic embitterment disorder". Psychother Psychosom 72 (4): 195–202.

Alas, sometimes our paradigms are incorrect. This can become painfully obvious when our beliefs don't match our reality. For instance, we may believe that our parents love us and take good care of us, that our teachers want us to succeed, that our doctors' primary goal is to help us get better, or that our society is fundamentally fair and caring. Our day-to-day life, however, may demonstrate otherwise. Maybe our parents love us, but they are not very good at taking care of us. Maybe they love the person they want us to be, but they don't like us the way we are. Maybe our teachers only care about how our grades affect their jobs. Maybe they enjoy watching some students struggle. Maybe our doctors care more about their positions as authorities than about the impact of the care they provide. Maybe they believe that some of their patients don't deserve medical care. Maybe they just care about their paychecks. Maybe our society requires a lot of people to have less than they need, so a few people can have more than they could ever possibly want. Maybe our government would prefer it if people like us just didn't exist.

When our beliefs clash with our reality, the resulting **cognitive dissonance** can be very unpleasant. Unfortunately, changing our basic beliefs – i.e., undergoing a **paradigm shift** – can be very unpleasant, too. However incorrect or even dysfunctional our basic beliefs may be, uprooting one of the cornerstones of our worldview is a big deal. Paradigm shift can be hard enough when it turns out that our beliefs were overly negative, because most people don't like being wrong. When we have to accept that reality is worse than we believed it to be, the process can be harrowing. We have to accept two unpleasant things: that we were wrong, and that our reality is shittier than we thought.

We have already looked at making a change that, for many of us, will require a paradigm shift: embracing our neurodivergence instead of working against it. For those of us who were brought up with the belief (not fact!) that neurodivergence is a problem that should be overcome, or that our neurodivergent traits are personal flaws, making this switch can be a big deal. In order to do that, we may have to accept that our parents, caregivers, teachers, doctors, and other adults who took care of us were also wrong about neurodivergence, and treated us badly as a result. We may have to accept that our families, friends, and loved ones are still treating us badly now. We may have to realize that they have no intention of ever treating us any better. Accepting these kinds of realities can require us to make several paradigm shifts, all of them unpleasant. This type of work is not easy, and can be profoundly upsetting and draining.

Threats or violations to basic beliefs can have such profound effects on some people as to leave them with Post-Traumatic Embitterment Disorder (PTED)[166] – the existential version of PTSD. Where PTSD is often caused by threats to our lives, in PTED the threat is to our basic belief system: "an existentialist, metaphysical, value-systems attack."[167] PTED occurs when an event clashes with deeply-held basic beliefs and results in prolonged and disabling feelings of embitterment. People with PTED can experience helplessness, self-blame, rejection of help, suicidal ideation, dysphoria, aggression, depression, pain, loss of appetite, sleep disturbances, unspecific somatic complaints, and phobias. These symptoms can be long-lasting and impair normal functions.[168] While PTED is not an inevitable result of paradigm shifts, the fact that these shifts can potentially cause such a reaction should clue us as to how significant they are.

The alternative isn't great, either. If we are unable or unwilling to make a necessary paradigm shift, we might get stuck in a **paradigm paralysis**. Paradigm paralysis keeps us in a constant state of cognitive dissonance, which is highly unpleasant. It also keeps us stuck in our current situation.

5. Processing Adverse Childhood Experiences (ACEs).

Processing ACEs is also not a standard feature of most anxiety- and stress-busting programs. However, for many of us, it's going to be an essential part of the process. When that's the case, it should be prioritized.

ACEs are a neurodivergent issue because neurodivergent children, like other marginalized children, are at disproportionate risk of experiencing them. Being neurodivergence puts us at greater risk of being subjected to "regular" ACEs like maltreatment (abuse or neglect), violence, coercion, forced adjustments (e.g., going into care, being forced to change schools or quit school altogether), prejudice, household adversity, and inhumane treatment (e.g., institutionalization). It also puts us at risk of being subjected to ACEs that don't affect neurotypical children, such as being forced to endure painful physical sensations as part of ill-fated "desensitization" attempts, or being put through behavioral "therapies" that are specifically designed to force us to hide our sensory pain, repress

---

[166]http://www.zpid.de/pub/tests/PT_9006580_PTED_Testbeschreibung_Manuskriptfassung_en glisch_2013.pdf
[167]Linden M (2003). Posttraumatic embitterment disorder. Psychother Psychosom 72 (4): 195–202.
[168]http://www.karger.com/Article/Abstract/70783

our natural expressions, and deprive us of our bodily autonomy. The impact of ACEs is cumulative, so the more ACEs we are exposed to, the more likely we are to suffer some long-term consequences.

Furthermore, if our caregivers don't share our neurotype, they might be unable to understand that we are being exposed to ACEs, or to provide us with the support we need to deal with them. On the other hand, if our caregivers are neurodivergent and struggling, they might be unable to help us because they simply lack the resources to do so.

If you resemble these remarks, processing ACEs is likely to be a key part of the work required to tackle anxiety, stress, and trauma. Childhood is the time when we should be developing a reasonable sense of safety, security, acceptance, and approval. If our circumstances do not allow us to do that, we are likely to develop some anxious patterns of thought and behavior instead. Dismantling those patterns is likely to require us to address how we came to develop them – i.e., to address the ACEs we were exposed to. That process of self-discovery can be grueling, but it may help us understand our behaviors, triggers, wants, and needs.

Some ACEs can have a direct impact on our stress and anxiety. Studies have shown that the way we experience and cope with stress and anxiety depends on a mixture of genetic factors, parenting, and trauma. If our parents or caregivers were chronically or excessively anxious, that will increase our chances of being anxious, too. If they are our genetic relatives, we may share their propensity for anxiety. If they modeled anxious behaviors for us, we might have picked them up from them. If they had an actual anxiety disorder, their functioning might have been impaired enough to have an impact on the quality of the care they could provide for us. Growing up under the care of people suffering from any kind of mental illness is in and of itself an ACE, regardless of how hard they might have tried to shelter us from it. This can be hard for us to accept, but doing so is a necessary part of our healing.

Healing from the impact of ACEs usually includes a mixture of different kinds of work. The work we will need to do will depend on the ACEs we were exposed to and their impact on our development, but it's likely to include some of the following:

- Developing self-care skills. These may include basic physical self-care skills such as ensuring that we are getting adequate sleep, nutrition, and exercise, but also social self-care skills, such as boundary setting.

- Developing emotional self-regulation skills.[169] We have already looked at a couple of them: breathing exercises and NVC. However, there is a whole bunch of them, which is really helpful as some neurodivergent traits make us constitutionally unsuited to using some of them. For instance, if our interoception is poor, focusing on skills that require interoception may be less than useful. While in the long-term focusing on the skills we struggle with may help us develop as individuals, in the short-term it's better to focus on what we can actually do.

- Learning how to weather neurophysiological crises. We have already covered this in the last two checklists – woo-hoo!

- Healing toxic shame – the feeling of worthlessness we develop in childhood.[170] Unlike guilt, which is a reaction to something we did, shame is a reaction to who we are – or, rather, to who we believe we are. If we grow up being constantly told or shown that there is something fundamentally wrong with us, we are likely to develop toxic shame, and this will affect (or infect) every aspect of our life.

- Tackling our inner critic.[171] Exposure to ACEs can result in the development of an overly harsh inner critic, either because we blame ourselves for our misfortune, or because we internalize the critical messages we are bombarded with. In order to get better, we have to learn to treat ourselves better, and that requires us to develop self-compassion.[172]

- Developing self-esteem, self-respect, and self-confidence. Some of this will happen naturally as we tackle our toxic shame and inner critic, but some of us may need to do some specific work in this direction. Embracing our neurodiversity is an essential part of this process.

- Carrying out inner child or reparenting work. This type of work allows us to explore how and why our childhood trauma occurred, what coping mechanisms we developed as a result, and whether there are better ways for us to protect ourselves from future trauma. In order to do this, we have to emotionally and mentally travel back to the traumatic event, and revisit it.[173] Needless to say, this can be very helpful, but is no fun at

---

[169] https://www.betterup.com/blog/emotional-regulation-skills
[170] https://www.webmd.com/mental-health/what-is-toxic-shame
[171] https://www.theguardian.com/lifeandstyle/2021/jan/06/silence-your-inner-critic-a-guide-to-self-compassion-in-the-toughest-times
[172] https://www.betterup.com/blog/self-compassion
[173] https://www.betterup.com/blog/inner-child-work

all.

- Learning specific techniques for processing traumatic memories stored outside of conscious awareness, such as the Floatback Technique.[174] This technique is usually performed in a therapeutic setting, and is not widely recommended as a self-help tool. To use the Floatback Technique, first we need to identify the negative self-beliefs, emotions, and physical sensations associated with certain negative states of mind, such as anxiety attacks. Once we have done that, we need to "float back" to a time in the past when we felt something similar. By repeatedly floating back to earlier and earlier memories, we might uncover the earliest cause of certain traumas. This can help us heal those traumas and manage our reactions to triggers. However, this process is risky and potentially re-traumatizing.

There are a number of programs designed specifically to help us process and recover from ACEs. The one I prefer is **"The Adverse Childhood Experiences Recovery Workbook: Heal the Hidden Wounds from Childhood Affecting Your Adult Mental and Physical Health"** by Glenn R. Schiraldi.

This book isn't perfect. However, it's the best book about dealing with cPTSD I have found to date, and I've looked at a bunch of them. A lot of the techniques suggested will also help with anxiety, stress, and in general. I could only find two notable issues. Firstly, the book suggests that ACEs cause ADHD. They don't. However, a difficult childhood will have an impact on whether we learn the coping strategies necessary to manage some of our less helpful ADHD traits, so disadvantaged children may look "more ADHD" than those who had a supportive childhood. Secondly, in the intro, the author speaks against blame, and states that "Harsh judgments and criticism just keep us stuck in bitterness and deflate motivation." I nearly dropped the book right there and then. When our trauma is caused by structural issues and stigmas – ableism, sexism, racism, homophobia, transphobia, you name it – placing the blame where it belongs is an essential part of our recovery.

There are many other programs out there designed to achieve similar goals. The trick is finding one that meets our specific needs. As this type of work is both difficult and potentially dangerous, it is best undertaken under professional care. However, if a suitable specialist isn't available,

---

[174] https://emdrtherapyvolusia.com/wp-content/uploads/2016/12/Floatback_and_Float.pdf

going solo may be better than putting ourselves in the hands of self-styled specialists.

As Tom Robbins said, "It's never too late to have a happy childhood." And this time, we can be the adults we needed when we were kids. We can fix this shit. It doesn't matter how long we have lived with the impact of our ACEs; we still have the rest of our life to do better. The work is hard, but doable, and it can have profound positive results that will impact every aspect of our life

6a. Managing our anxiety

I put managing anxiety before managing stress because of the type of work it requires. As I've mentioned enough times to bore everyone silly, anxious feelings that originate in our brain – i.e., anxiety – respond best to changes in **how we think.** Anxious feelings that originate from external stressors – i.e., stress – respond best to changes in **how we live.** Changing what goes on in our heads can be hard, but it's often easier than changing the world around us; if that's the case, prioritizing anxiety management can get us faster results, and those results can put us in a better position when it comes to handling our stress. If that's not the case for you, though, stress management can absolutely come first. If we want to maximize the benefits of our work, what we prioritize should reflect our situation at any given moment. As our situation changes in response to the work we do, our priorities may change, too.

Anxiety disorders are the most common mental health disorders. Over 30% of people are estimated to experience an anxiety disorder at some point in their lives.[175] This popularity is reflected in the number of programs and products designed to help people cope with or reduce their anxiety. There is so much out there that it can be hard to pick where to start.

Most successful anxiety-busting programs will include a mixture of the following:

- **Cognitive work.** This type of work aims at identifying the thoughts and beliefs that underpin our anxiety, and challenging them.[176] Anxiety disorders are often linked to a number of recognizable **cognitive**

---

[175] https://www.ncbi.nlm.nih.gov/pmc/articles/PMC4610617/
[176] https://medicine.umich.edu/sites/default/files/content/downloads/Cognitive-Skills-for-Anxiety.pdf

distortions, which may include:[177]

o Black-and-white thinking.

o Overgeneralization.

o Jumping to conclusions and mind-reading.

o Catastrophizing.

o Negative mental filters.

o Excessive internal criticism and toxic self-talk.

o Automatic, excessive self-blame.

Addressing these cognitive distortions and replacing them with more accurate ways of thinking can put the brakes on between what's going on in our life and how much anxiety we experience because of it.

Cognitive work may also address broader beliefs about the world and our place within it. These may include addressing issues like perfectionism,[178] people pleasing,[179] impostor syndrome, or an external locus of control.[180] We may also need to address anxious mental habits like over-planning.

- **Behavioral work**. This work aims at changing how we behave in response to our anxiety. Unlike stress, which is reduced when we avoid our stressors, anxiety usually worsens if we avoid what makes us feel anxious. The only notable exception is the aftermath of a traumatic event, in which case avoidance of triggers is a reasonable short-term strategy. However, over time trigger avoidance can cause natural post-trauma reactions to evolve into full-blown phobias or PTSD. Preventing phobias from taking roots is easier than uprooting them, and in any case, the cure inevitably includes exposure to triggers.

  Anxiety can also worsen if we perform ritualistic behaviors that assuage our anxious feelings. Those behaviors may give us short-term relief, but in the long-term they can develop into OCD.

- **Somatic therapies.** These aim at teaching us to manage our anxiety by

---

[177] https://www.health.harvard.edu/blog/how-to-recognize-and-tame-your-cognitive-distortions-202205042738

[178] https://www.goodtherapy.org/learn-about-therapy/issues/perfectionism

[179] https://www.webmd.com/mental-health/what-is-a-people-pleaser

[180] https://www.simplypsychology.org/locus-of-control.html

managing its effects on our body.[181] We've already looked at some aspects of this work in the section about how to manage emergencies and the section about relaxation. However, this type of therapy can go a lot deeper, strengthening the connection between our minds and our bodies. For those of us who have poor interoception or default to dissociation when stressed, this type of work can be invaluable.

- **Exposure therapies.** This type of therapy is used to address our reactions to specific phobias and trauma triggers. Over a period of time, we are encouraged to tolerate an increased level of exposure to whatever triggers our phobias or flashbacks. The aim is to slowly disconnect a traumatic memory or phobia trigger with our neurophysiological reactions – in a nutshell, we get used to tolerating the trigger without having a full-blown flashback or anxiety attack. This work has to be carried out extremely carefully, particularly when it's used to manage trauma triggers. If done badly, exposure therapy can be retraumatizing, or even physically dangerous for all participants.

One of the most popular treatments for all anxiety disorders is **cognitive behavioral therapy (CBT),** which combines cognitive and behavioral work. We have already addressed the pros and cons of CBT – in a nutshell, it's a great tool when used right, and a potential disaster when it's not. CBT is definitely something we can learn and do for ourselves, though. Doing so can enable us to notice if therapists are misusing it, which can nip a lot of problems in the bud.

CBT doesn't cover all the bases, though – in particular, it doesn't involve somatic work. As anxiety doesn't just happen in our heads, we are likely to have to find additional therapies to address the physical aspects of our anxiety.

My favorite all-round program for handling anxiety is presented in "Anxiety for Dummies" or "Overcoming Anxiety for Dummies"[182] by Charles H. Elliot PhD and Laura L. Smith PhD. This book includes a detailed explanation of various types of anxiety disorders as well as structure programs on how to manage them. It also includes an introduction to a way of managing anxiety that cannot be carried out through self-help: the use of **anti-anxiety medications**.

Anti-anxiety meds have a proven track record of working, and can

---

[181] https://www.choosingtherapy.com/somatic-therapy/
[182] Titles vary between countries.

provide a great degree of relief to some patients. However, like other psych meds, anti-anxiety meds should only be prescribed by qualified specialists. Family doctors are sometimes able and willing to prescribe psych meds, but their training on the subject may be limited, which can lead to problems. Some meds interfere with therapy, rendering progress impossible. Some have been shown to increase the chance of developing PTSD after a trauma. That doesn't mean that anti-anxiety meds aren't useful! We just have to make sure that we get the right sort, and a family doctor may lack the knowledge and experience required to make that call.

A note for ADHDers: for some of us, ADHD meds reduce both stress and anxiety. On the surface, this result may seem surprising: most ADHD meds are stimulant meds, which are supposed to *increase* anxiety, not reduce it! However, this point of view neglects two key facts. First of all, the ADHD brain's response to stimulant meds is nothing like that of neurotypical brains. Secondly, for a lot of us, ADHD meds actually work.

ADHD meds have a proven, measurable impact on how ADHD affects our daily life. The greatest improvements are shown in our ability to maintain focus, to start tasks, to keep on task, and to finish tasks. Meds literally make us able to get stuff done where we otherwise couldn't. This has two main effects: it makes our lives easier, which can reduce our stress, and it increases our ability to trust that we can cope with daily life, which can reduce our anxiety.

ADHD meds don't treat anxiety; rather, they remove one of the causes of our anxiety. That's much better, when you think about it. As a result, many ADHDers are able to cut down on anti-anxiety meds when they start taking ADHD meds. Similar effects are shown in relation to antidepressants, for the same reason.

Unfortunately, these facts are not as yet embraced by the medical system. Many doctors refuse to treat ADHD in patients with anxiety and depression until said "conditions" are under control. The received wisdom is that stimulants make people more anxious and impulsive, so we have to get our anxiety and depression under control before we can touch them. Unfortunately, this means that those of us whose anxiety and depression are caused by unmanaged ADHD can end up stuck in the system. Instead of getting the ADHD meds that could address the underlying causes of our anxiety and depression, we get anti-anxiety and anti-depressant meds that do little more than paper over the cracks.

There are other ways in which our neurodivergence may impact the work we do to manage our anxiety. The specifics of this will depend on our neurotype, but the bottom line is that treating our neurodivergent traits and coping mechanisms as symptoms of a mental illness is profoundly unhelpful. We need to make sure that our "generalized anxiety" or "phobias" are not actually responses to specific stressors. We also need to be able to differentiate between ritualistic behaviors, which could be a symptom of OCD, and stims or coping mechanisms like checking things several times to compensate for our distractibility and memory problems. This is particularly important if we are working with a therapist who doesn't share our neurotype and is not well-informed on neurodivergence. We shouldn't have to be the ones teaching our therapists how to support us, but we might have to.

6b. Managing our stress

If we want to look at stress in the simplest way possible, we can visualize it as the result of an equation:

Our demands – our coping abilities = our level of stress

The closer our demands come to matching our coping abilities, the higher our stress level will be. If our demands exceed our coping abilities, we will experience toxic stress, plus the consequences of failing to meet the demands in question. If we want to decrease our stress levels, we either have to reduce our demands or increase our coping abilities.

For a simple example of this concept, we can apply this model to an easily quantifiable and common type of stress: financial stress.

Expenditures – income = financial stress

According to this model, if our expenditures are significantly smaller than our income, we will experience little or no financial stress. The closer our expenditures come to swallowing up our income, the higher the financial stress we experience. And if our expenditures are greater than our income, we will experience both financial stress and actual financial hardship. If we want to reduce our financial stress, we need to either lower our expenditures, or increase our income.

This model ignores an additional factor: our level of stress is also affected by our beliefs about our coping abilities and the world at large. If we believe that we can weather the stressors we are exposed to, the result will be a lowering of the stress level we experience. On the other hand, if we believe that a stressor could make our entire world crumble, that belief will increase our stress levels.

Sometimes the beliefs that affect our stress levels are a reflection of our reality. We might know that we have access to internal or external resources that mean that, no matter what happens, we will be alright in the end. On the other hand, we might know that we lack certain resources, and that lack will have an impact on how bad things will go for us if we don't manage to overcome our stressors. We may also fear or hope for the intervention of factors that aren't in play yet, but are realistic and on the horizon, and could have a huge impact on how events will unfold.

In the example above, for instance, our equation could look like this:

Expenditures − (income + potential support from family members) = financial stress

If our circumstances are different, however, it could look like this:

(Expenditures + needing to save for an essential cost that's coming up) − income = financial stress

Or this:

Expenditures − (income + job promotion we have been promised) = financial stress

Or this:

(Expenditures + job insecurity) − income = financial stress

Sometimes the beliefs that affect our stress levels are based on our reality. We know that our family is able and willing to support us. We know that our vehicle is long overdue a service, and that we need to do something about it ASAP. We know that our manager thinks the world of us, and has put us up for promotion in the next quarter. We know that our employer has been making layoffs, and that our position is not secure. Including this kind of consideration into our mental risk assessments makes very good sense, because they are relevant and impactful.

Sometimes, however, our beliefs are just that: faith-based statements we hold on to, regardless of whether they reflect reality or not. For instance, we might have internalized negative messages in childhood that make us doubt our ability to cope with difficult circumstances. If that's the case, we might have a proven track record of coping with all manners of things, but still believe that we will fall apart whenever we are faced with a stressor. We might have absorbed certain anxious ways of thinking from our family, such as catastrophizing and all-or-nothing thinking. If that's the case, we might think that it's perfectly normal to expect the absolute worst to happen, and to react accordingly.

It can be hard for us to tell whether these additional mental stressors are real or imaginary. This is particularly true for beliefs we have absorbed in childhood and never measured against reality. It can be even harder for third parties to make this kind of call. People whose lives do not include certain risks may discount or ignore their significance, because they just don't understand their implications. For instance, people who have supportive families may not realize what life is like for people who lack that safety net. People who have a guaranteed income may not realize what life is like without financial security. I think of it as the difference between falling from a height when we know that there is something or someone to catch us, and when we don't. We might not enjoy falling regardless, but we are likely to fear it way more if we know for a fact that we'll splatter on landing, and that fear is not uncalled for.

Sometimes, however, it pays for us to look at how other people, in particular people we trust and respect, react to the same kind of situations or view our circumstances. Would they jump to the same conclusions? How would they respond to them? If the people who know us best have no doubt whatsoever that we will be able to cope with something, they might be right. If they are able to identify coping resources that we have access to but simply didn't consider, it may pay to listen to them.

In some circumstances, however, playing around with our stress around stressors may only bring limited benefits. If our demands are real, we have correctly quantified our coping abilities, and the resulting equation leaves us with too much stress, there are only two possible solutions:

- Decrease our demands, or

- Increase our coping abilities.

This may sound like a very daunting prospect, or like straight-up bullshit: if we could make our lives less demanding or make ourselves more resourceful, we would have done so already! However, there is often something we can do. Maybe we can ask for help, delegate, or drop some of our commitments. Maybe we can lower our standards or expectations. Maybe we can divert some of our time and effort on doing stuff that can lower our anxiety; while this won't have a direct impact on how much we have to cope with, it may make us better able to cope with it. Maybe we can run off into the woods, join a gaze of raccoons, and forget about human woes. Maybe we aren't able or willing to do much, but that doesn't mean that we are doomed: as stress is cumulative, the tiniest shifts in the right direction can add up to a significant reduction in our overall stress levels.

What we need and can do will depend on our circumstances. Generic advice about this issue has a tendency to be either not very useful or positively annoying; glib catchphrases like "work smarter, not harder" are unlikely to magically fix anyone's life. However... for many of us neurodivergents, that can be sound advice.

We have already discussed doing something that can both lower our demands and increase our coping abilities: embracing our neurotype. Trying to function as if we were neurotypical creates a ton of extra stress and reduces our coping abilities. Ignoring our needs, limitations, and strengths forces us to work harder. If we want to live a less stressful life, we need to stop doing that.

Embracing our neurotype won't magically make all our stress go away; in fact, it might add a few extra stressors, because discrimination is real and pervasive. It might not be safe or feasible for us to go all out at all times and in all situations. However, I'm willing to bet that all of us can make at least some adjustments. Until we do so, our inability to accept ourselves is going to be just another stressor we saddle ourselves with.

7. Managing our responses to triggers

In recent years, the concept of "trigger" has been popularized and stretched to breaking point. It is now used in popular parlance to describe anything that could upset or offend someone. While it's unarguable that people have the right not to be surprised with shocking material they haven't consented to be exposed to, the expansion of the meaning of "trigger" is not without potential negative consequences. On the one hand, it encourages people who aren't actually susceptible to triggers to avoid anything they find unpleasant or upsetting. While this kind of avoidance isn't harmful to most people, in susceptible individuals it can blossom into anxiety or phobias. On the other hand, the use of "trigger" as a throwaway term can trivialize the struggles of people who are genuinely susceptible to triggers. So, what's a "real" trigger?

We have already discussed the word "trigger" in four different contexts:

- **Environmental triggers**: environmental factors that can trigger or exacerbate medical conditions such as asthma, rhinitis, migraines, epilepsy, gastrointestinal conditions, chronic inflammatory diseases, autoimmune diseases, and many more.

- **PTSD triggers**: anything that forces a traumatized person to mentally or physically re-experience a traumatic event.

- **cPTSD triggers**: anything that forces a traumatized person to emotionally re-experience a traumatic situation.

- **Meltdown/shutdown triggers**: anything that triggers meltdowns or shutdowns in a susceptible individual.

Other issues, such as selective mutism, also have triggers.

The fact that the same term can be applied to all these situations is seriously unfortunate, because there is a critical difference in how different types of triggers respond to **exposure**. Over time, managed exposure to trauma triggers can lessen their impact; exposure to environmental triggers, on the other hand, either does no good at all or can actually increase our sensitivity to them.

The modern zeitgeist often paints trauma triggers as insurmountable obstacles. Happily, that's not the case. Overcoming trauma triggers is doable. However, it's neither easy nor pleasant.

The protocol for learning to manage our reactions to trauma triggers is called **trigger desensitization** or **trigger inoculation**. In essence, this is a type of exposure therapy in which the thing we are exposed to is a trauma trigger. Trigger desensitization can be a long, grueling, and potentially dangerous process. The program needs to be planned and managed very carefully to ensure that each instance of exposure is pitched at just the right level. If the exposure is excessive or the situation is mishandled by the facilitators, this type of therapy not only won't work, but it can result in serious psychological or physical harm to all involved. Every part of that process should be completely up to the participant. They must agree that they are willing to undergo the process, decide the methods that will be used, and have the right to stop or dial down the treatments if they so wish. Professional support is recommended in order to manage both the process and its aftermath.

Over time, successful trigger desensitization results in a progressive reduction of the neurophysiological responses associated with the trigger in question. As recovery progresses, triggers stop producing automated protective reactions or immersive PTSD flashbacks, and move on to generating strictly emotional reactions, like discomfort, annoyance, sadness, frustration, etc. These feelings are unpleasant, but they are manageable. This progressive reduction in the level of havoc wreaked by triggers can make a huge difference in people's quality of life.

None of this applies to environmental triggers. There are no training protocols through which we can become less sensitive to whatever triggers our conditions, and exposure most definitely does not work. If we are routinely exposed to environmental triggers, the best we can hope for is that our conditions will be triggered routinely. However, repeated exposure can increase our sensitivity; this is particularly true if our bodies aren't given the chance to return to homeostasis between exposures. For instance, routine exposure to respiratory allergens won't make us less allergic. Over time, rather than suffer from occasional bouts of allergic rhinitis, we might end up with chronic rhinitis or sinusitis. This, in turn, can cause permanent physical changes to our nasal passages and sinuses, which can interfere with our breathing and make us more prone to other respiratory conditions.

The only reasonable, safe way to deal with environmental triggers is to protect ourselves from their impact. This generally entails one of three strategies:

- Avoiding the areas where those triggers are likely to be present.

- Shielding ourselves from the triggers. For instance, if we are sensitive to respiratory allergens, we might wear a suitable face mask. If we are sensitive to noises, we might wear noise-cancelling headphones. If we are sensitive to certain social situations, like crowds, cutting out some of the stimuli may be enough to make the situation tolerable.

- Taking steps to mitigate the impact of the triggers on our health. For instance, if we have been exposed to respiratory allergens, we might use antihistamines, nasal sprays, or inhalers. If we are sensitive (but not allergic!) to certain foods, we may occasionally opt to eat something we shouldn't, and take the appropriate remedies to stop our guts from exploding as a result.

Physiologically, the safest way to deal with known environmental triggers is to avoid them. However, this isn't always possible or practical. Depending on the trigger in question, avoidance can severely restrict our lives. It can also result in anxieties or phobias around our triggers or the associated situations.

What about triggers for meltdowns and shutdowns? Alas, that's where things often go wrong for us. If our episodes are caused by triggers that have a physiological impact or cause us pain, exposure therapies have zero chances of working. However, if our episodes are caused by strictly psychological triggers, we *might* be able to become less sensitive to them through well-designed, consensual, progressive exposure therapies. This distinction is critical in theory; sadly, in practice, other factors come into play. The main factor is agency, or the lack thereof. As the vast majority of desensitization therapies aimed at neurodivergent people are not consensual, they are inherently doomed to fail.

One of the cornerstones of any desensitization therapy is that the patient should be fully in control of the activity. Depriving patients of their agency while exposing them to triggers can never achieve desensitization. The best one can hope for under those circumstances is that the patients in question will learn to suffer in silence. That's not therapy; it's abuse. Over time, it is likely to result in long-term trauma.

If you think this sounds disheartening, I have got some relatively good news for you. We might never overcome our environmental triggers, and we might need help to overcome our trauma triggers. We can, however, start using triggers as feedback. Our reactions to environmental triggers may really suck, but they are designed to warn us that we are being exposed to something that's harmful to us. Many neurotypicals aren't as lucky; they may only find out that daily exposure has damaged their health when they are diagnosed with the resulting medical condition. Our reactions to trauma triggers also suck, but we can use them as road markers in our recovery. Every trauma trigger is an indicator of unfinished issues; it tells us that there is work that needs to be done. As our recovery progresses, we will become less and less reactive. We can use what we learn from our triggers to guide us, both in our recovery and in life.

8. Dealing with slow or no progress

Changing the way we experience and cope with anxiety, stress, and trauma is hard work, and not only because of the heavy mental furniture we may have to rearrange or set on fire. The work can be hard at times because, despite of the effort we put in, we seem to be making slow progress, or no progress at all. Hell, sometimes the work seems to push us backwards. This is often the case when we uncover a nasty bit of childhood trauma we now need to unpack, process, and heal from.

This kind of thing sucks, but it's inevitable, and we have to learn to deal with that. Healing mental wounds is just the same as healing physical wounds: it takes time and effort, and it can't be hurried. The work takes the time it takes, and trying to push for accelerated healing can hurt us.

While we are working towards our healing, we will have to live with our symptoms. This can be hard to do, particularly if we were used to ignoring them or dissociating away from them. Now that we are paying attention to them, it can be easy to allow them to take up way too much space in our life.

Railing against our symptoms is natural, but it doesn't help. Obsessing about our symptoms doesn't help either. Constantly reviewing them or how we feel about them doesn't help. People with a physical injury are not encouraged to spend every waking moment fixating on how it is mending and how they are feeling about it. Picking at scabs does not speed up healing. The same applies to psychological recovery. We need to learn to embrace that the process of healing can suck, and to accept that suck as a normal part of our recovery process.

If we keep on pushing, our symptoms will improve. If they don't, we now have the skills to work out why, and to work out a new and improved strategy for managing them. If we truly believe that our recovery isn't going as it should, it might be time to consult a professional, if we are able to. Having said that, no professional can tell us how long this process should take for us. The given "normal" timeframes for recovery tend to be broad because people's recovery times can vary hugely. Recovery is not a competition, and it's definitely not a race.

Time doesn't heal all wounds; but time and appropriate care can make wounds a hell of a lot better. We just have to trust in the process, and in our ability to stick with it.

9. Dealing with pushback

Sometimes the problem isn't that our recovery is slow or stalled; quite the opposite, in fact. Everything is going swimmingly for us. We are making changes for the better, both to ourselves and our lives. Those changes are sticking, which enables us to make even more changes with less effort. Everything is getting better! That should be just great, right? Except that not everyone is happy about it, and they're letting us know that.

Whenever we change ourselves or our lives, those changes have an impact on the people around us. Sometimes those changes benefit them, too; being less anxious and stressed, or less affected by past traumas, can make us easier to live, work, and play with. Sometimes, however, the changes we make to improve our lives mean that other people will have to change a bit, too. Not everyone is going to appreciate that.

When we encounter pushback against our healing from the people around us, it can be difficult to decide what's going on. Are we in the wrong? Are we being self-centered, selfish, or just too demanding or difficult? If we are used to accepting responsibility and blame regardless of the circumstances, we might jump to this kind of conclusion. If we are habitual people pleasers, we might find the idea that we are letting people down intolerable. If we suffer from rejection sensitive dysphoria, dealing with that kind of interpersonal friction can be excruciating. There's a chance we're not the problem, though. Other things could be going on, and it pays to be willing to explore them.

People may be scared of the changes we are making because of their potential impact on our relationship with them. If we stop being anxious or stressed, what else is going to change? Will we still need them? If we don't need them, will we still want them? Will we realize that they're not good for us, or not good enough for us? Will we finally realize the part they play in our problems?

People who want to exploit or victimize us might not want us to get stronger. Taking advantage of anxious, stressed, traumatized people is easier. Our new boundaries and our willingness and ability to look after ourselves may be extremely inconvenient to them.

Some people derive great benefits from our perfectionism, over-planning, and people pleasing, and might not want to see them go. Taking the weight of the world on our shoulders often entails taking on more than our fair share of work. If we start relaxing and letting responsibilities fall where they actually belong, other people may have to start pulling their weight. That might not suit them.

People who thrive in chaos, or are simply used to it, might not want us to reach any kind of inner peace or balance. They want us chronically overwhelmed and dysregulated, because that's what they enjoy, or what makes them feel at home. The calmer we get, the harder they might work at creating dramas and emergencies around us.

For people whose self-esteem hinges on being the strongest half of our relationship, seeing our capabilities increase can kick off all kinds of insecurity. If we become their equals, they won't have anyone to feel superior to.

People who self-identify as our caregivers might not want us to get better. If we start being able to look after ourselves, we will erode that part of their identity. This doesn't just apply to parents; anyone close to us may take on a caregiver identity, whether we want them to or not.

People who are as anxious as we used to be may see our change as a challenge or an accusation. If we can get better, does that mean that they should try, too? That prospect might frighten them, and so might the prospect of being judged negatively if they fail to match our progress.

People who shared our problems may not be willing to see us heal and grow. They might want us to stay as they are, so we will remain their anxiety buddies. They might simply not want us to have something they don't. If they believe that they absolutely cannot get better, they might see our progress as a slap in the face. What right have we to get better if they cannot? This crab bucket mentality[183] may even cause them to try to sabotage our progress, consciously or unconsciously.

Anxious people who care about us might experience increased anxiety in response to our behavioral changes. We may be doing more things, including things that scare them. The fact that we worked at reducing our anxious feelings around those activities doesn't lessen their anxiety. If they are unwilling to work on their anxiety or at the very least to own it as their responsibility, they might try to guilt us into "staying safe" for their sake. This problem is particularly noticeable in anxious people who have an enmeshed relationship with us, as they may genuinely believe that they have the right to a vote on how we live our life.[184]

There are myriads of reasons why people might not like that we are healing, and many of them aren't really anything to do with us. They are about the fact that said people don't like the real or perceived impacts of our changes on their life. We need to be mindful of this possibility, or we risk getting sucked into other people's narratives, where our efforts to heal may be reframed as offenses against those around us. That's bullshit, plain and simple, and we need to be able to treat it as such.

---

[183] https://www.developgoodhabits.com/crabs-bucket/
[184] https://psychcentral.com/lib/tips-on-setting-boundaries-in-enmeshed-relationships

The people who really love us and care for us will want us to feel better, do better, and be better. That's all there is to it. As Heinlein said, "Love is that condition in which the happiness of another person is essential to your own." People who want us to continue being anxious, stressed, and traumatized may be very attached to us, but that attachment isn't love. Unfortunately, that's unlikely to make dealing with them any easier on us.

If we were able to manage our mental processes like Vulcans, we could see people's reactions as a type of feedback. Said feedback would be classified as either truthful or untruthful. Truthful feedback can tell us a lot about ourselves. Untruthful feedback can tell us a lot about the person providing it.

In that Vulcan frame of mind, even deliberately damaging feedback would be incredibly useful. That kind of behavior lets us know that the person in question is being an asshole, which is a useful data point. If we saw the world like that, we would be emotionally insulated from other people's behavior, and treat all interactions as learning opportunities.

Alas, most of us are plagued by those pesky things known as "feelings." We care about our relationships. Because of this emotional investment, we end up classifying feedback and all other interactions as "negative" or "positive" depending on how they make us feel.

This is not a sign of weakness on our part. Our brain chemistry is affected differently by negative and positive interactions. Negative interactions, such as those involving criticism, stimulate the production of cortisol, the stress hormone responsible for so many health issues. Cortisol causes us to think less clearly and to be more sensitive and reactive, which can cause us to overreact to further criticism, sending us into a downward spiral.[185] Positive interactions, on the other hand, cause us to produce oxytocin. This hormone not only makes us feel good, but also increases our ability to communicate and collaborate. This makes us better able to interact with those around us, increasing the chances of further positive interactions.

This does not mean that turning negative feedback into a positive force is an impossible task; on the contrary, it means that, although difficult, this process can bring huge rewards. It's a skill to be cultivated, like any other worthwhile skill.

---

[185] https://hbr.org/2014/06/the-neurochemistry-of-positive-conversations/

10. Social connections

I left this section for last not because it's unimportant or shouldn't be prioritized, but because I have no useful advice to give you.

Healthy social connections are a cornerstone of good physical and mental health. Social isolation and loneliness are linked to serious mental and physical health risks.[186] In the context of anxiety, stress, and trauma, healthy social connections are resilience factors[187] – they enable us to cope with stress, reduce our anxiety, and help us overcome our traumas. We all need and deserve strong, healthy interpersonal connections, based on honest interactions and shared interests and values.

That's all very well and good; the problem is that I can't tell you how to get them. For some of us, making new, true friends can be relatively easy; it's just a case of, yannow, going out and meeting people. All we have to do is take advantage of the social opportunities that are out there waiting for us, and bingo! New friends and new communities await us!

For some of us, however, making connections is not so easy. Maybe those opportunities just aren't there or aren't accessible to us. Maybe we are multiply marginalized, and we struggle to find spaces that welcome and accommodate all of us. Maybe we don't trust our social skills, and that makes social interactions so excruciatingly stressful that we avoid them. Maybe we enjoy deep connections but loathe superficial ones, and we can't work out how to get the former without suffering through the latter.

If we lack the opportunity to meet like-minded people, chances are that we will be socially isolated, and may feel lonely. I don't have the magic wand that can fix that.

Going online can help, particularly if we are brutally strict in how we curate our experience. The interwebs give us the chance to meet people who share our neurotype, to drop our neurotypical mask without incurring social repercussions, to join communities that share our needs, wants, values, and struggles, to find a place where we truly belong. That feeling can be wonderful, and it can do a lot to dispel unpleasant and limiting beliefs we may still hold about ourselves. The world is full of people who like us and love us just the way we are.

---

[186] https://www.cdc.gov/aging/publications/features/lonely-older-adults.html
https://www.apa.org/monitor/2019/05/ce-corner-isolation
[187] https://www.feelinggoodmn.org/what-we-do/bounce-back-project-/5-pillars-of-resilience

Sometimes, however, online interactions just don't cut it. Online friendships are just as real as irl ones, but the lack of physical connection can be an issue. It's hard to get an online hug, and our online friends may struggle to give us practical support if we ever need it.

I'm sorry I can't do or say more. I promise you, if I ever manage to crack this, I'll be shouting the answer from the rooftops

.

Conclusion

If you think that what you've read up to now was horribly gnarly but at least you got to the end of it, I've got some bad news for you. Re-evaluating and restructuring our lives at a practical and cognitive level can be very difficult, but it's not the end of the job. Feelings matter, too, and the work described in this book is likely to bring up a whole load of them. Not all of them are likely to be pleasant. This is particularly true for those of us who come to realize that our childhood was a minefield of ACEs, and that our adulthood was marred as a result. We may come to realize that what we thought of as personality faults or neurodivergent traits were actually symptoms of profound, long-term distress, and that our distress had specific causes. Some of those causes have names, and claimed to love us or at least to want the best for us. Some are still hurting us.

This type of reframing can lead to radical changes in our lives-. It can make us want to travel back in time and beat the snot out of our teachers or relatives. We might feel anger, peace, joy, grief, hope, or hopelessness. We may also feel anything in between, or a bit of everything, all at the same time. We are likely to feel something, anyway, and that something might be pretty substantial.

As a result, some of us will go through what is popularly known as "the Stages of Grief." These are often seen in people going through the grieving process after a death, but they can be associated with any kind of major loss or radical change in worldview. Following a reframing of our past and present, we may grieve at the shift in our self-image, or in our opinion of our support systems or the world at large. This grief may vary in duration and intensity, and can manifest in various ways at various stages.

Please note that the Stages of Grief are a model, not a checklist. They are a very generic summary of what people *may* experience. We do not always go through the stages in order, or even experience all of them. Sometimes we go through the same stage(s) more than once. We may not experience any of this at all. Having said that, if we are going through the stages of grief, knowing about them can help. They are: [188]

- **Denial, numbness, and shock:** the event does not seem real, or has "not registered."

---

[188] http://www.drchristinahibbert.com/dealing-with-grief/5-stages-of-grief/

- **Bargaining:** characterized by circular thoughts about what could have been done to prevent the event.

- **Depression:** feelings of emptiness, despair, or deep loneliness.

- **Anger:** towards people, society, God, ourselves, or life in general.

- **Acceptance:** the event becomes integrated into our set of life experiences.

The bottom line is that whatever you feel is the correct feeling. And if your feelings change, the new ones are correct, too. There is literally no wrong way to feel about this. There are, however, feelings that are more or less helpful, and more or less toxic. If your feelings are causing you distress and do not appear to pass, I would advise you to look for professional support. If that's not available to you, you could grab an emotionally competent friend. If that's not available to you either, I'm really sorry. That sucks. There are community support options out there, most notably online, but if you are in a vulnerable emotional state, I struggle to recommend any. Most internet communities are not vetted, so not all participants can be trusted. That also sucks.

Your feelings are not wrong, and they should not be disallowed. You have the right to your feelings. However, you do not have to wallow in them, although that's more easily said than done. You also do not necessarily have the right to act them out. You might need to express them, but that expression might require a degree of filtering.

You might find yourself particularly resentful towards people who did not support you adequately in your childhood – parents, relatives, teachers, doctors, you name it. That can be hard to navigate, particularly if those people are still in your life. If you need to take a break from them, that's allowed. They might resist that, though, which is likely to open a new and exciting can of worms.

If you find your feelings overwhelming (which is perfectly normal) and you are worried about the risk that you might take them out on innocent bystanders, it may be a good idea to practice explaining yourself to people. If you don't trust your words in the moment, written messages may help. It may all seem a bit over-the-top, but it beats losing control and damaging your relationships. A minimalistic explanation can be enough to let people know that you have a momentary problem, you are working at it but you are still struggling, and you are concerned you may be acting below your normal standards. Most people worth having around will understand and support you, or at least stay out of your way until you have had a chance to rebalance yourself. However, this is meant to be a temporary arrangement. Do not turn your processing into an excuse for becoming permanently toxic – unless you want to become a toxic person, that is. I would not recommend it.

If through your journey of self-discovery you realize that you have been or are still suffering from neglect or abuse, please seek help. There are organizations out there that might be able to help you – they might provide you with a competent listener, or offer practical and legal support. I cannot tell you what to do because local provisions vary wildly, and your needs will depend on your situation. But competent support can make anything easier to deal with, even this.

If people in your past have done you wrong, you might find yourself having to decide whether to forgive them or not. In our culture, we have a very broad view of what forgiveness should entail. This can make forgiveness not only more difficult or even impossible to achieve, but also unhealthy or counterproductive.

Different people will have their own standards, and that's OK, but it pays to consider the following:

- Forgiveness is a possibility, not a requirement.
- Forgiveness must be your decision and yours alone.
- Forgiveness should be on your own time; nobody should try to rush you into it.
- Forgiving the person and forgiving the act are two different things.
- Forgiveness does not mean that the relationship is restored.
- Forgiveness does not entail giving the offender another chance.
- Forgiveness does not mean that what happened was OK.
- Forgiving does not mean forgetting.

Forgiveness should be ultimately about you, not the person you are forgiving. It can be an effective way of detaching from your past and moving on. If it isn't coming, though, forcing it is unlikely to work.

Forgiveness may be hard, or even impossible, if the people in question are in denial about what happened. Denial can take many shapes:

- Denial of fact: using lies or omissions to evade painful or inconvenient realities. "I didn't do it!"

- Denial of responsibility: shifting blame for an action, or justifying it, as in victim blaming. "She made me do it!" "He deserved it!"

- Denial of impact: refusing to accept the consequences of a certain action or its effect on others. "It's not that big a deal!"

- Denial of awareness: claiming impaired awareness in order to minimize one's responsibility. "I didn't know what I was doing!"

- Denial of cycle: refusing to accept the decision-making process that lead up to an action. "It just happened!"

Denial is a natural self-protective response that many people default to. However, that doesn't make it any less harmful for those at the receiving end of it. While the people who harmed us are in denial about it, we might be able to forgive what they did in the past, but we cannot trust that they will do better in the future. That's a treacherous foundation on which to build a relationship.

These are all worst-case scenarios. Working out the underlying causes of our stress and anxiety can make our lives better, and it can make us feel better, too. It might make us feel validated to know that our struggles are real. It might make us feel less alone, because other people share our problems. We might feel positive about our improved ability to take care of ourselves. We might feel optimistic about how much better our future will be than our past. We might just understand ourselves better, and that might make us treat ourselves better, and that might make us like ourselves more – and, if you ask me, that's the best possible result. We have to live with ourselves. The only voice we can never escape is our own. We might not feel that we have much control over our lives, but we all have the power to make ourselves feel worse. Life is better when we don't.

Feelings aside, the work does not have to be over. This book is a brief introduction to a very broad subject. A myriad of tomes have been written about stress, anxiety, and trauma, and the research is still ongoing. If you have the spoons for it, you might benefit from checking out what else is out there. The sheer volume of it should prove that we are not freaks and we are not alone.

Stress, anxiety, and trauma are a natural part of the human condition. That doesn't mean that they don't suck, or that we don't have the right to wish that they would just go away. We don't have to reach a minimum quota of suffering to earn the right to wish for a better life. We don't have to hit rock bottom to earn the right to change.

The opposite is also true: however banged up we might be from our past misadventures, we can get better, feel better, and do better. It might take a while and require a ton of work, but we can do it. In the immortal words of Matthew Stover, we can keep our heads down and inch towards daylight.[189] It might take a while, but we can get there.

---

[189] https://www.amazon.com/Acts-of-Caine-4-book-series/dp/B074C71NMX
The series is absolutely full of violence, gore, and general awfulness, but it's probably the best therapy I ever got. The Horse Witch changed my life. For realses.

Further reading

This section has been really hard to write, for a simple reason: no book is perfect (and yes, that includes this book). Writers are human, humans are fallible, and their fallibility is reflected in their work. This might not matter if we have the chance to consult several sources on the same subject, but we don't always have the time and resources to do that. Also, sometimes we would have to consult books on entirely different subjects to discover where the mistakes lay.

Many fields of study are so insular and insulated that information discovered in other fields never seems to break through. For instance, books written by therapists routinely present "facts" that have been conclusively disproved by neuroscience, yet they stand unchallenged. I guess neuroscientists and therapists don't go to the same parties.

Some fields are also biased by their very nature. For instance, military science holds a certain view of the value and values of state-sanctioned users of lethal force. This view is unlikely to be shared by those who live in constant fear of unjustified violence from said state-sanctioned force users, and rightly so.

And then there's how you package it. There is a lot of guff spewed about how people learn best from stories, hence stories – engaging stories, vivid stories, stories that bring a subject to life in all its glory and gore – are essential to our learning. And yeah, that's cool and all, but the truth of the matter is that this type of writing makes books inaccessible to those who need them most, because every story is a potential trigger. There are books out there written specifically for trauma survivors that no trauma survivor could ever read without being triggered. I'm sure that the fact that trauma porn sells doesn't have anything to do with this.

Then there are fields like self-defense, where a host of subjects come together to form new and wonderful concepts. It might not be obvious to those who aren't involved with it, but successful self-defense requires us to engage with reality. Engaging with reality requires us to understand it first. This requires us to dabble in a variety of fields: biology, physics, psychology, sociology, neurobiology, and many more.

Unfortunately, superficial dabbling can give us solutions without giving us a real understanding of how they work. As a result, many self-defense experts come up with strategies that work reliably and consistently, but not for the reasons they think. That's how we ended up with so many one-punch-knockout techniques that only actually work for people who are 6'6" and built like a brick shithouse. This guaranteed technique is 100% reliable... as long as you can put 200lbs of muscle behind it. No refunds.

When a person like me – under 5' and built to scale – tries those techniques and fails, the cause may be obvious to most of us. Unfortunately, the same issues can apply in other, far less obvious ways. There are plenty of allegedly one-size-fits-all strategies that don't actually fit all sizes, both literally and metaphorically. Assertiveness and boundary setting, for instance, are not the cure-alls for interpersonal conflict they are hailed to be. They only work reliably if we use them to deal with people who regard us as their equals – and, as often as not, those are not the people against whom we need to be assertive or set boundaries. And if the people who are pushing those strategies are unwilling or unable to admit that societal biases exist, and that they have a huge impact on what will and won't work for us, they will continue to peddle crap that not only can't help us, but can put us in serious danger.

This doesn't mean that no book can help us – if I thought that, I wouldn't keep writing. It does, however, mean that books written by people who don't share our issues might not help us deal with those issues, or might only help us if we adapt the content to suit us. It means that sometimes we have to wade through toxic slurry while we pick and choose the tools that will actually help us. It means that we might have to process the fact that some authors' view of the world doesn't include us, or includes us as villains. All of this takes extra time and extra effort, and most of this is painful.

So, yeah, writing this section wasn't easy. Do I include books with great factual information or practical solutions but toxic biases? What about trauma triggers? What about the stuff that works, but all for the wrong reasons? The stuff that works great in one setting, but could get us killed if we misapply it? The stuff that works for me but might not work for you? What about the fact that I'm also a person, with limited life experiences, a considerable amount of privilege, and a ton of biases? What am I missing?

Anyway, I did my best. Please proceed with caution, if at all. And if you think that I got something wrong, I can promise you that you're probably right.

Essential resources

- **"The Adverse Childhood Experiences Recovery Workbook: Heal the Hidden Wounds from Childhood Affecting Your Adult Mental and Physical Health."** By Glenn R. Schiraldi.

The best book about dealing with cPTSD I have found to date, and I've looked at a bunch of them. This book is concise and packed with clear information and helpful suggestions. A lot of these techniques will also help with anxiety, stress, and in general. I could only find two notable issues. Firstly, the book suggests that ACEs cause ADHD. They don't. However, a difficult childhood will have an impact over whether we learn the coping strategies necessary to manage some of our less helpful ADHD traits, so disadvantaged children may look "more ADHD" than those who had a supportive childhood. Secondly, in the intro, the author speaks against blame, and states that "Harsh judgments and criticism just keep us stuck in bitterness and deflate motivation." I nearly dropped the book right there and then. When our trauma is caused by structural issues and stigmas – ableism, sexism, racism, you name it – placing the blame where it belongs is an essential part of our recovery.

- **"Anxiety for Dummies" or "Overcoming Anxiety for Dummies."**[190] By Charles H. Elliot PhD and Laura L. Smith PhD

A clear and comprehensive introduction to anxiety, how to manage it, and how to resolve it. I used the audiobook version, which is delightful.

Sources I can recommend without reservations:

- **"Overcoming Low Self-Esteem, 1st Edition: A Self-Help Guide Using Cognitive Behavioral Techniques."** By Melanie Fennell. (There is a second edition, but I haven't read it.)

I put this book on top of the list on purpose. For most of us, and particularly for those of us with cPTSD or RSD, self-esteem is an issue. Lack of self-esteem can increase our anxiety and decrease our ability to cope with stressors and stress. And while our self-esteem is poor, it can be very hard for us to allow ourselves to get better, to help ourselves, to recognize our achievements, and so on.

---

[190] Titles vary between countries.

This book does include some stories which can be triggering to susceptible people, but it doesn't get into details or sensationalize the experiences. Also, it's a damn good introduction to CBT – which, while not a cure-all, is a damn good therapy if applied correctly and to the right problems. CBT skills are highly transferrable, so it's worth learning about them, and this is a good way to do so safely and cheaply.

- **"How Emotions Are Made. The Secret Life of the Brain."** By Lisa Feldman Barrett.

An excellent introduction to modern neuroscience, engaging and easy to process even if you know nothing about the subject. It dispels a lot of myths about how people function (or fail to). It will change the way in which you evaluate and process the rest of the books on this list.

- **"Hardcore Self Help: F**k Anxiety"** and **"Hardcore Self Help: F**k Depression."** By Robert Duff.

These books are, as you might guess from the titles, peppered with swears, which won't suit everyone. However, they are short, accessible, and immediately useful, which is not all that common for self-help books. They both provide a good starting block to set you up for success on the road to recovery, and they won't require much of your energy or time. I particularly enjoy the audiobook versions.

I also strongly recommend that everyone should read the Depression book, because it includes an excellent explanation of suicidality and good practical suggestions for how to reduce risks. Given that the vast majority of popular advice available on the subject starts off by making no distinction between suicidal ideation and suicidal intent, and ends up by reeling off a bunch of uninformed platitudes, this book could save lives.

- **"Ice Cream for Breakfast: How rediscovering your inner child can make you calmer, happier, and solve your bullsh*t adult problems."** By Laura Jane Williams.

It's full of swears and bad ideas. What's not to like? But seriously, it's a one-stop-shop for adding joy to your life. One caveat: when Williams says "everyone," it needs to be translated into "everyone who sees you as an equal and does not have a personality disorder."

- **"Emotional Abuse: A manual for self-defense"** by Zak Mucha.

Explains in a succinct yet comprehensive manner the mechanisms and impacts of emotional abuse and how a history of abuse can facilitate future abuse. Currently only available as an audiobook on Audible.

- **Guided journaling**

Journaling doesn't do it for me, but this is my favorite guided journal creator. If you don't like bright colors, look elsewhere.

https://www.etsy.com/uk/shop/SelfLoveRainbow

- **"Down the Rabbit Hole. The world of estranged parents' forums."**[191]

A free online resource for children (of any age) of estranged parents who are either abusive or dysfunctional, aiming to explain the mentality of the estranged parents and why dealing with them can be a frustrating waste of time and effort. Extremely triggering in places, but needfully so. I would say that it's an essential read for those of us who need or want to go no contact or limited contact with our relatives.

- **"Fear is the Mind Killer: How to Build a Training Culture that Fosters Strength and Resilience."** By Kaja Sadowski.

Only tangentially relevant, but it's a good tangent. This book is aimed at helping martial arts and self-defense instructors build a training environment that helps all their students grow. In order to do so, the book clearly breaks down the requirements of a good learning environment, and how it should be run. For those of us who are not instructors, it's helpful to know what we can and should expect from our instructors, what might be holding us back in our learning, and the terminology and rationale with which we can present requests for change. We shouldn't have to teach our teachers, but we might need to nonetheless.

---

[191] http://www.issendai.com/psychology/estrangement/

Sources that are really useful, but also kind of suck:

- **"Nonviolent Communication – A Language of Life."** By Marshall B. Rosenberg.

A useful resource for learning to self-de-escalate and express needs in a non-challenging way. Despite its claims, it will NOT work in all situations. NVC only works as intended when we are in a social conflict with someone who sees us as equals and does not have a personality disorder or mental illness. This bug functions as a feature, though: when NVC fails, it's a good indication that we're entering dangerous waters.

Furthermore, NVC can also be misused to manipulate people in the context of emotional abuse, and that misuse is becoming increasingly common. That's just another reason to learn how it's supposed to work, though: so it can't be used against us.

- **"Conflict Communications – A functional taxonomy of human conflict"** by Rory Miller.

It's a powerful tool that can help you communicate more effectively while avoiding and navigating conflict. I recommend it to all humans who plan to interact with other humans, with two caveats. Firstly, the triune model of the brain has been thoroughly discredited, but it still works well as a model, in this context. However, the split is supposed to be reptilian complex (basal ganglia), paleomammalian complex (limbic system), and neomammalian complex (neocortex). Reframing it as lizard-monkey-human is incorrect. The human brain is the sum of its parts – if anything, the neocortex on its own would be better labeled "the Vulcan brain" – and, while they are wonderful in their own way, Vulcans are not human.

The lizard-monkey-human labels also devalue the paleomammalian brain, which is our social and emotional brain. As it happens, emotions and social impulses are actually pretty important. If you think I'm carping about semantics, try reframing it as lizard-wolf-human. Does it feel the same to you?

- **"Violence: A Writer's Guide"** by Rory Miller.

Although designed to explain violence to writers, it's a good introduction for anyone who has little or no first-hand experience on the subject. Still potentially a bit much for stressed or anxious people.

- **"Meditations on Violence: A Comparison of Martial Arts Training & Real World Violence"** by Rory Miller.

My favorite non-fiction book ever. This book is probably the best introduction to the complexities of violence and its potential effects on survivors. However, it's not a comfortable read, and it might not be ideal for people who are dealing with severe stress or anxiety.

- **"The Gift of Fear: Survival Signals That Protect Us from Violence"** by Gavin de Becker.

A good introduction to the role of intuition in keeping us safe and some of the common techniques predators use in order to get close to their chosen targets. However, the book starts with a graphic description of a violent crime, and is a triggerfest throughout. If the information it provides wasn't so good, or was available elsewhere, I would not recommend it.

- **"The Tao of Fully Feeling. Harvesting Forgiveness out of Blame."** By Pete Walker.

Within the first five minutes, Walker, a licensed therapist, states that "habitual lateness and forgotten commitments" are a passive-aggressive way of "acting out" our subconscious anger. In case you're wondering: no, they are not. They are external manifestations of how our brains function, or fail to. If therapists actually bothered to learn any neuroscience, that'd be swell. Unfortunately for us, the strategies he describes can be useful. I'd suggest borrowing it if you can, because he does not deserve our money.

- **"Complex PTSD. From Surviving to Thriving."** By Pete Walker.

This is generally hailed as THE text on cPTSD. Unfortunately, it's written by the same Pete Walker who wrote the book listed just above. In this book, Walker states categorically that ADHD and ADD are misdiagnosed trauma responses. So, yeah, the dude is clearly well-informed about neurodivergence <insert eyeroll>. The book is also a minefield of potential and rather unnecessary triggers, which also reveal some concerning biases. Again, the public library might be your friend.

- **The "Overcoming Books" series.** By various authors.[192]

A series of guides on how to use CBT to deal with a variety of specific problems. I haven't checked the whole series, but I have checked several of the books and found them very useful.

The usual caveats about CBT apply here. I'd also steer clear of the volumes that try to use CBT to handle recognized medical conditions (e.g., Chronic Fatigue Syndrome – seriously, what???) or are entrenched in biases (e.g., fatphobia).

CBT books won't replace a good CBT specialist. However, if you pick up a bad book, you can chuck it out of the window and forget about it. If you do that to a therapist, you'll get in trouble.

Sources I can't recommend, because I wrote them:

- **"Facets of Neurodivergence: Our Brains, Our Health, Our Lives."** By Ash Banks

The results of the public survey I ran to try and quantify the prevalence of neurodivergent traits and co-occurring conditions. Not a scientific text, but if you want to know more about some of the most common issues that affect the ADHD corner of the neurodivergent community, this may be a good place to start.

- **"Going Official! On getting a diagnosis of adult ADHD, and what to do with it."** By Ash Banks.

About ADHD, but also about the societal and medical biases that prevent so many neurodivergents from accessing the diagnoses and treatment they need, and the potential impacts of being undiagnosed.

- **"Creepology: Self-defense for your social life."** By A.R. Banks.

An introduction to non-violent sexual predators, how to spot them, and how to get rid of them.

---

[192] https://www.amazon.com/dp/B09PYZC5DZ

- **"A Woman's Toolkit for Recovery from Violence and Trauma."** By A.R. Banks.

A short, principles-based guide for recovery in the immediate aftermath of interpersonal violence and trauma.

- **"Trauma-Aware Self-Defense Instruction: How instructors can help maximize the benefits and minimize the risks of self-defense training for survivors of violence and trauma."** By A.R. Banks.

Useful (hopefully) for survivors of violence and trauma who want to know what they can and should expect from their self-defense instructors.

Sources I've picked information from but cannot recommend:

- **Lt. Col. Grossman's work on "killology."**

This is where I learned about stress inoculation, and I am grateful for that. However, Grossman's work is steeped in the American hero complex, and constantly glorifies state-sanctioned users of lethal force.

In case there is any confusion about it, Black Lives Matter.

If money is a limiting factor

I've deliberately stayed away from really expensive books, but none of the books on this list are free. If money is a limiting factor and your local library can't help you, you might be able to find what you need in used bookstores like AbeBooks. Alternatively, the two required readings are currently available for free to Audible members. Audible memberships aren't free, but you can sign up for a free month's trial and get one free book credit (I'd recommend using it on "Overcoming Low Self-Esteem" or "How Emotions Are Made"). If you cancel the trial *immediately*, you won't risk forgetting about it and getting charged at the end of the free period, and you'll still have access to the Audible Plus catalogue for a month.

About the author

Hi! My name is Ash. I picked it myself. You might know me as Modgoblin from The ADHD Gift.[193] I have written some non-fiction books[194] and a blog[195] about self-defense and recovery from violence and trauma. I also write sci-fi and fantasy.[196] Most of my characters are neuroqueer, but that's not a deliberate slight against the neurotypical community; I just have no idea how their brains function. I do, however, have at least two straight characters in each book, because representation matters!

I currently live in rural Lincolnshire with an unreasonable number of dogs. I have had several careers, including agriculture, genetics, nature conservation, and animal care. Evidence suggests that I have to go through a life reboot every 5-10 years. I am currently overdue. It's uncomfortable.

My path to finding out that I am neurodivergent has been convoluted, to put it mildly. I started showing signs of hyperactivity as a fetus – no, seriously. My mom reckons that once I started moving, I just didn't stop. My behavior did not improve until I was made to develop a paralyzing degree of social anxiety. That, combined with my family's belief that 100% was the passing grade, meant that I had a whole load of fun in school.

I discovered that I have a number of sensitivities in my late teens, when moving into a university dorm caused me such a bad reaction that I ended up in the emergency room. I discovered that I'm dyslexic in my early 20s, when I started tutoring students with learning difficulties. I discovered that my mother had known all about it in my mid-30s. I would say that put a crimp in our relationship, but our relationship was mostly crimps anyway. Shortly after that, I discovered that I am dyspraxic, which is jolly good fun when you are trying to learn martial arts. The working memory issues and sleep disorders became apparent a couple of years after that, when my insomnia caused me a level of cognitive decline so profound that I ended up being referred to the local dementia clinic. While all that was going on, I signed up with a life coach to try and get my life into a resemblance of order. I didn't realize it at the time, but a lot of the work we did was around unmasking and addressing my needs, rather than my

---

[193] https://www.facebook.com/TheADHDGift
[194] https://www.amazon.com/A-R-Banks/e/B09JHP4FT5
[195] https://godsbastard.wordpress.com/
[196] https://www.amazon.com/Robin-Banks/e/B01MU5VWGL

"faults." The process was pretty rough at the start, but it got easier over time, and now it's good fun. I enjoy my own company now. It's great.

There I was, trying to fix my real life while writing fiction to escape it, when an idea occurred to me: what if the part of me that craves spontaneity and adventure and the part of me that needs to overplan everything were two separate people? And what if they met, and instead of detesting each other like they do in my head, they fell in love? That caused me to drop the perfectly good manuscript I was working on and embark on a two-year-long escapade with my two favorite characters to date. Yes, I wrote a love story between my ADHD and my anxiety. And at the time, I didn't know that I was neurodivergent and anxious.

Those discoveries were made at the behest of an Autistic friend, who suggested that my brain didn't quite work as most brains do, and that I might want to look into that. A hyperfocus and a whole bunch of tests later, my life suddenly made sense.

The funniest thing was telling my friends about it. With no exception, their reaction was utter surprise... at the fact that I had only just found out. I'm still not sure if the issue was that I don't mask around them or that most of them are also neurodivergent. We sure have a way of finding our own, even when we don't have a name for what we are looking for.

It took me another two years to get a diagnosis valid in this country. I didn't see the point, to be honest: I am self-employed, so workplace adaptations are all up to me, and I absolutely did not want meds. I didn't need meds. I had been without them all my life and had managed perfectly well. I liked my brain the way it was, thank you! Then something shifted inside me, and I started to listen to what other ADHDers had to say on the subject. A lot of stress and an exorbitant diagnostic bill later, I discovered what all the fuss was about. Shortly thereafter, I discovered that meds are not for me: I can adult better when I'm medicated, but I can't write. That's not a trade-off I am willing to make. I'm glad I got to try them, though, and it's reassuring to know that they are there when I need them.

I really hope that reading this book will help you at least as much as writing it helped me. The world can be a pretty gnarly place, but life can be better – or, rather, we can make our lives better.

Keep your head down, and inch towards daylight.

Printed in Great Britain
by Amazon